Werner Poscharnigg:

AUSTRIAN ART OF RIDING

Five Centuries

XENOPHON PRESS

Copyright © 2015 by Xenophon Press

Idea, German text, private images, photos: © Dr Werner Poscharnigg 2013, Goessendorf, Austria, Europe

Translated by Dr Werner Poscharnigg

Edited by Sabine Winter, Canton, TX, and Richard F. Williams, Franktown, VA

Author's photo by Christa Kainz

All rights reserved. No part of this work may be reproduced or transmitted in any form or by any means, electronic or mechanical, including photocopying, or by any information storage or retrieval system except by written permission from the publisher.

Published by Xenophon Press LLC
7518 Bayside Road, Franktown, Virginia 23354-2106, USA
XenophonPress@gmail.com
1/757.414.0393

ISBN: 9780933316645

e-book ISBN: 9780933316744

I owe thanks to the following: Heinrich A. Gawlik, Christa Kainz, First Chief Rider Klaus Krzisch, Maria and Heinrich Lehrner, Sylvia Loch, Chief Rider Karl Mikolka, Walter Pirnath, Renate Prietl, Ulrike and Peter Weiss, Richard F. Williams, Sabine Winter, Günter Zeman, Heeresgeschichtliches Museum Vienna (HGM) who helped me form this book.

Dr. Werner Poscharnigg

Xenophon Press Library

Xenophon Press is dedicated to the preservation of classical equestrian literature. We bring both new and old works to English-speaking riders. Available at www.XenophonPress.com

30 Years with Master Nuno Oliveira, Henriquet 2011
A New Method to Dress Horses, Cavendish 2015
A Rider's Survival from Tyranny, de Kunffy 2012
Another Horsemanship, Racinet 1994
Art of the Lusitano, Yglesias de Oliveira 2012
Austrian Art of Riding, Poscharnigg 2015
Breaking and Riding, Fillis 2015
Baucher and His School, Decarpentry 2011
Dressage in the French Tradition, Diogo de Bragança 2011
Description of Modern Manège, D'Eisenberg 2015
École de Cavalerie Part II, Robichon de la Guérinière 1992, 2015
Equine Osteopathy: What the Horses Have Told Me, Giniaux 2014
François Baucher: The Man and His Method, Baucher/Nelson 2013
Great Horsewomen of the 19th Century in the Circus, Nelson 2015
Gymnastic Exercises for Horses Volume II, Russell 2013
H. Dv. 12 Cavalry Manual of Horsemanship, Reinhold 2014
Handbook of Jumping Essentials, Lemaire de Ruffieu 1997
Handbook of Riding Essentials, Lemaire de Ruffieu 2015
Healing Hands, Giniaux, DVM 1998
Horse Training: Outdoors and High School, Beudant 2014
Legacy of Master Nuno Oliveira, Millham 2013
Methodical Dressage of the Riding Horse, Faverot de Kerbrech 2010
Racinet Explains Baucher, Racinet 1997
Science and Art of Riding in Lightness, Stodulka 2015
The Art of Traditional Dressage, Volume I DVD, de Kunffy 2013
The Ethics and Passions of Dressage Expanded Ed., de Kunffy 2013
The Gymnasium of the Horse, Steinbrecht 2011
The Italian Tradition of Equestrian Art, Tomassini 2014
The Maneige Royal, de Pluvinel 2010, 2015
The Portuguese School of Equestrian Art, de Oliveira/da Costa 2012
The Spanish Riding School & Piaffe and Passage, Decarpentry 2013
To Amaze the People with Pleasure and Delight, Walker 2015
Total Horsemanship, Racinet 1999
Wisdom of Master Nuno Oliveira, de Coux 2012

CONTENTS

Foreword by Karl Mikolka iii
Foreword by Charles de Kunffy iv
Foreword by Sylvia Loch v
Introduction vii
Maximilian I and the end of heavy knightly cavalry 1
Equestrian art of Renaissance and Renaissance of equestrian art 6
Federico Grisone, godfather of equestrian art 20
Spanish-Neapolitan becomes Austrian 29
Giovanni Battista Galiberto and Vienna's first equestrian book 37
The classical era of Austrian equestrian art: Johann Christoph von Regenthal, Adam von Weyrother et al 51
Campaign-riding and Anglomania 89
Mechanistics and equestrian practice: Maximilian von Weyrother 100
Rider's spirit and exercise manual for the Austrian cavalry 111
Mathäus von Niedermaier and the vigour of high school 124
Sovereign riding: Francis Joseph I and Elisabeth 133
Cavalry and Spanish Riding School: Holbein and Meixner 137
Doom of the Austro-Hungarian cavalry 151
Final habitat of Austrian equestrian art: The Spanish Riding School 158
Hopeful retrospections: Koch, Josipovich and Dreyhausen 162
Alois Podhajsky: survived the barbary of war and new heyday 168
Austrian equestrian art: radiant source of identity 183
Summary: playful proof that riding is an art 187
Endnotes 197

Foreword by Karl Mikolka

Rarely in the conception of a book has such thorough research and commitment to historical accuracy provided a better understanding of the subject presented. Dr Werner Poscharnigg's Austrian Art of Riding not only leads the reader on an exciting journey through the Cultural History of Austria, but illuminates five centuries of equestrian advances. The Spanish Riding School in Vienna, the European cradle and sanctuary of classical riding since the Baroque era is masterfully documented in text and illustrations.

Poscharnigg manages to present the contents of the book in such a well-written, captivating manner that the reader is reluctant to put the book down. He harmoniously melds historical events with equestrian highlights of the Riding Masters of the past that would be otherwise forgotten.

Austrian Art of Riding acknowledges Austria's role in bringing equestrian art to the highest possible level preserving it for future generations. It is a tribute to man's centuries-long dependency on his partner, the horse during both peacetime and war.

The book is must for the professional horseman and for any student or aficionado of classical horsemanship and it is an honour for me to recommend this translation to the English speaking audience along with the original German version.

Gloucester, Massachusetts, August 8, 2014

Image 0 - Karl Mikolka and Neapolitano Strana, Levade, Spanish Riding School 1967. Courtesy of Karl Mikolka

Foreword by Charles de Kunffy

Austrian Art of Riding is a major contribution to the understanding of classical riding principles. His richly illustrated and elegantly written text traces the evolution of the classical riding tradition. This tradition culminated in the safekeeping of the Austro-Hungarian equestrian institutions. There it thrived for over 300 years.

The principles of the Classical Riding Tradition developed by understanding gained from the experiences of thousands of riders through the centuries. They experimented with various schooling methods and, what survived as worthy was passed on to those of us devoted to the well-being of horses. The training and taming principles were those that worked well for most horses most of the time. The classical principles we inherited are pragmatic. To survive, training methods had to be horse-friendly and promote the well-being of the horse, thereby extending his serviceable years.

The Austro-Hungarian riding institutions were among the surviving "temples" that carried on the civilized equestrian culture that represented the best in the relationship between horses and their riders. The best practitioners of this ancient art could be likened to a "priesthood" of those who understood the values of classical riding principles and remained dedicated to their promotion.

Dr. Poscharnigg eloquently exposes many important principles of classical riding and training methods in his richly illustrated text. The taming of the horse elevates the rider's character. Important human virtues are internalized by daily contact with horses and by riding experiences. Acceptable exercises used in daily training must be rehabilitative, therapeutic and only ultimately gymnastic to unfold and maximize the horse's inborn potential.

To increase the horse's weight bearing on his haunches results in collection and preserves the forehand. Through appropriate exercises, the rider can increase the horse's strength and multiply his skills, enabling amplification of his gaits. The correctly trained horse moves with maximum efficiency with minimal effort, preventing exhaustion. Horses that submit the energy of their haunches to the rider show engagement. A classically trained rider will induce and guide his horse's tranquillity of mind while inspiring physical activity. A horse whose trust is cultivated remains tranquil in mind, even during spectacular physical performances. A supple horse in elastic motion with seamless energy carries his rider with ease and elegance born of harmony.

The Austro-Hungarian custodial trust in classical training methods continues. It is without fear of force, artifice and cruelty. Instead, it is a monument to impeccable trust between horse and rider. The result is harmonious interaction—both in mind and body—between horse and rider. The horse ennobled by becoming able to move better than he ever could have had he been left alone in nature. And the rider is elevated in character, his virtues multiplied and his spirit illuminated.

Palm Springs, California, November 18, 2014

Foreword by Sylvia Loch

Dr Werner Poscharnigg has written a very important book. It fills in the missing links of so much of our understanding as to how the equestrian art evolved in Europe and how it inspired not only those great horsemen of the past, but also the riders of today and tomorrow. When I first set foot in Vienna, it was not difficult to understand how this extraordinarily beautiful and grand city had become the cradle of equitation for the civilised world. All around, the influence of the Classical and Baroque eras dominate the great squares, avenues and architecture—but it goes much further than this.

Gazing up at the lofty equestrian statues, proudly etched against the clearest of skies, one is overcome with a sense of awe and wonder. Endeavour is the word that springs to mind. It is embedded in each block of granite, each turn of the sculptor's hand, each silhouette, each spire—so much that you know, deep in your heart that this was where art and equestrianism combined to give us what we understand today.

To train horses, to observe their behaviour and to appreciate the principles of equitation one cannot dismiss their history. For me, a young rider, in love with the idea of the white stallions long before I met them, who later watched the famous Spanish Riding School of Vienna either on film or at their performances in England, there was always a desire to know more. It required a leap of faith to board a plane and fly to Austria to see how it had all evolved.

As so often in life, especially in history—the formation of the School came down to a stroke of good luck. Was it chance, or divine intervention that led to two great dynasties—that of the Spanish and the Habsburg royal families coming together through marriage to combine their vast empires and their cavalry so many centuries before? Whatever the influence, it was Emperor Charles V of Austria who, in 1516 succeeded to the Spanish crown to become all at the same time King D. Carlos I of Spain. Through the influence of his Spanish mother and his success in the field of battle, he prized the horses of the Iberian Peninsula above all. He was not the first to fill his empire with them and, happily for us, that legacy lives on.

These hot-bloods had already infiltrated the royal courts of Europe, largely due to their importation from Naples—another Spanish outpost—as their courage in the face of danger and their manoeuvrability in combat was legendary. Far away in Brunswick, the court equerry Von Lohneysen wrote in 1588 'the Spanish [horses] are the most intelligent, the most likeable and the gentlest.' In England, it was the Royalist, Duke of Newcastle, who developed so many of the High School exercises that would '...settle the horse mightily upon the hand, make him light in front and put him on his haunches which are all useful, especially for a man in armour.'

So what of that heritage now? The Spanish Riding School of Vienna is literally the last bastion of this unique culture in the world today since the breeding of the Lipizzaner has remained largely intact despite the interruption and horrors of war and particularly those of the 20th century. Equally important, there still exists an unbroken method of raising and training these horses in keeping with the techniques and secrets of the Grand Masters of Equitation who lived and breathed their Art. The well-being of the horse is at the forefront of all training since it would be wasteful and harmful both to his limbs and psyche to rush or overburden.

It is all too easy for people to say that much of this work is irrelevant today and that dressage has moved on. Yet if you take the art out of dressage and turn it into just another sporting discipline, you lose the very essence that draws the crowds. Spell-bound and mesmerised by the sheer beauty of the work at Vienna, you do not have to be an expert to see what is good and noble, and what is right.

I often wonder if we returned to the principles laid down at The Spanish Riding School and those scores of academies that once filled the lands of Bohemia, Hungary, Burgundy, Alsace, Friesland, the Spanish Netherlands, where horses were ridden with the utmost care and precision and where strict guidelines prohibited any attempt to hurry the schooling, we might enjoy more interaction from the wider public. As Xenophon so famously wrote in the 4th Century BC 'Anything that is forced or misunderstood can never be beautiful....' and you do not necessarily have to be versed in the gymnastics of dressage to recognise this simple truth.

Dr Werner Poscharnigg's stunningly produced Austrian Art of Riding is special for many reasons, first, because many of us may not have had the pleasure of seeing many of the incredible illustrations before. They tell us so much about the guardians of the art of classical riding. They show a good balance in both man and horse in different situations and this inspires us, in turn, to try to replicate Nature as they have done. Out of them shines pride of achievement, commitment of endeavour and desire for perfection.

These milestones are important since they follow the great Masters and innovators of equestrian art through their journey which leads the riders of today to re-examine. Only then, may we come to the conclusion that the schooling of the horse is a fine and fragile thing. To do it well, we must discipline ourselves through study, observation and self-examination. Only through this humbling process, can we begin to understand and protect that extraordinary animal beneath us. Once we have taken this on, the results may be quite extraordinary. Who knows where it may lead?–but of one thing we can be sure: in the words of Colonel Handler – 'If training has not made a horse more beautiful, nobler in his carriage, more attentive in his behaviour, revealing pleasure in his own accomplishment with a twitching of his ears and a lively expression in his eyes, he may be been dressed, but he has not been schooled, in the classical sense of dressage.'

Eden Hall, Kelso, Scotland, January 25, 2015

INTRODUCTION

A voyage of discovery not undertaken so far

Sarajevo, June 28, 1914: The assassin had run into the street. From the distance of a few feet his second shot hit the Austrian heir to the throne, Franz Ferdinand, into the jugular vein and trachea. Much blood flowed. The murder triggered World War I.[1] Franz Ferdinand was not shot in the saddle but in an automobile. The Danube Monarchy's demise was to be parallel to the victory of motor vehicles, and with it – apart from some remainders – Austria's equestrian art which had decisively shaped the achievement of a cultural territory.

Austrian equestrian art – something distinctive, special and superb in its quality, as Sigmund von Josipovich describes: "Typical of the Austro-Hungarian equestrian style was always the horses' swinging, elastic gait and the rider's pliant, elegant seat in harmony with it. This was the Austro-Hungarian school, envied abroad. This was the school whose art, based purely on mechanism of gait, on correct placing of feet, putting the feel of swing above form, but choosing form individually. Moreover the typical feature of the riders' seat was not so much the outer conformity that convinced but the implicitness by which each rider could adapt to his horse's movement, thus encouraging the gait and expressing the uniformity of all Austro-Hungarian riders."[2]

Man becomes one with the horse, relaxed, unconstrained elegance of horse and rider according to an education preserving the horse's nature in spite of all artificiality. Such awareness of the originality in Austria's equestrian art reminds one of the assessment of the Vienna Philharmonic as Europe's best orchestra by a most prominent international music critique: "For music aficionados, Vienna is the most irresistible orchestra, the one that inspires a desire to give all. And it is not necessarily the most regular concerning quality. But there is nothing more beautiful in the world. And it is without comparison."[3]

Josipovich describes Austria's equestrian style as if it were one of natural horsemen. However, in the land of the Spanish Riding School, art had become second nature. Perhaps old Austria ascribed the same high role to equitation as the Mongolians or Mohammed's Arabs. Austrian equitation of yore has its roots in a great tradition from which it draws its strength.

It is rewarding to explore this long tradition. Where are the beginnings? What are the foundations? Will the secrets of this beautiful, easy, seemingly effortless and playful elegance be discovered? The journey is, as almost always in life, the reward. And we shall dwell on fascinating milestones, and in the process, notice that there are obstinate misconceptions in the commonly accepted history of European equitation. We are in for an exciting expedition. We will discover the essence of Austrian equestrian art by accessing written documents and images dating back nearly 500 years – some of them never published and difficult to access – with the goal of critically discerning and comparing their characteristics. This voyage of discovery has not been previously undertaken.

This book offers treasures of equestrian culture even for those not especially interested in Austria. It was for the international community who adore fine equitation that I selected carefully the best material without allowing scientific correctness to suffer.

I wish to inspire those who are on a quest for subtle, soulful, rich association with the horse in order to help them realize they are not alone in their passion.

Image 1- Official seal of the Imperial First Equerry. (Archive Lipizzanermuseum, Stallburg, Vienna)

MAXIMILIAN I AND THE END OF HEAVY KNIGHTLY CAVALRY

Alliance with Spain

In order to understand the fundamentals of Austrian equestrian tradition, we need not go further back than Maximilian I (1459-1519) crowned Holy Roman Emperor in 1508. He is commonly known as the "last knight and first cannoneer," thus ruling at a time of transition in military techniques and equestrian approach. His sophisticated marriage policy finally led to the fact that today's Viennese riding school bears the name "The Spanish Riding School." Spanish equitation constitutes the foundation of everything that occurred in Austrian equestrian art substantially more than in other European countries. Anybody can recognize the Lipizzaner as an Iberian horse.

In 1495, Charles VIII of France conquered Naples. Maximilian reacted by founding a "Holy League." King Ferdinand II of Aragon was a member of this league. Maximilian married his daughter, Margarete to Ferdinand's son, the heir of Aragon and Castile. Maximilian's son, Philipp espoused Ferdinand's daughter, Joanna the Mad. With such an alliance, France faced an awkward position from the East and South. The onset of French-Habsburg differences shaped politics and consequently, equitation for the next two and a half centuries.[4]

"Bella gerant alii, tu felix Austria nube. Nam quae Mars aliis, dat tibi regna Venus."

Others may make war, you, happy Austria, marry. For kingdoms that Mars gives others, Venus bestows on you.

Because of such strategy, strikingly drafted by an anonymous writer, Maximilian's grandson, Charles V, became ruler of a realm "where the sun never set." Since 1442, King Alfonso V of Aragon ruled over a territory, later called Kingdom of the Two Sicilies, namely Naples and Sicily. Charles VIII of France ruled Naples only from February to July 1495. Then Ferdinand II of Aragon, the Catholic, reclaimed his heritage. With his army, a new style of cavalry evolved and Naples became the Mecca of European equitation with many

Image 2 - Tournament, Hofburg, Vienna 1565. (Private archive.)

noteworthy pilgrims. Like Sicily, Naples became a country associated with the Spanish crown, a part of Spain nearer to Vienna.

Theuerdank's Tournament Realm

Maximilian I closed himself to the new strategy of war; for in his heart he stayed true to the heavily armoured knighthood and its culture, a dreamer of middle-age phantasies. What then was taxpayer's woe is now art lover's joy. Maximilian not only incurred debts for military enterprises and a most pompous lifestyle but also acted as a great patron of celebrities of humanism and renaissance, of literature and sciences. He initiated several poetic works that he wrote in collaboration with other authors and had them illustrated by artists with xylographs, such as the "Theuerdank" (who directs his thoughts to the high) and the "Weisskuning," relating Maximilian's deeds. The "Freydal" was intended to describe the emperor's tournaments but remained a fragment. All of this, and much more, was financed by the "house banker," Jakob Fugger.

The emperor gathered the best intellectuals and artists of his time around him, such as Albrecht Dürer, whom he granted an annual pension of 100 guilders. In return, contributions concerning Maximilian's immortality were expected. In Georg Rüxner's "Thurnier Buch" (Frkft., Feyerabend and Hüter, 1566) a woodcut from 1565 by Jost Amman depicts in a nutshell the old world of knightly tournaments under the emperor's auspices at the Viennese court: We look into a bailey with a massive fence able to withstand the impact of even the mightiest equine chargers. Width: Only about ten horse's lengths! This means the steeds had to strike off at the canter, preferably from a standstill, in order to gain momentum that destroyed the adversary, a considerable performance of power and education. These horses needed both mass and mettle. An aggressive trait was probably an important aim of breeding, comparable to fighting bulls. The well-tempered, cold-blooded heavy horse was out of place here, as can be noticed from a battling group in the centre where not only knights and squires fight with swords and maces, but also the stallions, incited by the atmosphere, attack each other of their own volition.

Doubtlessly veterinaries and surgeons were in demand after the show. Even though the knights wore sophisticated bandages and paddings under their armour, their assistants fought without armour or helmets, thus leaving them more exposed to injury. Socially disadvantaged persons were worse off, an ageless fact. It was necessary to train the stallions in a way that they cantered selflessly against their opponents on a straight line despite several clashes a day. As can be seen, helpers, both mounted and afoot supported keeping the line straight. A horse that turned back was deemed a disgrace. In order to conceal the danger, horses were blinded by head armour with various bells near the ears masking the opponents' noises. A knight's honour and life depended on his charger's dressage, vigour, and reliability. Luxury prices were paid for top quality. Breeding, training, and maintenance were according to rigorous criteria.

Imagine the bailey in this woodcut filled with tremendous, reverberating noise from drummers and trumpeters, rattling armours, the crack of breaking lances, caws of the wounded, pounding and bawling stallions, and the screams and cheers the audience emitted. Just behind the fence "groundlings" gather in droves, while noble men and women crowded balconies and windows. To the right, a knight rides on the fence, his helmet on the ground. For "who was convicted of lie, breach of promise, extortion, or marriage below his class got bashed not only by the knights but also by the servants until he paid ransom by giving away his stallion. Then he was placed on the tournament's fence and had to stay there during the entire fight under the most excessive derision."[5]

From the central loge – in company of dames décolletées and court jester – obviously the emperor himself, hands the knights their lances which usually were approximately twelve feet long. To facilitate directing such poles effortlessly at the opponent, supportive hooks were attached to the armour. There were also lances with tridents, suitable for pushing the adversary out of the saddle or throwing the helmet from his head. Those who speared the falling helmet received extra admiration. Even today, the Gardians, the cowboys of the Camargue, use the trident skilfully to bring fighting bulls to the ground. Moreover, the Gardians' saddles and riding manners remind one of the age of chivalry.

The knight who lay in the sand was defeated. If both riders fell, they continued combat afoot using the dull sword. To miss the opponent with the lance was considered a great disgrace. An even worse disgrace was to injure his horse. Usually both lances broke if the riders were not thrown out of their saddles. Only after all lances were broken, did the knights resort to their swords. During less noble tournaments, a bad custom developed: Servants armed with iron-studded clubs seized the adversary's reins in order to stop him. Then, he was regarded as caught and had to pay ransom.

Ladies' Abundant Show of Appreciation

The tournament's winner received "thanks" in the form of a wreath, ring, falcon, or kisses "from a number of more or less desirable ladies."[6] Winning became even sweeter because the loser had to pay a ransom for his charger, its equipment, and his own armour. Only very rich organizers of tournaments agreed to pay the ransom for the prisoners. Professional jousters who had become skilful in the use of their steeds and arms, almost always winning, proved especially unpleasant for the defeated. Their terms of combat were often aimed at ruthlessly maximizing profits. Ladies' helpful hands cared for the bruises and the beaten limbs of the winners, and assisted in washing away sweat, dust, and armour rust. Often the winner could not join the coveted evening dance because he needed medical attention.

Taking part in jousts and the involved pomposity placed a massive financial burden on the participants and their subjects. In addition to accommodation expenses, came the armour, the manufacture of which was considered high technology. Purchasing or breeding chargers cost a pretty penny, and turning a foal into a charger took much work.

Flaunting Light Parade Horses

Furthermore the knight needed splendid, highly trained parade horses to carry him through festive occasions in the appropriate manner. At that time, such a horse was less costly. Different from the charger, the parade horse had beautiful conformation and light, elegant gaits were a must. "The most desired gait for these horses was a short, highly elevated canter with deeply bent hocks, the parade canter. The shorter the bounds, the more perfect the gait was considered. A horse capable of such a parade canter, had to be thoroughly ridden.[7] This parade canter was likely what was later called "mézair", a sort of half courbette, a "moitié air," or half school, where the horse rises more than in the terre-à-terre, but not as high as in a courbette.

Maximilian's Triumphal Procession

In comparison to the heavy charger, the lighter type of parade horse was apt for the new, more manoeuvrable warfare. It is depicted in a work Maximilian I commissioned. The

Image 3 - Albrecht Altdorfer, Detail from the Triumphal Procession for Maximilian I. (Private archive.)

Triumphal Procession, a series of 147 woodcuts to which major artists such as Albrecht Dürer and Albrecht Altdorfer (1480-1535) contributed. The emperor's idea never really took hold and went to print only in the following centuries.[8] Altdorfer's page shown here was only reproduced in the 19th century, as the paper shows. Parts of the wooden block had warped in the course of time. Horses and riders were resplendent in the emperor's honour. The horses – not exactly beauties – are of a tenacious, mobile, tough sort with high action and an obvious desire to move forward with hard hooves, strong joints, fine heads. The reins show slight slack, though long-levered curb bits guarantee effect if required. Two horses wear chain reins, something an enemy could not sever easily. The riders proudly present their banners, cherishing the age of knighthood, but they and their light stallions herald a new age.

EQUESTRIAN ART OF THE RENAISSANCE AND THE RENAISSANCE OF EQUESTRIAN ART

The Rider as a Monument

Riding as a display and to represent is a by-product of martial equitation. Consequently, equestrian training constituted "a main subject in the education of the Middle Age's noble youth. Both boys and girls were soon trained in the fine art of equitation, for the brave man had to stay in the saddle firmly and know how to handle a horse. Thence every knight was also a true horseman." [9]

To become an elegant rider was a necessary part of general education for all political leaders until World War I (1914-18) and longer. Emperors, kings, heir-apparents etc. who cut a poor figure in the saddle were regarded as regrettable aberrations from the ideal. For he or she who could not control a horse without effort, was suspected of not being able to rule his country. Thus the great many equestrian statues worldwide signal, "I have my stallion under control, consequently the situation in general is under control, my enemies as well as my subjects." The ruler's pose turned out more or less presumptuous, depending on era, artist, and commissioner. Even in the 21st century North Korean dictators are presented triumphantly to their hungry people in larger-than-life bronze equestrian sculptures.

The Natural Grandeur of Marcus Aurelius

No equestrian statue can match the natural, ceremonious nature of Marcus Aurelius. In the year 165 AD, an artist created a bronze statue of this Roman emperor whose gesture emanates grandeur from within. It breathes the spirit of Marcus Aurelius' "Meditations," where he sees himself as a man and soldier on his post, always recallable by life.[10] Hence this matchless imperial lack of constraint. All imitations of this statue for other rulers appear wooden, posed, and cramped in comparison to the original and cannot reach its elegance. Today we would call the horse an Iberian, Neapolitan, or Lipizzaner. By the way: The Renaissance (about 1400-1600) encouraged the study of original sources. And so a

Image 4 - Marcus Aurelius, Statue Tulln. (Photo Poscharnigg.)

scholar of the Vatican found out that this statue did not depict Constantine the Great, as had been believed for a long time, but instead, Marcus Aurelius.

Noble Lack of Constraint

Such was the quality Baldesar Castiglione (1478-1529) called "sprezzatura" in his epoch-making "Libro del Cortegiano" (1528), i.e. the indispensable necessity for the nobleman to handle things gracefully, to do the cumbersome apparently without effort, just as befits a rider of rank. Here, we investigate the deep roots of the Austrian equestrian style, as described by Josipovich, and its natural elegance. Castiglione postulates the universally educated, active personality of the Renaissance: Grace, balance, spirit, and art are cornerstones in this idea of humanity.[11] The "Cortegiano" influenced the equestrian academies of

Naples and Italy. Its translation was an international standard work for the modern nobility. A central skill was optimum equitation, as Castiglione stated, "So I wish our courtier to be an accomplished and versatile horseman and, as well as having a knowledge of horses and all matters to do with riding, he should put every effort and diligence into surpassing the rest by just a little in everything, so that he may always be recognized as superior."[12]

Riding As School of Character

Accepting the notion that Castiglione's ideal of the noble knight and cavalier deeply influenced Europe's courts, we understand why cultivated nations put so much effort towards equitation. At that time, the skill of riding was deemed much more desirable than reading and writing. Hence the proliferation of equestrian academies of Naples and their later affiliates in Austria, France, Germany, etc. Today, in the 21st century, we might be surprised about such eminent importance put on riding. Considering how riding and handling horses can build character, this development is completely understandable. At that time, gentlemen did not find it necessary to castrate their stallions. To ride a gelding or mare was considered unthinkable, unworthy, and even fainthearted.

Graceful Dexterity in the Saddle

Castiglione highly appreciates Italian equitation of his era:

> "Thus it is the peculiar excellence of the Italians to ride well with the rein, to handle spirited horses very skilfully, and to tilt and joust; so in all this, the courtier should compare with the best of them…But, above all, he should accompany his every act with a certain grace and fine judgement if he wishes to earn that universal regard which everyone covets…I think no less highly of performing on horseback, which is certainly very exhausting and difficult but more than anything else, serves to make a man wonderfully agile and dextrous; and apart from its usefulness, if agility on horseback is accompanied by gracefulness, in my opinion it makes a finer spectacle than any other sport."[13]

Castiglione's cavalier is a balanced Renaissance polymath, and Leon Battista Alberti (1404-72) was considered its incarnation. He worked as an important architect, mathematician, author, but did not consider his abilities in these fields higher than his equestrian skills,[14] unbelievable for the people of the 21st century. Castiglione, by the way, died as a papal nuncio in Toledo, a fact that emphasizes the connection of the Italian and Spanish spheres of culture in this context.

Cavaliers of the Golden Spur

Two facts constituted the final blow for heavily armoured knightly equitation: The invention of the pistol and the removal of the French from Naples by the Spanish. The French occupants and their brutality had not made them popular in Naples.[15] In 1496, the Spanish defeated the French under the leadership of general "Gran Capitán" Gonzalo Fernández de Córdoba y Aguilar. The French used heavy cavalry with sufficient vigour but little manoeuvrability. This disadvantage opened the gate for the Spanish "caballeria d'espuela dorada," or cavalry of the golden spur.[16]

The general nobility of Castile rode Andalusians, horses showing ideal manoeuvrability, intelligence, discipline, fast reaction, and intuitive response to the rider. They proved ideal in the fight against the Moors, were highly esteemed, carefully bred and trained, and moreover, were considered a military secret: In 1490, a law prohibited the sale of foals without mayoral consent. Even today, the Spanish Ministry of Defense administers the studbook.[17] The French called the Andalusian horses "genets d'Espagne." This comes from the Spanish jinete, rider, from jineta, the rider's short lance.[18] The Spanish riders rode a la jineta, with short stirrup leathers and wore only light armour, with a lance and a scimitar. "They used a Moorish curb bit with a stiff chain and one pair of reins."[19]

The Spanish Conquistadores also used such curb bits in America. They are called "ring-bits" because they sport a metal ring instead of a chain, with the mouthpiece having a kind of spoon-shape influencing the palate.[20] In poor riders' hands such bits can become brutal tools, whereas an expert handles his horse with the lightest contact. Even today, some riders in California cherish the Spanish-Mexican tradition of the vaqueros. There are competitions where the Spade or Chileno Bits are only tied to the reins by a few horsehairs. The winner is the one who rides with the fewest horse hairs.[21] Talking about tradition, Moorish bits have been used in North-Cameroon ever since the 18th century. In a fantasia, horses are stopped from a full gallop to a standstill with the flicker of the hand, resulting in bloody mouths,[22] due to the severe bits.

Compared to the knights' jousting-saddles, the jinetes had relatively low cantles. The rather short stirrup leathers allowed the rider to stand up and employ their sabres from a higher position, compensating for the smaller size of their Andalusian horses in comparison to their adversary's mightier chargers. The caballeros ("cavaliers") could attack their relatively inert opponents with lightning speed, could stop, throw their speedy genets around, gain a safe position, attack again, and escape the enemy skilfully in order to attack him again until the battle array became confused and the heavily armoured knights on their less manoeuvrable chargers ("coursiers") were defeated. Ever since, in Europe, the concept of "Spanish rider" has come to mean the acme of intelligent, efficient, artful, elegant, and

Image 5 -Moorish ring bit. Museo dos Coches, Lisbon. (Photo Poscharnigg.)

exemplary handling of the horse. What was Spanish and had to do with horses, received high respect for over 250 years, especially in Austria with her close relations to Spain. Hence terms like the Spanish Riding School and Spanish stable in Vienna, Spanish trot (passage) were coined; the Lipizza Stud bred "original Spaniards." Spanish riding masters trained the court; archdukes were taught equestrian art in Spain.

Lust to Kill and Sense of Art

Seen from a Darwinist point of view, the faster ones, using their equestrian intelligence, defeated the slower ones who stuck to bullish riding straight ahead. The Iberians had developed their martial skills on horseback in mounted bullfighting. While ordinary men fought bulls afoot, their masters faced them as riders to prove their bravery and virility with elegance and "sprezzatura." If they wanted to leave the arena alive, certain conditions had to be fulfilled. Imagine horse and rider enclosed in an arena with a 1,000-pound heavy, nervous fighting bull, separated from the idyll of his pasture, and now surrounded by a beastly, roaring crowd. With justified anger, he would attack the visible evil and chase the horse to the best of his ability.

The flight animal would do what nature commands, until the final breakdown. But man compelled the horse to a community of interests and schooled it in such a sophisticated way that it runs up to the wild bull, enabling the rejoneador, the mounted bullfighter, to place his banderillas (skewers) in the bull's neck. This takes the best of horses, most skilful training, extreme courage, and absolutely fast reaction, if one wishes to leave the arena alive.

Image 6 – Monogrammist, Rejoneo. (Private archive.)

However deeply one despises the mounted bull-massacring, and rightly so, the endeavour demands an equitation surpassing all others with its quality and speed. Human lust to kill and a high sense of art are closely intertwined in irritating and unpleasant ways. In 1991, Fernando Sommer D'Andrade codified the basic movements of mounted bullfighting. Even a casual glance at some sketches of the fighting technique shows that utmost equestrian skills are demanded.[23] Breathless silence fills the arena when the rejoneador requests the bull to attack. Horse and bull gallop at each other. But in the last moment, before the impact, the horse tightly avoids the bull, and riding past, the rejoneador places his banderilla in the poor bull's neck.

The art of mounted tauromachy takes years of training with many horses being sorted out because they cannot meet the physical and mental requirements. A good bullfight horse is the rejoneador's life insurance. Absolute discipline and immediate reaction to minimal aids of the rider also guarantee the horse returns to his stable without injury. In mounted tauromachy the antique myth of the centaur becomes reality, for with thorough training,

Image 7 - Pluvinel's Riding School for the King. (Private archive.)

horse and rider form a unity in front of the dangerous, strong, and fast opponent, the bull. The Spanish caballeros applied such refined equestrian techniques to the battlefield, thus defeating the heavily armoured knights' tactic of primitive confrontation aboard weighty chargers.

Nevertheless, medieval jousting still belonged to the standard education of noblemen. In his book "The Maneige Royal" of 1623 [Xenophon Press, 2010] Antoine de Pluvinel (1555-1620) instructs his king, Louis XIII of France, the exact right way of breaking the lance:

> "King: On which part of the body do you think / Is it best to break the lance? Pluvinel: The commonest place to break the lance on / is from the eyes to the left-hand shoulder / but it is best to hit the head."[24]

Other forms of traditional knightly combat are related to the king in detail, too. Perseverance and consciousness of tradition belong to the formative factors in equestrian history. So there is no other explanation that still by the end of the 17th century an English copper

Image 8 - Richard Blome, The Manag'd Horse. (Private archive.)

engraving by Richard Blome for the squire John Cutts depicts what "The Manag'd Horse" must perform: Apart from airs above the ground and ring jousting, we still see knightly combat with lance and sword. Such spirit of perseverance later on was to preserve the Lipizzaner breed and the continuity of the Spanish Riding School of Vienna.

Pistols and Spirals

The deadly shot for heavy armoured equitation came from the firearm. Armour hardly protected one from bullets and hence became useless or inconvenient. The rather heavy harquebuses proved apt for riders, especially when they alit and fired afoot, though shooting with long firearms was also practiced in the saddle. The handy pistol, suited much better for cavalry in Spanish style, was used since 1510, then still with matchlock. Equestrian literature commonly describes the pesade, the lifting of the horse's forehand or low, controlled rearing, protected the rider from the enemy's bullets that hit his poor horse instead. That may have held true in those times for it took a while until a shot actually dispatched.

From 1517 on, ignition occurred faster and safer by wheel lock. "The upcoming corps of cuirassiers was equipped with pistols in the 1540s. Pistols were first used on a larger scale in the battle of Mühlberg in 1547.[25] Usually the cavaliers rode up to the enemy, fired once or twice, and returned. This was called "caracolla" (in Spanish caracol means snail; in Italian caracollare is riding voltes), with the purpose to weaken the opponent's pikemen before attacking anew with rapier or lance. Pikemen were an inexpensive, efficient weapon against the cavalry that faced a wall of spears and had to break it up.

Image 9 – Pesade in battle, Heydebrand, op. cit.

Image 9a – Capriole in battle, Heydebrand, op. cit.

Finally, when in the course of the battle the arrays got into disorder, a well-trained dressage horse, perfectly manoeuvrable through chaos, was at least worth a kingdom. For he who fights has little time to control a crazy mount. Riding a volte, the cavalier tried to protect himself against the enemy from the side or back. With a half volte he could reach the opponent's left side or back. The fleeing enemy could be overtaken, and, after a half pirouette, attacked frontally. "Even the most difficult of all airs, the capriole, a jump where the horse strikes out horizontally with his hind legs, was applied to hurt a pursuer or his horse severely or to deter him."[26]

In mounted bullfight, manoeuvres are much more complicated and sophisticated than in High School. Nevertheless, High School is part of the mounted bullfight and therefore constitutes a branch of martial equitation, because not every bull acts in constant aggression. If he senses to be in a bad position, he starts waiting. The rejoneador, however, wants to provoke him, remind him there is still an enemy to deal with, and show off his skills in front of the audience. Piaffe and passage, canter in place, gallop terre à terre, and pesade suit this situation because, out of these airs, a sudden attack can be started. Caprioles or courbettes only take place when no immediate attack is on the agenda. During such manoeuvres, the bull can regain aggression.

In mounted combat, in which man fights against man, movements of High School indicate, "I have my stallion under absolute control, every inch of him. And I will control you, too, opponent! I am not afraid of you. I play with my horse in your presence." This is virile ostentation, testing the limits, intimidation before the actual confrontation, High School as part of psychological warfare and self-expression, Combat as an aesthetic adventure, Romanticism leading to death or disability.

"The Neapolitan, Pasqual Caraccioli became founder of the High School, and probably the cavorting of military horses was called 'caraccoling' after his own name," Heydebrand speculates.[27] More obviously this means the playful spectacle of equitation during the "caracolla": After having fired their pistols, the riders show off their skills in High School during the preliminary retreat with noble "sprezzatura."

Equestrian Art and Intimidation

During the conquest of Mexico Hernán Cortés intelligently applied such ostentation of martial riding skills in order to avoid battles with potentially heavy losses, by demonstrating for the Indios (who had great fear of horses to begin with) his cavalry's skills: "So that they could report to their lord of our warriors' way of combat. I paraded all of my cavaliers in a large place and let them race, fence, and joust."[28]

In his novella, "The Gold of Caxamalca" (1923), Jakob Wassermann (1873-1934) narrated how conquistador Francisco Pizarro took possession of the Peruvian realm of the Inca's by shrewdness and impertinence, but also by equestrian ostentation: "We did not dismount because we felt safer and instilled in the Peruvians more fear from the saddle, as was our experience. So, De Soto realized that the Inca attentively watched the spirited animal on which he sat that chewed the bit restlessly. De Soto had always been vain with respect to his riding skill; he was keen on showing off. He thought this would intimidate the opposing ruler. He let the reins fly, spurred his horse and galloped over the paved place. Then he threw himself around and stopped from full speed gallop, setting his horse almost on his hocks so near to the Inca, that some of the foam covering the horse's nostrils sprayed onto the kingly attire. The trabants and courtiers were so affected by the never-here-to-fore-seen spectacle that they spread their arms involuntarily retreating in fright at the boisterous approach of the animal. Atahualpa himself remained quiet and calm as before."[29]

Such kind of equitation not only impressed the Indios, but also the Europeans. Spanish riders generally were considered the model of modern mounted warfare, and with them, the Spanish Andalusian horse was best suited for this new kind of riding. The European nobility of the 16th century was eager to adopt this novel equestrian art in perfection.

Boomtown of the Spanish-Habsburg World Empire

Most young cavaliers were not sent to Spain, but instead to Naples. This region had a strong attraction, being in intensive economic relation to Spain and developed into a radiant centre of the Italian Renaissance. Certainly, one of the important goods in demand was Spanish horses which were bred to heavier local stock, from them, developed the most influential Neapolitan horse. Even today one of the Lipizzaners' stallion lines bears the name "Neapolitano." In today's Italy the Neapolitan horse is unfortunately almost completely extinct.

In 1550 AD, Naples was Italy's largest metropolis and – after Paris – the second largest city in Europe. The population had grown from 40,000 inhabitants in 1450 AD, to over 200,000, and a boomtown of the Spanish-Habsburg world empire. Viceroy Pedro Àlvarez de Toledo thus had a new quarter of the town built in chequered design, the *quartieri spagnoli*.[30] Geometry was viewed as an array of life, an idea that had not been implemented since Roman antiquity. A city with such a dynamic evokes intellectual life. During the following centuries, the equestrian art of Austria became rooted in Naples, more so and differently than was the case with other nations.

Hippologic treatises concerned with the history of equitation are haunted with chimerical "art-riders" said to have come from Egypt to Constantinople: "Decisive for the Renaissance of equestrian art were so-called 'art-riders' of the East-Roman empire. With the fall of the city of Constantinople in 1453 AD Byzantine artists mainly fled to Naples. As early as 532 AD, art-riders settled in Naples' after Belisar, general under the East-Roman emperor Justinian I, conquered the city. By 1134 AD, an equestrian school was founded in Naples."[31] Good ideas in need of scientific proof.

Barb horses, though, imported to this day to Malta, Sicily, and Campania, were suited for the equestrian art of the era. During the Reconquista (718-1492), the Spaniards made sufficient acquaintance with mounted equestrian martial art of Arabian-Moorish origin, and adopted the techniques successfully for warfare.

Image 10 – R. Dalton, Arab rider. (Private archive.)

R. Dalton's etching shows Islamic riders in combat, galloping at their target at full speed, abruptly stopping to throw the lance, throwing the horse around before galloping away. If we replaced the Arabian in this picture with a Spaniard, there would be little difference. The type of horse is what we call today, "baroque"; the stirrups, the curb bit, the saddle appear unmistakably Spanish. This equestrian technique corresponded to Renaissance equitation. Such manner of warfare, though, was brought to Italy by the Spanish.

Equestrian Art in the Concert with Sciences

In order to train combat with spears, there was the "juego de canas," where two riders tried to hit each other with blunt, light spears.

> "The challenge was to avoid the thrown spear. Whoever got hit was defeated. But the utmost efficiency was proven by the rider who succeeded in getting hold of the thrown spear in flight by hand. Such a game required both highly trained, fast, agile horses, and especially skilled riders. By training their horses in the High School, the Spaniards achieved such dexterity that their reputation as eminent riders spread all over the world." [32]

Thus the highly respected art of riding in Iberian style could compete in concert with the other sciences in Naples.

Prominent intellectuals of the era who came from Naples included: The poets Jacopo Sannazaro, Pietro Summonte, Giambattista Marino, and Laura Terracina; the architect Pirro Ligorio; the alchemist and writer Giambattista della Porta; the philosopher Giordano Bruno; the mathematician Luca Valerio. The energetic field of intellectual prowess, economic power and demographic explosion made Naples a most desirable destination for young people eager to widen their horizons. They came from all over Europe to get educated without being deterred by the severe eye of inquisition. Inspired by the renaissance in classical studies, the humanist Antonio Beccadelli founded the first academy of modern age already in 1433 AD. Later, it was called "Academia Pontaniana" because of the engagement of Giovanni Pontano (1426-1503).

Knightly Academies and Character Building

"… a different kind of High School claimed the status of an academy, as well. It was the 'High School' of equestrian art prevalent in Italy that not only offered equestrian training but also knightly education…The academy of knights is always a place for the knightly art of riding. It is also always an institution for education, reserved for young men of knightly rank, very often equipped with professors and courses in university style. The academy of knights is not a society, but sometimes sports the appearance of a Platonic academy or even an academy of sciences…As means of communication in cultural civilization, academies for knights can be found similarly in several European countries."[33]

Such academies trained their students in an array of sciences that were considered decent and useful. But since war was omnipresent in Europe at that time and returned again and again, things had to be taught which have their place in military academies today. Concerning equitation, the focus was on training mounts apt for war and willing to face any danger. The obedience had to be absolute. It took highly trained riders who obviously had their horses under control, and who also fought victoriously or at the very least returned from battle alive. The use of diverse weapons was trained intensively to aim for virtuosity in their use.

In conjunction with this remained the artistic element of High-School movements, partly for immediate use in mounted combat, but also for virile, romantic ostentation to intimidate the opponent and to represent the ego. Of additional importance was to show off these skills in front of audiences and subjects. The character-building component should not be forgotten: To learn how to educate young stallions, ride them, carry out difficult airs on trained mounts, is a challenge not to be underestimated. It demands courage, reaction without delay, skill, correct and rapid assessment of the situation, modesty toward nature, and knowledge of one's own abilities.

Perhaps parents who sent young nobles to the vibrating metropolis Naples thought as Winston Churchill expressed in his autobiography "My Early Life" of 1930:

"Don't give your son money. As far as you can afford it, give him horses. No one ever came to grief - except honourable grief - through riding horses. No hour of life is lost

Image 11 – Eugène de la Croix, Mounted battle. (Private archive.)

that is spent in the saddle. Young men have often been ruined through owning horses, or through backing horses, but never through riding them unless of course they break their necks, which, taken at a gallop, is a very good death to die."[34]

FEDERICO GRISONE, GODFATHER OF EQUESTRIAN ART

Humanism without Humanity?

The attractiveness and quality of the Neapolitan academies must have been extraordinary. Why else would Antoine de Pluvinel have studied there for years, if he were later to become riding master and adviser of the French king? For six years, Pluvinel studied under Giovanni Pignatelli, who had founded Naples' first academy of knights in 1532, reportedly together with Federico Grisone (also Federigo Griso).[35] Grisone's mentor was "Colas Pagano, son of the Neapolitan king's riding master."[36] Such connection with the equestrian art at the Spanish viceroy's court certainly would have promoted Grisone's popularity and prestige. The "unforgettable, most famous cavalier Nicola Pagano" was an idol for him.[37]

However, Grisone is notorious as founder of the "school of violence,"[38] because his book "Gli ordini di cavalcare" (Naples 1551) sports instructions of cruelty which appal any civilized person of the 21st century. It seems to be humanism without humanity toward the horse. The translation by Johann Fayser into German, published in Augsburg in 1570 AD, offers pretty depictions when compared to the Italian original. Grisone advises to nip any resistance in the bud immediately by means of most brutal methods. He is unforgiving in the choice of the means: If the almost completely green horse does not move to a desired spot it gets whipped everywhere, only the eyes are avoided. Hollering is a standard measure. Unwillingness to go ahead is punished by lurking men with

Image 12 - Federico Grisone, Gli ordini di cavalcare. (Private archive.)

Image 13 – Stefano Della Bella, Miniatures. (Private archive.)

sticks, throwing stones, or using a wild cat tied to a pole, or a hedgehog tied to the tail. Horses that throw themselves to the ground in desperation or contumacy are motivated to get up by burning objects.

To Grisone's credit, it should not be forgotten that he prefers equestrian solutions to these problems. Permanent spur attacks are sanctioned in response to aggression toward other horses or unwillingness to turn. The horse, for fear of more punishment, is to bleed and feel pain in order to work willingly the next day. But as soon as the horse surrenders, he gets caressed. Repeatedly, Grisone disapproves of beating the horses too much.

In order to learn such horse torture, the European aristocracy's elite would not have had to go as far as Naples, and because of it there would not have been unauthorized copies and several translations into European languages. Michel Henriquet asks in desperation how such a setback of humanitarianism could have happened in an era of brilliant literature, antique studies, refinement of arts, and how Xenophon's legacy could have been forgotten.[39] What was it that made Grisone the godfather of European equitation in the centuries to come?

Treasury of Equestrian Knowledge

Those not specifically looking for animal abuse in Grisone's book will find a treasure trove of equestrian knowledge. No author before could hold a candle to Grisone when it came to concrete advice for artistic and martial riding, and in relatively systematic manner. This is Grisone's humanistic-scientific achievement. It is unlikely that any rider in today's world could carry out the wealth of knowledge that Grisone taught.

The most important equestrian authors in Europe before Grisone were: The famous Greek, Xenophon (ca. 426-355 BC): "On Horsemanship," "Hipparchikos." Rusius: "Hippiatrica sive Marescalia" (ca. 1300 AD), published in Rome 186 years later. The Portuguese Mestre Giraldo: "Arte de Alveitaria" (1381 AD) The Portuguese king Dom Duarte: "Livro de ensinanca de bem cavalgar," manuscript (1434 AD).[40]

The impact of the above authors on European equitation in the so-called modern age was minimal in contrast to Grisone's influence. Regrettable and somehow embarrassing that almost 2000 years after Xenophon, who demanded sensitive handling of horses, just a brutalist opened new doors for European equitation, paving the way from riding to equestrian art.

Image 14 – Stefano Della Bella, Miniatures. (Private archive.)

In apology to Grisone, social interactions among humans were anything but humane, as anyone can observe in museum paintings of that period. Therefore, we cannot expect horses to have received better treatment than their masters granted each other. Although a good horse certainly counted more than a simple man. Moreover, war horses had to be absolutely obedient to carry their masters home victoriously and unwounded. To achieve this, any means were fair. Some of today's so-called "sport horses" are hardly less tortured. And today it is not about survival, but ridiculous vanities such as winning shows or getting prize money. Therefore the poor creature has to bear mean spurs, bits, "auxiliary" reins, rollkur ("low, deep, and round"), electric shocks, poling, fencing, nailed tendon boots et al. And not even Grisone would have come up with the idea of placing thumbtacks in gloves to sting the withers, which is thought to bring nicer passages. Horse torture of the 21st century is only passed on orally and is executed in secret.

Presenting the Knighthood a Well-Schooled Horse

Federico Grisone offered a comprehensive approach that combined science and practicality. At his academy and in his book the new equestrian art for modern warfare and ostentation could be learned. He describes the final product of his training: "How a well-schooled horse coming from training ought to be shown and ridden for the knighthood."[41] "Knighthood" for Grisone represented princes, kings, emperors. Clearly he trained both horse and rider for the utmost high demands. He carefully considers from which side the "princes" should watch the rider in order to gain the highest prestige.

> "Therefore every diligence and art is to be applied to present the horse's virtues when cavorting in a skilful and laudable manner. So commence at a trot, with the whip pointing toward the right shoulder…And when you reach the end of the track, lower the whip, take a half volte to the right and hesitate awhile. Then ride a horse's length and speed past the princes on the racetrack…When you have come to the end and you stop as expected, take the right lead after the pesade."[42]

Image 15 – Stefano Della Bella, Miniatures. (Private archive.)

Keeping the Horse in a Good Spirit

Thus the rider exercises his horse in front of the princes rapidly and with virtuosity on the repellon, a riding track. After this, he stops. "And if the horse were strong, he could do this six times."[43] This can be followed immediately by a redopped volte, in conjunction with a capriole or courbette, and again exercising at a redopp in the repellons. Grisone considers this only apt for horses of "utmost strength;" "all their movement should appear light and slight, apt for right use in warfare, where to all these instructions are meant and useful." The horse must show "more courage and power than is in him." Riding in front of the princes is also to display how to act in wars and battles, how to attack the enemy with the lance, and to make use of the sword. "Finally obey my rule: Whenever you ride the horse, leave him in good spirit, so that he does not finally become gruff when you want to use him, but he should stay in the same constant willingness."[44]

The Sensible Rider

Grisone recognizes his historic mission: "Therefore I do not doubt, that when my report is read with diligence and judgement, perfection in this art (equitation) can be achieved, more than ever."[45] He proceeds systematically and presents a general "Argumentum" before each "book."

In the first chapter the author describes horses' temperaments, colours, and characters systematically and in depth. Moreover he describes the assessment of age by the teeth, then principles of breeding, keeping of foals, feeding, grooming, which he wants to control completely so that the personnel do not spoil horses with carelessness or violence.

The second "book" deals with breaking the colt and training him on the track, called "ring-riding." If the colt resists, he gets severely punished. From the beginning the rider drives him into a trot or gallop on a circle, again with abundant use of the crop. Cavesson and curb bit are used, but no stirrups for the time being. As far as the seat is concerned, Grisone teaches stretched legs as if the rider were standing on the ground.[46] The author considers the trot to be the most important gait in training. He works the horse predominantly on a figure eight, consisting of two circles of about 35 metres (115 feet) in a field, increasing the demands, and finally also includes voltes. The training to condition the horse takes time and effort to bend and school him. Finally the cavesson is taken off and "auxiliary" reins are attached to the curb bit. Grisone prefers the use of spurs sooner rather than later, so that the horse cannot develop any habit of resistance.

Image 16 – Stefano Della Bella, Miniatures. (Private archive.)

Releasing the Aids

Bringing the horse to a full stop is developed by repetitive backing and halting, ending with a pesade, in order to make the forehand light and to impress. When the horse offers the pesade well, Grisone commences to make the haunches light, developing the capriole, which he considers only apt for sufficiently strong horses. He insists the rider spur and hit the croup until the horse understands: "And as I said repeatedly, do not forget to stop hitting and caress the horse immediately as soon as he does what you want."[47]

From the pesade, he develops a half volte with rhythmically exact jumps, which is later expanded to a complete volte. This takes place, among most things, on the *repellon*, a straight line at the ends of which he turns his horse, goes back, and turns again. Advanced horses can ride *repellons* in serpentines. For all of these exercises, Grisone offers elaborate, practical instructions, more educational and applicable than many authors after him. Again and again, he admonishes not to strain the horse, and to carry out the training in a consistent, methodical manner. Grisone's scholar must not be a beginner, but instead must have his body under complete control and possess a secure seat. After the implementation of voltes, the author proposes to ride pesades and caprioles on the *repellon*. When riding on the curb only, he demands a light, certainly not too firm, contact on the bit and emphasizes the calm position of the horse's head.

He definitely refuses sagging, dangling reins, but warns against tolerating the horse pulling on the rider's hand. Grisone devotes his third book to the *redopp*, although he deals with other matters, such as subtle spurring. His principle is to cease aiding the horse, or to release the aid, when the horse carries out the required action. In the 18th century Guérinière will call this *"descente de main."* Following his mentor Nicola Pagano, Grisone recommends gallop and canter only after training at the trot for at least 6-12 months.

Hephep! Ola Ola, Haha!

Grisone offers a special chapter for voice aids, probably more profound than any other before or after him. So "hephep!" is for encouraging and pesade, clicks of the tongue are for making the horse attentive. Every spoken word must come in the same cadence, lest the horse could be confused, because the rider's voice is a strong orientation for him. "Ola, Ola, haha, Dreyditor, Haribaldo!" is to be hollered in a terrifying voice when the horse commits an "error," with the voice pitched higher or lower, depending on the offense. As soon as the horse has been "won" again, he should be patted and caressed, using a smooth, soft voice. For any sort of training, special words and pitches of voice could be used, such as "eia, eia" or "uia, uia" or smacking the lips.

> "In all this you may use good common sense, so that you can choose or use from these proposed ways and lessons that seem to you most apt and best for your situation."[48]

This advice already sounds much like the "thinking rider" of later times.

Grisone strongly warns to refrain from excessive demands that harm the horse, especially in his early years. He develops the redopp from pesades in a tight volte, slowly first, then faster, until the redopped voltes work on both hands. "If you want to show something new and beautiful with your horse, also his grandeur and skill, it appears better trained and admirable."[49]

Image 17 – Stefano Della Bella, Miniatures. (Private archive.)

Not a Prophet of Torture Bits

The fourth book deals with bits.[50] Even the young, green horse is ridden with a curb bit, even though made more appealing with honey and salt. In cases of resistance Grisone recommends more severe models, "provided that a sufficiently intelligent rider knows how use and handle them effectively."[51] This caveat does not let him appear as the reckless prophet of torture bits for which many people have accused Grisone. Certain bits even Grisone considers too severe. "But I admonish that you avoid them because of their brute force."[52] And at the end of the "book" he insistently warns about severe bits, "Thus the poor creature is completely wounded,"[53] gets mad, and cannot recognize the rider's will any longer.

The fifth book is about horses' "vices and bad habits."[54] Again, Grisone advises in detail against the abuse of severe bits, chin rings and chains. "By the way I also admonish you, as so often, to maintain the hand in a beautiful and calm manner…according to the nature of the horse's mouth."[55] He describes a number of equestrian problems, offering concrete, calculated, in-depth solutions, some of them hair-raisingly brutal.

Never Ride Before the Age of Four!

The sixth book, "of daedal instructions,"[56] is devoted to techniques of equitation. Grisone cites "Emperor Frederick": Horses must not be ridden before the age of four years! The horse in training should be worked daily, the educated one only every third day. According to Grisone, most horses take about half a year for the described training; some, however, considerably longer.

Grisone emphasizes that he masters equestrian art thoroughly and in a scientific manner, and that "so far, no one has undertaken to publish it in writing."[57] Therefore, he expects much criticism but also gratitude. He considers High School exercises not necessary for war: Though "*Capreola, Corveti, Volta inganiata, Volta Dancka, Radopiata* in double or threefold rings, *Galop Recolto, Salto dom passo, Salto di do passo, Salto di monton*"[58] are not absolutely necessary, "no one can deny they make a horse better ridden and add to his beauty."[59]

Horse and Rider: One Body, One Sense, One Will

In order to desensitize the young horse, Grisone advises against bashing and encourages tenderness to give the animal confidence. He recommends riding the horse in moonlit nights and during the daytime in town among metalworkers, farriers, and butchers. Getting used to other horses, soldiers, and cannon thunder must be practiced, too. Grisone disapproves of riding without collection, demanding correct work and "sweet contact"[60] with a perpendicular forehead. For him, the art of a "dear rider" is when the horse understands the reason for the aids and punishment, so that, in the course of time, the audience thinks "you and he were of one body, one sense, and one will."[61] Grisone acknowledges that the most complicated airs are almost indescribable in a book, even if musical notes are added to the verbal description. Hence he postulates the thinking rider, "So that a docile rider with decent skill and good intellect may carry out the not-so-obvious after diligent pondering."[62] The seventh book[63] discusses knightly fighting techniques and tricks.

Modern Medium of Printed Book Instead of Oral Tradition

Rightfully, Federico Grisone's "Ordini de cavalcare" gained the reputation of a bible for the novel equestrian art, because he wrote and systemized what had heretofore, only been passed on by oral lessons. His detailed instructions and his will to solve almost any equestrian problem made the book an efficient tool for practical riding. What he described was usually viable and applicable, hence the great international success. His translators, plagiarists, copyists, and developers spread the Spanish-Neapolitan equestrian art fast and wide, so that it soon became a European standard. Last but not least, this was due to the growing popularity of the medium of the printed book. This is another testament of Grisone's modernity.

On the other hand, Grisone became disreputable over time because of his often harsh methods and the depiction of inhumane bits, since people of all epochs generally prefer to judge instead of reading carefully or reading at all. A new translation from the Italian original is available in English, The Rules of Riding translated by Federica Deigan and edited by Elizabeth Tobey, (ACMRS Publications 2014) and is worthwhile for riders seeking knowledge and practice from Grisone.

Image 18 – Stefano Della Bella, Miniatures. (Private archive.)

SPANISH-NEAPOLITAN BECOMES AUSTRIAN

European Centaurs

Because of the political and dynastic connections between Austria and Spain, Iberian-Neapolitan equitation in the manner of Grisone is one of the roots of Austrian equestrian art, and even more than in other countries, as we shall see. Moreover, the desire for playful elegance – anything equestrian should appear "light and slight" – complies with the Viennese School's style. And the thinking rider as a principle will become evident repeatedly during our quest for the essence of Austrian equitation. Castiglione's ideal courtier and Grisone's cavalier became established as a European cultural asset in the epoch of Renaissance-Baroque, forming an image of man worthy of being followed. In "A Lover's Complaint" (1609) William Shakespeare (1564-1616) brilliantly describes this type of man as most desirable for a lady, and centaur-like equestrian skills play a vital role:

> "Well could he ride, and often men would say
> 'That horse his mettle from his rider takes:
> Proud of subjection, noble by the sway,
> What rounds, what bounds, what course, what stop
> he makes!'
> And controversy hence a question takes,
> Whether the horse by him became his deed,
> Or he his manage by the well-doing steed."[64]

Grisone puts it in a similar way. Horse and rider must be "one body, one sense, and one will." Federico Grisone inspired other Italian riding masters to publish their philosophies in book-form: Cesare Fiaschi: *Trattato del imbrigliare, maneggiare, et ferrare cavalli*. Bologna, A. Giaccarelli 1556. Claudio Corte: *Il Cavallarizzo*. Venice, Ziletti 1562. Pasquale Caracciolo: *La Gloria del Cavallo*. Venice, Giunti, Ciotti 1562. Marco Pavari: *L'Escurie de M. De Pavari*. Lyon, de Tournes 1581.[65]

Spanish Italy emanated this equestrian culture to the north. Margrave Francesco Gonzaga of Mantua had begun breeding Barbs from North Africa, and his son bred Spanish and Turkish blood horses to them. Such horses were also exported to England's Henry VIII and his successors.[66] The proliferation of the Iberian type of horse was followed by the art of riding a more manoeuvrable and hotter horse with skill, even virtuosity. This required

Image 19 – Crown jewels Iberian horses. Museo dos Coches, Lisbon. (Photo Poscharnigg.)

the rider's will to devote himself to equitation by means of a novel, written science. The *manège* became a location of academic engagement. The ideal expressed by Grisone – "one body, one sense, and one will" – evolved into a central task:

> "In Italy, France, and in the whole of Europe, thousands of men devoted their entire lives – sometimes in extreme poverty – to the quest, the testing, the aberrations and eventually finding of the animals that have and can fulfil this ideal…, an image of their era, and, on the other hand, links in a long chain, while still expanding their knowledge."[67]

Non-Habsburg Europe had to put forth considerably more effort to purchase optimal Iberian-Neapolitan horses for the new equestrian art. For the countries outside of this empire, there was only indirect access to correct academic training that would enable them to be ridden efficiently with apparent effortless elegance. For example, Antoine de Pluvinel

Image 20 – Playful martial equestrian art. Fresco in the former winter riding school, Salzburg. (Photo Poscharnigg.)

studied first in Naples, before he could work as a tutor and riding master to the French king. Thus the King of France – like most of his colleagues – could only indirectly approach the sources of academic modernity in equestrian art.

Casa de Austria in Charge of Equestrian Art

The connection of the Habsburg dynasty with the topic, however, was direct and without mediators: "Equestrian Art is Spanish heritage and its preservation duty of the *Casa de Austria*."[68] Because "with the House of Habsburg, in Spain called *Casa de Austria*, the Spanish horse began his triumphant procession throughout Europe. The worldwide realm of Emperor Charles V (1500-1558) was also the Spanish horse's empire," namely in Europe and America.[69] Fostering the equestrian art, provisioning the world's best horses and riding masters were a private matter. Therefore, the publication of written, printed riding instructions seemed dispensable.

Between the Spanish and the German-Austrian line of Habsburg, an intense exchange took place. Austrian rulers were born or raised in Spain, where, as is generally known, equestrian training was central to courtly education. Spanish equestrian art ran in the blood of each ruler of the *Casa de Austria*. Anything else was unthinkable. Strong, unbending awareness and the adamant preoccupation of being in charge of the best horses and equitation on earth contributed to the Spanish Riding School of Vienna surviving the French Revolution and the altered methods of military riding. Conversely, many riding schools of the courtly Spanish method disappeared in other European countries.

A Spaniard Is Emperor in Vienna

Emperor Ferdinand I was born near Madrid in 1503 AD, died in Vienna in 1564. He did not speak German when he came to Austria. Thanks to his advisor, Gabriel de Salamanca, he asserted himself bloodily and became extremely unpopular with the Viennese population. Andalusian horses and Spanish equestrian culture must have been his source of comfort and strength in his politically difficult, hostile environment. He possessed what other European courts craved: Spanish equitation and horses of the highest quality at his disposal.

The diplomat, Pedro de Cordoba acted as Supreme Equerry, then Don Pedro Lasso di Castilia from 1528-48. A stud in Himberg near Vienna was run by Juan Maria until 1541, then by Pedro de Rada until 1549, followed by Alfonso de Mercado until 1564: Skilled personnel for the Spanish "genets" was at hand.[70] Ferdinand I "also had a 'planta de la traca de la cavalleriza', a plan for the ideal layout of a riding stable," sent.[71] Spanish trainers of the era were Luis Acardo, Antonio and Bartolomé Moreto and Juan de Salazar.

Since Ferdinand I liked to surround himself with courtly Spaniards, everything Spanish became increasingly fashionable. "The prestige the Spanish language and the behaviour displayed by the Spaniards at the court in the middle of the century are shown by the description of a tournament held in Vienna in 1560. Its 'star' is Philipp II's ambassador, Don Claudio Fernández de Quinones, Conde de Luna, appearing in great splendour, thus underlining the fascination radiating from the Spanish culture at the Viennese court."[72] It should not be forgotten that, in the military sector, everything Spanish was held in highest esteem. Charles V is said to always have been accompanied by 500 riders![73]

"The presence of Spanish culture at Ferdinand's court and of Spanish soldiers in the Empire was increasing continuously from the years 1521/22 until the middle of the century and was to decrease only one hundred years later because of Spain's loss of supremacy after the Thirty Years' War and the Treaty of the Pyrenees, to die out completely with the extinction of the Spanish Habsburgs (1700) and the result of the War of Spanish Succession. The last extensions of Spanish culture in Austria appear at the time after the death of Joseph I

These facts, as we will see, were to shape Austrian equestrian art sustainably.

Image 21 – Playful martial equestrian art. Fresco in the former winter riding school, Salzburg. (Photo Poscharnigg.)

Importing Andalusian horses directly from Spain was certainly a luxury even for an imperial budget, because overseas transport was costly and was risky, and the over-land route was long and marked by chicanery. Therefore, Neapolitan and Turkish horses became a popular second choice.[75] Thus, logistic problems were solved to meet the ever-increasing demand for Iberian horses. For, as mentioned, Naples was the closer Spain.

A Kingdom for Andalusians

Emperor Maximilian II (1527-76) was born in Vienna, but he lived in Spain for about three years during his youth. It is unthinkable that he did not get the most thorough equestrian education while there. In 1552, he returned to Vienna in triumph, bringing the elephant, Soliman, camels, parrots, and of course, Spanish horses with him.[76] But the supply of Andalusians in Vienna still seemed unsatisfactory: "Maximilian even wrote to south-Italian dukes and earls to obtain horses from Naples, for Vienna lacked good horses. Furthermore, in Naples there were good instructors of equestrian art. Generally, Spaniards were put in charge of acquisition and breeding of the animals. Rodrigo de Barragán and Lope de Mardonés, monitored the selection of horses in Naples."[77] Maximilian II commissioned Vienna's Stallburg, the first example of Renaissance architecture constructed in

Image 22 – Playful martial equestrian art. Fresco in the former winter riding school, Salzburg. (Photo Poscharnigg.)

1569. Ever since, the horses of the (later so-called) Spanish Riding School have been stabled there. Maximilian's wife, Maria, liked to be surrounded by all things Spanish. "Adam von Dietrichstein, Diego Manrique de Mendoza, Agustín de Alexandro, and Luis Saboyano were in charge of her horses."

After accepting his father, Ferdinand I's, inheritance, Maximilian had to cede territories of the German Habsburg line to his two brothers. One of them, Archduke Charles of Inner Austria (1540-90), ruled from Graz down to the Adriatic Sea. He solved the logistics problem with the Andalusians and Neapolitans perfectly by choosing an area of his territory that corresponded geologically and climatically to the horses' countries of origin: sparse, rocky, hot in summer, icy in winter. For centuries the Karst stud of Lipizza near Trieste has proved ideal to maintain the qualities of precious Spanish-Neapolitan-Arabian horses: noble, dry, hard, hot, tough, light-footed. Geography's grace did not allow the horses to become lethargic and heavy there as they did on Kladrub's lush pastures. Halbthurn/Mönchhof never yielded Lipizza's brilliant breeding results in the course of history.

Image 23 – Playful martial equestrian art. Fresco in the former winter riding school, Salzburg. (Photo Poscharnigg.)

Manneristic Treasure Trove Stable

Emperor Rudolph I (1552-1612) received a very strict catholic education in Spain (1563-1571) that formed him forever. He proudly showed off his Spanish affectation and was considered "a relatively skilled jouster"[79]. He his brother, Ernst returned to Austria in 1571 and brought 180 Spanish horses that built the foundation of the imperial stud in Prague. However mentally unsound Rudolph II may have been, he had the talent and means to surround himself with objects of beauty, interest, scientists, artists, artifacts and gorgeous horses. He is said to have owned both 3000 paintings and horses and spent a great deal of time in his stables.[80] Great lords were in the habit of reveling in the sight of their sumptuous steeds as if visiting a gallery or treasury. Guests were presented these living treasures, indulging in knowledgeable conversation. In 1588, Georg Engelhard von Löhneysen (1552-1622) published his "Neu-eröffnete Hof-Kriegs und Reitschul," reprinted in 1729 and embellished with Valentin Trichter's beautiful copperplate engravings. In his book is a depiction of an ideal, semi-elliptical stable, bright, high, and elegant. In this way the lord can observe all horses at a glance. Best suited for flaunting to selected visitors were the spectacular pintos, skewbalds, piebalds, leopards, and rare colours such as grullos[81], which unfortunately became unpopular later on. In Europe, they are almost always re-imports from the Americas. Pinto horses sporting blankets with spots, for instance, can hardly be found in today's equestrian competitions. And the Lipizzaner of our time is mainly grey, seldom bay and rarely black. With his taste for the unusual, and astonishing, Rudolph II made his court a pole of mannerism.[82]

He, who regards the horse as an artifact, will likely eventually develop riding into something artistic, artificial. "The connection of nature and art is of utmost importance in the mannerism theory of art."[83] Up until the French Revolution in 1789, a hyper-refined equitation developed beyond mannerism that alienated itself more and more from the battleground, being only art for art's sake, a skill which had little to do with war. For example, if reverse courbettes were teased out of horses, they hardly would have been of military use. Above all, mannerism was about evoking something unnatural from a natural creature in order to achieve astonishment. Such artificiality became one facet of equestrian art.

Image 24 – Valentin Trichter's ideal stable for great lords. (Private archive.)

GIOVANNI BATTISTA GALIBERTO AND VIENNA'S FIRST EQUESTRIAN BOOK

A Swordsman as a Professor

In the rough world of war, horse and rider had to prove themselves in the virtues of classical Iberian equitation. The Thirty Years' War (1618-48) gave plenty of such opportunities. To create new political facts, the long-lasting mass-slaughter of (un)involved people, displacements, destruction of resources, and annihilation of cultural values saw many people drawn in.

One of these was the author of the first equestrian textbook for the Viennese court, the Neapolitan Giovanni Battista Conte di Galiberto (also Giambatista Galiberti or Galimberti)[84]. Likely it was not his intention to set this eminent milestone in the history of Austrian equestrian art. Galiberto was a man of action, a swordsman, dragoon-colonel under the Imperial General, Tilly. Why he wrote is an exciting story.

In 1632, Tilly appointed the Neapolitan Galiberto commander of Bamberg and sent him there leading forty Croatian riders. Galiberto proved himself to be an "extremely efficient and capable officer."[85] During a night in May, Colonel Galiberto raided Margrave Johann Georg von Brandenburg's field camp with his Croats, citizens of Bamberg, and students, all tolled over one thousand men, armed with cannons. "The assault on Johann Georg's camp succeeded before midnight, the citizens put down the sentinels, dispersed the men, and took possession of the baggage. But instead of using the victory, they plundered the enemy's baggage despite Galiberto's insistent appeal, thus giving the margrave's troops opportunity to gather. By means of more troops the citizens of Bamberg, most of whom had set aside their muskets, were now themselves surprised and massacred without mercy."[86]

Galiberto was sent to Bavaria in the autumn of the same year by Prince Elector Maximilian I of Bavaria, taking part in a winter campaign under the command of Imperial Field Marshal Johann von Aldringen in Oberschwaben. During an attack by the Swedish Field Marshal Horn, Galiberto was wounded in January 1633. Imperial riders fled from Horn's troops, and the Elector wanted to have this punished. The men tried to dodge this inquiry, pretending there was no time to investigate the matter because of heavy marches. They asked for an authorized commissioner to clear the case up. But the Elector demanded

Image 25 – Antonie Palamedesz, Mounted battle. (Private archive.)

exemplary punishment. The outcome is not exactly known. But "Galiberto had to defend himself in Munich and quit the army because of differences with Cronberg. Galiberto defected to Italy. From there he offered his services to Bernhard of Saxony-Weimar."[87] Bernhard was the commander on the side of Sweden's King Gustav Adolf, and received the duchy of Franconia from him in 1633, which mainly consisted of the dioceses Würzburg and Bamberg.

Did Galiberto want to become commander of Bamberg again, this time under a different regime? Was he treated unjustly? Anyway, "in the winter of 1633 he was arrested on his way back to the Empire and was imprisoned in January 1634 in the Castle of Burghausen in Upper Bavaria."[88] There, Galiberto had leisure time to draft his equestrian doctrine. Thus the first book about equestrian art published in Austria was written by a likely wrongly-imprisoned Neapolitan in Bavaria. He may have had an interesting conversation partner in Swedish Field Marshal, Gustav Duke of Horn also jailed in Burghausen from 1634-1641. Galiberto succeeded in escaping in 1637. Giovanni Battista di Galiberto was in Emperor's Ferdinand III (1608-57) service not only as an officer but also as riding master. In his book's introduction "*Al lettore*" of 1648 AD, he recommends himself as "*professore di*

Image 26 – Van der Meulen, Mounted battle. (Private archive)

perfetto cavagliere" (teacher of the perfect rider). In 1650, under imperial privilege, "Giovanni Giacomo" (Johann Jakob) Kyrner published in Vienna the work:

"IL CAVALLO DA MANEGGIO.

Libro Doue si tratta della Nobilissima Virtù del caualcare; Cioè, Come il Cauagliere deue star à Cauallo; and come si deue domare, gouernare, inferrare, imbrigliare, and ammaestrare ogni sorte di Caualli; Et in che tempo si deuono pigliar li Polledri per ammaestrarli; della razza de' Stalloni, de' pelami, and de' segni buoni, e cattiui. DI GIO: BATTISTA GALIBERTO Conte Napolitano, e Colonello della Sacra Cesarea Maestà di FERDINANDO III. Diviso in tre Parti; Nella Prima si tratta del conoscere li Caualli; Nella Seconda il modo di Caualcare; Nella Terza la regola di medicar ogni sorte d'infermità, che li puo accadere. Con tre copiosissime Tauole. DEDICATO ALLA SACRA REGGIA MAESTÀ DI FERDINANDO IV. RÉ D'VNGARIA, E BOEMIA, & c."

This might appear unusual amount of Italian for Vienna, but Ferdinand III, as a highly educated ruler, wrote Italian poems. And his third wife, Eleonore Gonzaga (1630-86), Princess of Mantua, energetically pursued the Italianization of the Viennese court.[89]

Together with the Emperor she stood in the centre of the Italian Academy founded by himself."[90] As a compromise, Galiberto was a likely choice out of all competing parties at the court: as a Neapolitan Spaniard, and, nonetheless, Italian.

Lest we forget that the House of Gonzaga was the home of horses that strongly influenced Austrian horse breeding. And the court's Chief Equerry, Duke Don Annibale Gonzaga (1602-88), acted as Commander of the City of Vienna.[91] The Chief Riders of the era were Italians: Vicenzo Rizzi (1635-52), then Giacomo Baron del Campo, Hannibale Rocci (1679-95), and Pietro Capitolo (1695-1709).[92] After all, 6% of the court ladies originated from Italy, 5% from Spain; 10-15% of the chamberlains and councillors were Italians from 1620-57.[93] In 2014, the first edition of Galiberto's equestrian masterwork cost the price of a new car. Does its dignified quality indicate a readership in the upper echelon?: The parchment cover sports golden stamping, presenting the Emperor's coat of arms on the front side, the back cover shows the Austrian Archdukes' coat of arms; the book has gilt edging on three sides and a number of copperplates.[94] Galiberto dedicated his oeuvre to the Emperor's son, Ferdinand IV, who, in the year of publication, was King of Bohemia, Hungary, and Croatia, was elected Roman-German King in 1653, but died of pox only one year later.

The first edition of an equestrian text for the Viennese court is clearly considered a remarkable historic novelty.

> "No imperial Chief Rider or Equerry in the 17th century had published his riding doctrines or had stood out in one way or another. There was no Pluvinel or Löhneyßen here, no Newcastle or Solleysel. The representatives of equestrian culture at the Viennese court were only the Emperor and his Equerry."[95]

Extraordinary and different from the rest of Europe, Galiberto, not a didactic person of the *manège*, appeared on the scene, nor was he an artistically-minded riding school professor, but instead, a man of war, an equestrian colonel who nonetheless knew all of the finesse of Iberian riding. This synthesis of martial equitation and High School became the hallmark of Austrian equestrian art well into the 20th century.

Galiberto's *Il Cavallo da Maneggio* definitely caught on in Vienna, for a second Italian edition was released in 1659, during the rule of Emperor Leopold I (1640-1705), who was very fond of the Italian language. 1660 brought a German translation, with a second edition in 1682. It became an influential hippological bestseller in Vienna. Why? The Imperial Chief Riders were entrusted with the care of the ruler's horses and his riding. The rest of the empire aspired to copy the absolute monarch just as happened in competing France. Like a magnet, the absolute ruler attracted the nobility to his court and was a paradigm for his followers, who increased in number. The Viennese Court was increasing drastically and boasted 2000 persons in 1672, whereas 100 years earlier, 500 people had sufficed.

Image 27 – Galiberto's equestrian treatise, detail. (Private archive.)

This caused an enormous increase in the demand for court-suitable horses. Courtiers that felt important wanted to represent their status on noble steeds. The high standard set by the imperial riding school could not be approximated without immense effort, requiring both excellent horses and superb training in Spanish-Neapolitan equitation. Sufficiently qualified instructors were unavailable, hence the new mass media, printed books offered a solution. In this regard, French literature was deemed politically incorrect and would remain so until the 18th century. In contrast to other European dynasties, the Viennese Court did not see any necessity to seek equestrian expertise from the Sun King Louis XIV. Thus the equestrian system of Conte di Galiberto – a proven catholic and soldier – was the first choice to meet the demand for information. In 1660, Emperor Leopold I granted the book's German edition his "Privilegium Impressorium," a copyright for ten years:

Image 28 – Galiberto's equestrian treatise, detail. (Private archive.) *Image 28a – Galiberto's equestrian treatise, detail. Private archive.)*

"NEWLY-LEVELED ARENA AND OPENED RIDING SCHOOL."

In his introductory dedication, the Viennese publisher, Michael Rieger stated the German edition's purpose: to "help the noble youth, if not fluent in Italian, to learn to ride a well-trained, skilled horse by means of the highly renowned equestrian art, for the sake of joy, success in battle, at court for artful knightly games, as a pleasant pastime, and in the field against the enemy, where they would prove their prowess and innate bravery."[96]

What Rieger expressed here – not without baroque intricacy – would be announced seventy-five years later in the hall of Vienna's Spanish Riding School on a marble plaque with the same meaning, but more to the point: "This Imperial riding school was erected for the noble youth's education and exercise, as well as for the horses' training in equestrian art and war."[97] Austrian equestrian art was never understood as mere *l'art pour l'art* alone, but always also as military skill even in the inner sanctum of equestrian art, the Winter Riding School. It is no accident that Austria's first equestrian schoolbook was written by a cavalry colonel. The images in Galiberto's book seem inspired by Grisone's oeuvre, but were not copied. The horses look finer, and the riders' attire fits the era. Obviously, Galiberto knew

Grisone's book. But he created something entirely original in the Neapolitan-Spanish equestrian tradition. Unlike Grisone, who went into greater detail, Galiberto's text is shorter, in an effort to be comprehensive with an emphasis on equitation.

Give the Horse Good and Gentle Words

The first part, "Knowing the Horses"[98] deals with categories of horse-types according to the doctrine of the four elements, the colours, signs, and whorls, plus the supposed skills attributed to them. This philosophy stands in complete opposition to the idea that a good horse has no colour. In order to produce strong foals, breeding practice must not exploit stallions and mares. The young should be "raised and kept on mountains or in stony meadows and heath, so that they develop good feet and hard hooves and, at the same time, become light and trainable."[99] This suggested a territory like that of the Karst Stud in Lipizza. Only at the age of two should the foals be separated from their mothers, so that they do not remain "faint and weak." This is also the time to tie them up and teach them to lead in a halter. At 3 ½ years, the young horses are brought into a stable. "In the stable he should not receive rude and rough hollering, nor whipping nor beating, so that he is not frightened and does not develop vices or damage to his body; instead, one should give him good and gentle words."[100]

Such affection for horses completely dominates Galiberto's opus. Again and again, he recommends gentle treatment and advises against violence. A warrior wrote this, knowing that in a critical moment his life could depend on a reliable, affectionate mount. The owner must constantly watch and monitor whether his employees treat the horses correctly, according to the proverb, "The master's eyes make the horse healthy and fat."[101] Otherwise, he needs a reliable equerry and to "apply for good and true grooms and keep them in good obedience and will, moreover keep them in an honest and appropriate manner."[102] For, "a good horse is worth a big treasure" and should be "groomed with love." Malevolent personnel can massively spoil dear horses. Thus, fear led to employers' socially responsible behaviour even in the age of serfdom. Then Galiberto describes the features of a perfect, strong, fast horse, that he liked in beautiful shape, upright, straight, and light; the haunches even higher than the shoulders, like a stag, but with a Roman nose.[103] After this, he discusses the assessment of age according to the teeth as well as a short valuation of the horses of different nations.

The book's second part deals with "Bridling and Training of Horses, and How They Should Be Handled and Green-Broken in the Arena."[104] The four-year-old "foal or wildling" is to be treated nicely and coaxingly. The colt should get a saddle of straw or felt, along with "good words and stroking of the hand." The groom should treat him "tenderly" and give him – "without sharp hollering" – a snaffle bit into the mouth.[105] Then he can be led in hand, and Galiberto insisted on doing this without switch or whip, so as not to make the colt shy and unwilling.[106] Interestingly, illustrators at that time did not necessarily read the works they illustrated, for the corresponding copper engraving depicts all three persons armed with switches.[107] Galiberto emphatically warns against riding horses before their fourth year of age.

Ride the Distance of Some Muskets' Shots

The first mounting happens in a careful and tender manner and is rewarded with oats. In contrast to Grisone, who worked with brutal intimidation, Galiberto demands absolutely no whipping or beating. Before mounting, the rider shall pat the saddle, seat himself carefully, take the cavesson reins short, and follow a "waymaster," first at a walk, then at a trot "for a few muskets' shots." After a quiet dismounting, the colt gets a reward and is led back to his stable "quietly and without fear," being treated in the best possible manner.[108] After a while he is bridled with a straight curb bit, first without chin chain, and carefully ridden with it more and more, without making him hard in the mouth.

Once the horse is used to being ridden, he gets a school saddle; the rider wears spurs, but does not apply them. The horse must walk on a large circle as well as slightly flexed on a straight line. Soon after this comes – lo and behold – the pesade, which Galiberto assigns high importance, in order to lighten the forehand, and prepares the horse for the other airs. By the way, he develops pesades from a standstill and scolds riders who do not know how to make use of the pesade correctly. Generally today's strict separation of schools on the ground from those above the ground is absent from Galiberto's discourse because he clearly requires a light, easily manoeuvrable forehand.

The chapter "About Crossing or Side-Passing" describes – unfortunately rather vaguely – movements that could be shoulder-in, haunches-in, or just complete travers; all are forms of side-passing, which he discusses more precisely later on. Galiberto considers *mezair*, a very exalted, strongly collected canter, fancy, but impractical. For him, as a practitioner, a gallop must be safe over rough terrain as well, without tiring the horses. Like Grisone, Galiberto canters and exercises the horse on a *repellon*, a track with voltes at both ends. Again, Galiberto advocates punishing the horse only very seldom, and if done, to do it seriously and effectively. "And if he performs well, you should flatter him, so that he gets more love and desire to learn the airs."[109]

"The greatest masterpiece and science of a cavalier who thinks he can ride well," is to teach his horse to walk with a steady head.[110] Galiberto deems this more important than a horse performing all artistic schools without carrying his head steadily. When stopping colts, the author warns of hard handling, lest the horse's back becomes damaged. The rider should take the cavesson-reins, lean back slightly, standing firmly in the stirrups. The halt is followed by an immediate half-pesade. Galiberto likes to connect stopping with reining-back and starting from it, making the horse light and fine, supporting collection. As far as cantering is concerned, he advises smart restraint to avoid overcharging the horses. Galiberto describes courbettes in a low and high manner, straight or on the volte, also laterally, and even backwards. He develops this bow-jump from a pesade with energetic aids from the spurs and whip. When the horse has understood, the rider should "caress him, so that he does not become wild and peevish, but follows willingly."[111] A special topic are the *redopp-courbettes* on the volte: The horse jumps a two-beat-canter in a rocking-manner, alternating from forehand to hindquarters, while performing a pirouette.

Furthermore, Galiberto describes the croupade, the walk and jump (*passo e salto*), the mutton jump (salto di montone), and finally the capriole, schools above the ground, for which he demands horses with strong legs and backs. Even caprioles are ridden on a volte; the author recommends applying a stick with a spike as an "aid," which pricks the croup.

Shoulder-In Formulated in the Year 1635

Then Galiberto thoroughly explains travers [haunches-in] on the volte, developing it to passage and finally to a *redopp-volte*. Not only does he describe the travers, but also the shoulder-in, calling it "canton or angle,"[112] a movement he deems useful for strengthening the horse and training it in a lighter manner:

> "The reason, however, why a horse soon gets schooled and ridden like this is that, when you ride him properly in the 'angle', he will lighten up and obey in collection, build strength, arch and bend his neck, carry his head steadily, position his spine correctly, look into the turn, develop a good mouth, cross his legs and feet."[113]

All advantages listed here are generally attributed to the shoulder-in. In order to motivate the horse, Galiberto uses two walls forming an angle to which he rides in a straight line. And when the horse "reaches the angle with his head, one pulls the cavesson's inner rein and applies the inside leg at the girth. In this way, the horse will turn his neck, facing the circle, crossing the legs and feet."[114] Galiberto writes that this air can be ridden at all gaits.

Unfortunately the book's images do not show travers and shoulder-in. But Galiberto's words clearly prove: In Naples and Vienna shoulder-in was ridden about 100 years before Guérinière, who commonly is said to be the inventor of this movement. But this is not true. Guérinière is only the inventor of the term "épaule en dedans," meaning "shoulder-in," but not of the air itself. Time will tell if the truth will gain hold people's minds.

"Cantering to the side," meaning a canter in (almost) complete travers, can only be seen in the bull-fighting arena today, when the *rejoneador*, hat in his hand, parades past the audience almost at a right angle to the wall. In Galiberto's time, this air served a military purpose. In a mounted combat, one could always face the opponent's front in this way, without letting him attack from behind.

Judicious Rider and Gentle Hand

In contrast, the passage serves only to present. Galiberto develops it from rein-back into a collected, shortened trot, speaking softly and caressing the horse's neck with hand and switch, in order to make the horse proud. He warns of overstraining the horse with this exhaustive movement, appealing to the thinking rider's intellect:

> "Thus a horse can be brought to all possible movements and to whatever the judicious rider wants from him, with good words and a quiet hand for the reins, as well as patience in correcting and punishing at the right time and in the right place."[115]

After explaining each movement, Galiberto deals with general questions of training. Double pillars, as those still in use at the Spanish Riding School of Vienna today, are not mentioned by Galiberto. He considers a single pillar useful only for coarse, heavy-headed horses in the beginning of training, but not for the gentle, light, and willing ones. He corrects ruined horses with a honey-covered rope in the mouth, using a cavesson as well as generous ease and patience and by avoiding excessive demands.

In the chapter entitled "How to Punish," Galiberto repeatedly appeals to the rider's judgement, not to demand too much from the horse and not to punish him without reason because

> "a perfect rider must know how to handle the horse correctly, and know whence the error and the cause come, if he does something improper or evil."

He who mistreats his horse, is

> "worth getting all the punishments he gives his horse. For he lets anger master and embitter him, and knows neither how to control himself nor the horse. Thus, two insensible brutes are together, urinating side by side malevolently, for they fight, quarrel, and beat each other."

As an advocate of humane treatment, Galiberto demands:

> "Since equestrian art is such a noble virtue, it ought not to be 'botched'. Hence a horse should be handled lightly, so that he accepts and fulfils, with more joy and pleasure, what the judicious and skilled rider teaches and wants from him."[116]

In contrast to Grisone, who recommends sore-spurring, Galiberto advises against this because it eventually desensitizes the horse.

> "Thus any punishment should be given sensibly and moderately, so that the rider can be considered well-experienced and judicious in this art." "And it is certain, that a horse sooner gives in to gentleness and flattering, than to excessive beating and punishment."[117]

Like Grisone, Galiberto recommends adjusting the right stirrup leather a little shorter than the left one in order to facilitate mounted combat. Generally, he advises adjusting them neither too short nor too long. He especially disapproves of riding with stirrup leathers that are too long, a serious mistake made by the French cavalry. The French did not come off well in old Austria's equestrian literature, as can be seen repeatedly. The rider should sit in the saddle firmly, "close his mouth," "but stretch the knees and legs, as if they stood on the ground, though they should be kept slightly forward."[118] He holds the switch towards the horse's left ear, like a lance.

The question arises, if the advice "to close the mouth" refers to Emperor Leopold I. Several contemporaries report having often seen him with a hanging lower lip. In order to gain "perfection in all airs," the rider must allow the horse time and work toward everything thoroughly without superficiality. Steadiness is important for Galiberto: Mouth, ears, and tail should always keep calm.

Cavesson and Mild Curb Bit

Concerning the choice of the correct bit, Galiberto strongly advises the reader to use the cavesson until bending and forming are completed. Only then, can a curb bit be used without harming the horse and making him hard-mouthed. The curb bit should be the simplest and mildest available, the horse will be ridden with it all his working life. Galiberto warns of the misconception that bits could fix horses' natural shortcomings and weaknesses. If a "good and judicious rider"[119] finds out he cannot reach his aims despite stringency and diligence, he should give in wisely, without requesting anything his mount cannot give. Excessive demands can foster dangerous vices. With decency and diplomacy, Galiberto acts as horses' advocate, by showing repeatedly that "honour and laudation" cannot be achieved employing brutality. He strongly disapproves of experimenting with various bits because this will not bring proper results. For heavy-headed stallions, he recommends

Image 29 – G. P. Rugendas, Riding school. (Private archive.)

severe cavessons because these are "more helpful" in these situations. A remarkable word choice: The rider should be "helpful" to the horse, and not forcing him.

This is followed by the description of several cavessons and kinds of curb bits, and, compared to Grisone's book there aren't any mouthpieces that attack the horse's palate; progress. Galiberto offers principles and practical details of correct horse shoeing also to "help the horse." The veterinary chapter plays a large part in Galiberto's book and completes it. Perhaps homeopathic practitioners today could glean valuable information here.

2000 Years after Xenophon,

the Greek cavalry colonel, had written "On Horsemanship" with empathy and the horse's well-being in mind, a worthy successor appeared on the scene: In 1650, the cavalry colonel Giovanni Battista Galiberto published his book "Il Cavallo da Maneggio" in Vienna, a riding instruction doctrine encouraging thinking riders to train their horses with gentleness and without brutal methods and tools. Only in rare cases, does he consider violence justifiable. Thus, he became an advocate of horses at a time when humane procedures were anything but normal, as a popular riding school depiction by Georg Philipp Rugendas showcases:

"Man's art and diligence can bring to obedience the mightiest horse, if there is need. With whip, spur, and bit it can be forced by threats, So that he performs courbettes for war and pomp."

Eight years after Galiberto, in 1658, William Cavendish, Duke of Newcastle, published in Antwerp the most internationally influential equestrian schoolbook of the era, "A General System of Horsemanship." Fear is the cornerstone of his training, Newcastle states, not without humour:

"If the wisest man in the world were put into the shape of a horse, and retained his superior understanding, he could not invent more cunning ways (I question if so many) to oppose his rider, than a horses does: Whence I conclude, that a horse must know his rider to be his master, that is, must be afraid of him, and then he will obey him, which is what we call a dressed horse."[120]

With his concept of humane horse treatment, Galiberto exceeds the average writer of his era, thereby considerably influencing the equestrian art of a mighty nation. His book was published in four separate editions. Exceptional, too, is that Galiberto described in 1635 what Guérinière was to call "shoulder-in" one hundred years later. Galiberto named it "canton or angle," a term that did not catch on and fell into oblivion like Galiberto himself. At the latest, since 1791 the obstinate historic error got established by Ludwig Hünersdorf: "We owe this lesson exclusively to Mr Guérinière's invention."[121] Nevertheless, Galiberto did not become an unrecognised genius, because his book experienced a new edition in 1682, for "the aristocracy was besotted with equestrian art, as it was besotted with tennis, musical compositions."[122]

The Emperor Is Having a Ball

The marriage of Emperor Leopold I with the Spanish Infanta Margaretha Theresia in 1666 became a special cause for Viennese festivities that lasted almost a year.[123] Good mounts were needed to shine in the "highly renowned equestrian art" "because many people had to follow the Court's example or followed it voluntarily. Where so many horses trained for High School were needed all at the same time, equestrian art was to thrive."[124]

No wonder that Galiberto's book enjoyed great popularity then. Reportedly one thousand people took part in an equestrian ballet in the inner bailey in 1667. The Emperor himself rode a bay Andalusian called "Bravo" that allegedly had been bought in Spain for a fortune. Leopold performed courbettes on Bravo before his wife's loge. He was generally deemed to be an excellent rider.

"The Emperor had nine knights sitting on school horses as well, and carrying out the same lessons as their master."[125] Another forty-nine knights had their horses dance to the music, among them four capriole horses, nine courbette horses, and four redopping horses. The rehearsal time for the horse ballet was four months. Everything took place in a bombastic, baroque setting with specially composed music. "Alessandro Carducci invented the choreography."[126]

In his era, Emperor Leopold I acted as a patron of equestrian art and breeding. Georg Simon Winter von Adlersflügel, for example, was knighted. Winter personally dedicated to Leopold several of his works and, at the time, was among the leading horse experts in riding, breeding, and veterinary medicine.[127] In 1658, Leopold I decreed a detailed stud instruction for Lipizza, thus proving the regent's knowledge through concrete orders, which provided decisive directives for the development of this horse breeding jewel.[128] After all, the very best horse material was needed for the rapidly expanding court. On the other hand, excellent horses were also a military necessity at a time when both the French and Turks threatened the empire.

Image 30 – Wedding of Leopold I, festivities (Private archive.)

THE CLASSICAL ERA OF AUSTRIAN EQUESTRIAN ART: JOHANN CHRISTOPH VON REGENTHAL, ADAM VON WEYROTHER ET AL.

J. G. v. Hamilton: The Arena as a Place for "Highest" Demonstration

The era between 1648, the end of the 30 Years' War, and 1789, the year of the French Revolution, can be considered the zenith of a specifically European culture. Its distinguishing characteristic was the desire to unify both horse and rider as a living artefact. What Galiberto's publisher, Michael Rieger, called "highly renowned equestrian art," gradually became the educational standard for the nobility. In no other art form can the performer shine in such a way as when showing off exercising his horse. Furthermore, owning noble, well-fed exquisite horses demonstrated the rider's wealth. Each of the numerous gorgeous horses living in pompous stables during this time literally ate away starving people's food; it was merciless luxury. Each of these horses received optimal care around the clock. The equipment of finest cloth and leather, often golden bits represented unimaginable opulence for most people.

Image 31 – J. G. v. Hamilton, Palomino stallion of the Imperial Riding School. (Private archive.)

The rider's attire needed to befit his position. Johann Georg von Hamilton's famous painting "The Imperial Riding School" (1702) may serve as a paradigm: Concentration of prosperity and beauty. In a heroic and decorative setting, protected by soldiers, admired by simple people, imperial pomp unfolds, the elegance of which potentates of all times might hardly surpass. Exquisite horses pranced in the finest equipment, superbly ridden by gentlemen in the most luxurious apparel.

Young Archduke Charles, the later Emperor Charles VI, rode an effortless piaffe, which, in such perfection, would only be possible by few riders today. And what child can ride a capriole today? To achieve this high level of equestrian skill, a nobleman's education in the art of horseback riding had to start during his early childhood, otherwise he could not have reached a proficiency that can be seen today in only handful of riders worldwide.

The gifted painter, Johann Georg von Hamilton portrayed a number of imperial stallions in all their grandeur. These steeds appear with abundant temperament, seem more than well-fed, and display ostentatious saddles and bridles, obvious treasures of masterly craftwork. The musculature development indicates perfect training. Often the horses display high-spirited piaffe or passage, or are depicted in challenging movements, such as canter pirouettes or caprioles. All of this is full of self-evident, cheerful brilliance. In his technical perfection as a horse painter Hamilton remains unsurpassed, and together with Ludwig Koch and George Stubbs he forms a triumvirate in this genre. Hamilton, of a noble Scottish family, born in Brussels in 1672, was appointed to the imperial court as animal painter in 1712, and died in Vienna in 1737.[129] The most beautiful examples of his portraits can be found in the Rösslzimmer (horse room) of the Viennese Schoenbrunn Palace.

Image 32 – J. E. Ridinger, All airs in one picture. (Private archive.)

J. E. Ridinger: Riding Schools as Cultural Achievements

Johann Elias Ridinger (1698-1767), who studied under Georg Philipp Rugendas, is considered even today as one of the most popular horse-artists of his time. In contrast to Hamilton, he did not always depict horse and rider anatomically correctly in his engravings, a fact that has been frequently met with reproach. It should be considered, that according to the baroque theory of art, reality should represent the ideal rather than actual performance. Doubtlessly, Ridinger's horse depictions show elegance and expression. Ridinger's works, edited by his own publishing house in Augsburg, offer plenty of artistically designed information about equitation of the 18th century. Two of these copper engravings serve as examples.

The first features a large number of movements clustered on one page. From left to right: Ballotade, halt from canter, step and leap, *redopp* on a circle, passage, accustoming horses to shots, "head inward and croup outward," rein-back, half courbette; accustoming horses to the flag, drum, and trumpet; kicking out, pirouette *terre à terre*, pesade, halt from a walk. Several of these depictions appear as set pieces in other engravings by Ridinger. His sons assisted in the production. The background of the scene is the wall of a city or castle with a natural landscape. The movement "head inward and croup outward" resembles today's shoulder-in, which apparently was part of the standard repertoire of the era's equestrian art, and Ridinger therefore added it to his canon.

In the second engraving we view – in the midst of resplendent architecture adorned with sphinx, statues, peacocks, cypresses, and ladies in the background – a party of elegant gentlemen, proudly presenting to an amazed Ottoman delegation the cultural achievement that occidental equestrian art symbolized. The oriental guests watch something quite splendid: Passage with the croup or head to the pillar (here renvers, travers), *redopping* on small and large circles, passage toward the wall, half-pirouette at the walk, and *terre-à-terre*. Waiting horses sporting beautiful blankets are kept ready by polite grooms. Impeccably dressed riders on fine mounts show off their skills with apparent effortlessness. The image documents the social importance attributed to equestrian art; it is demonstrated with pride in the presence of the military opponent.

Image 33 – J. E. Ridinger, Riding school and oriental spectators. (Private archive.)

School for Men and Horses

High School riding played an integral part in the personal education of young noblemen. Valentin Trichter illustrated Georg Engelhart Löhneysens "Della Cavalleria" anew in 1729: School for both men and horses. We see well-clad, chubby-cheeked boys atop horses awaiting their riding lessons. One of them is already riding a capriole. Two others are fashionably sniffing tobacco, reproachfully overseen by a seasoned gentleman with a rapier. He who does not ride turns to unhealthy decadence. In this engraving, Trichter modernizes Löhneysen, whose first equestrian scholarly book dates from 1588. Riders portrayed in his book, as well as those of Grisone or Galiberto, only seldom had a "romping place" for exercising their horses. They rode in pastures and fields, blazing their own tracks, or "*repellons*," themselves. For certain movements they used the terrain or buildings at hand. Near cities convenient places were popular riding venues. In southern Austria's Graz there is a "Tummelplatz" even today, a slightly sloping square, which probably offered dry footing for the most part. The size was ideally suited for equitation. Only great lords had a special arena or even an indoor manège at their disposal. With the increasing sophistication of equestrian culture, the demand for riding arenas grew, a development that culminated in the construction of the "Winter Riding School" at the Viennese Imperial Palace, which has been considered a temple of equestrian art since 1735. Nowhere in the world can one ride indoors more beautifully than there. The best equestrian art on the best horses deserved the best ambience.

Image 34 – Valentin Trichter, Riding school scene. (Private archive.)

Riding Schools as Social Hubs

Elegant surroundings for riding were also in demand outside the Imperial Court. Ridinger portrayed his equestrian engravings with fantastic architecture. Fortunately we have a realistic depiction of a Viennese riding school by Salomon Kleiner (1700-61).

> "With his city views and depictions, Kleiner created works of utmost representative value for his princely and patrician clients. Because of their exactness and attention to detail, they are moreover eminent documents of architectural culture and urban layout. Today, in many cases, these engravings are the only sources showing the original form of buildings."[130]

As we can see, reality is in no way inferior to fantasy, since a mannerist rococo-style backdrop surrounds the location, the riding school of Count Joseph Ignaz von Paar (1659-1735) in "Alster Gassen," where equestrian art created a gallant realm of its own, shielded from the disdainful outside world. What is illusion and what architecture here? Everything serves only to offer a grand background for equitation, with obelisk, arcades, columns, gates, recreational park, fountains, and statues, a venue for subtle conversation and elegant courtesies. Exquisite equestrian movements: passage, capriole, ballotade et al., the arena as a social hub, where persons of quality meet.

Paar, who acted as General Postmaster, was said to be Europe's greatest horse keeper and a superb rider. His palace was Austria's post central.

> "On a site in the Alser suburb he had a riding school built, which was considered one of Vienna's most pompous buildings. The main edifice faced Alser Road, behind it there was a baroque garden with many statues."[131]

Image 35 – Salomon Kleiner, Count Paar's riding school, Vienna. (Private archive.)

Advancing Equestrian Art to a Point Maybe Still Unknown in France

Emperor Charles VI ruled from 1711-40, and under his reign Austria not only reached her greatest size, but also developed into a cultural world power, and outshone other nations in equestrian art. A renowned riding master and connoisseur of the era's international equestrian scene, Johann Baptismus von Sind (1709-76) stated:

> "The Baron of Paar, the Baron of Regenthal, the Prince of Dietrichstein, the Count of Trautmannsdorf, the Baron of Eisenberg, etc., whose scholars, even if they are few, further progress on these excellent masters' track and advance equestrian art according to their principles to a point perhaps still unknown in France."[132]

Sind owes recognition to the "great" and "famous men," Paar and Regenthal for leading him out of chaos and onto the right path through their lessons. Their talent for equestrian art was renowned, and Sind owes it to their kind-hearted spirit, that by means of their principles they "passed their torches on." "It is the sublimity of art whose veil I want to lift."[133] Sind also reports with enthusiasm about "true courbettes," which he only saw with Paar and Regenthal. Only few horses could manage this kind of courbette. "On the rider's part it demands a quiet seat and a fine and attentive hand."[134]

Image 36 – August Querfurt, Riding as self-presentation. (Private archive.)

Johann Christoph von Regenthal: Without the Slightest Movement in Perfect Unity and Complete Freedom

One personality essentially accounted for the fame of Austrian equestrian culture: Johann Christoph Regner, Baron of Regenthal, was appointed to become Chief Rider by Joseph I in 1709, confirmed by Charles VI, and remained in office until 1730, the year of his death. He gained international renown from his students: Emperor Charles VI who trained with him two or three times a week, consequently riding faultlessly and majestically in all functions.[135] Franz Stephan von Lothringen (as of 1745 Francis I Stephen, Holy Roman Emperor) was his most outstanding student. He also became the tutor of prominent riding masters, such as Friedrich Wilhelm Baron Reis von Eisenberg and the Baron von Sind, who spread his fame to England, Italy, Germany, and France.

Sind describes why Regenthal's way of riding impressed so much: He rides

> "without the slightest movement visible on the rider's part. The horse must work under him in perfect unity and complete freedom, as if he did his airs by himself. This is… the masterpiece of art. I saw it carried out that way by…the Baron of Regenthal."[136]

Regenthal himself reports:

> "There are many among my trained horses that are virtually led and reined by the rider's thoughts. You see no reins tightened or braced, but entirely vibrating, as if held by nothing, and nevertheless the horses stay in their most beautiful posture with the head remaining perfectly perpendicular. Now, if body or hand moves to this or that side only minimally, this [indicated movement] is carried out right away…I still have horses that are led and reined by the body. I take the curb reins at the correct length into my left hand, hold it steadily to my body and do not let it deviate from its position even the width of a knife's back. In such posture I canter my horse widely and closely, *redopp* him widely and closely, bring him to the smallest circles of a horse's length in diameter. I run at a fully stretched fast gallop and stop on the spot, all this alone with my body…, without the hand deviating a straw's breadth from its centre. All this…does not consist of any speculation, but of the true, correct fulfilment, as I often presented it to my audience."[137]

Image 37 – Bernard Picart, Regenthal and Le Superbe. (Private archive.)

One of the Noblest Trainers of Our Time

Regenthal must have impressed his contemporaries extraordinarily. Reis von Eisenberg, his famous student, describes him,

> "…who is one of the noblest trainers at our time…Indeed his way to train horses is infallible. I have had the honour to apply his superb school for some years to my advantage, and I cannot enough describe the virtue and friendship he showed me during this time and all my stay…Enclosed I publicly declare that everything I know about equestrian art, I have learned from him…I have never seen a man sitting more steadily on horseback…than him. It was a real pleasure to watch him exercising the horses on the circle…Furthermore, I must add, that his horses also went with an unusual lightness under others, and after my notion I have not been sitting on more pleasant animals."[138]

Not just Regenthal became famous, the horses he trained were equally renowned. He educated mounts for the emperors Joseph and Charles. A roan, for instance, called Peso d' Oro, carried out most extraordinary pirouettes and "indeed money could not buy him. He was such a rare piece, that a great connoisseur…said: This is a pulpit not for everybody to ascend. Nothing like him has been seen later on."[139] Charles VI had another horse trained by Regenthal brought to Spain, obviously to prove the high level of Viennese breeding and equestrian art. A capriole horse of the Emperor's riding school, called "Le Difficile" or "the Dangerous" or "the Evil," was unsurpassable, according to Eisenberg: "This horse has gained the Baron of Regenthal, who trained him, great honour, since a great many of foreign gentlemen attested that they had not seen such a jumper anywhere."[140] Regenthal won the greatest laurels for his black "Le Superbe," an outstanding, brilliant, arduous *passageur*, "so obedient, that there was no other horse in the world that would have deserved more to be mounted by His Majesty on such a ceremonious and pompous occasion."[141] Sind, too, reports, that Regenthal was famous for riding superb passages.

Bomb-Proof Horses for the Emperor

Indeed Regenthal had reason to be proud of his work. When Charles VI was crowned Emperor in Frankfurt in 1711, he needed a bomb-proof horse that cut an elegant figure even in a vast crowd:

> "A monarch, adorned with crown and sceptre, in an event, where more than 100,000 people shout the Vivat, swing flags, have drums, trumpets, and timbales resound incessantly; in such an extremely big bluster even the best horse could easily have come into confusion, and thus His Majesty into danger."[142]

Charles VI, having come from Spain without knowing Regenthal and his horses, had taken a risk, but everything turned out to his complete satisfaction. The Coronation-Diary registers Regenthal in the category "of high baronial comital rank and other persons of distinction…having come to Frankfurt…Sir Regenthal, Imperial Chief-Rider."[143] The "Imperial suite" consisted of several coaches and hand-horses: "The Imperial Chief-Rider Sir Regenthal / behind him sixteen precious Imperial hand-horses in black blankets / led by grooms."[144] As far as horses were concerned, Regenthal had made himself indispensable to the emperor, and therefore he went on his side during the coronation of the King of Hungary in Pressburg, in 1712. He assisted in coronations and ceremonies in Vienna, Prague, and Graz. Generally he led a life of prestige and wealth. He could afford to demand luxuriously high guarantee-sums for rented horses. In this way, one of Regenthal's mounts was killed during a carousel by the lance of the Count of Lengheim, and an enormous guarantee came due.[145]

Image 38 – J. E. Ridinger, Regenthal's favourite student, Emperor Francis I Stephen. (Private archive.)

Johann Christoph von Regenthal's "COMPENDIUM" "PRIMARY DIRECTIVES"

After half a century as a horseman of highest rank, he decided "to compose his experience in a compendium and to communicate it to the enthusiasts."[146] But he died in 1730 and left for posterity only a dictation, apparently, but no printed book. The leather-bound manuscript came into the hand of the antiquarian, Bengt Birck, and Bertold Schirg published it in 1996 under the name "The Primary Directives." Until then Regenthal had fallen into complete oblivion. Regenthal decisively contributed to the rise of Austrian equestrian art to utmost excellence. For the Casa de Austria it was unusual to document its equitation performed on highest levels in books, hence everything was left to oral tradition, a disadvantage to printed publications which generally last longer in the public memory.

Without French Influence

Thus Field-Marshal Holbein and Chief Rider Johann Meixner regarded Pluvinel and especially Guérinière as the Viennese Spanish Riding School's spiritual forefathers in their "Directives" of 1898.[147] Regenthal definitely is not mentioned there, though contemporary connoisseurship estimated that the equestrian art at the Imperial Court of Charles VI was held in higher esteem than that of France. Thus the historic error, that the art of the Viennese Spanish Riding School might be traced back to Guérinière, solidified until the 21st century. But Guérinière's work did not become known in Austria until the end of the 18th century, and did not influence equestrian art in Austria until the beginning of the 19th century. And if Pluvinel had any influence on the Viennese School then it was only indirectly through Guérinière, who was only noticed long after Austrian equestrian art had passed its prime.

Image 39 – Balthasar Ferdinand Moll 1781, Francis I Stephen, oldest Viennese equestrian statue, Burggarten. (Photo Poscharnigg.)

Empirical Procedure

Johann Christoph Regenthal introduces his "Compendium," now called "Primary Directives," with a description of his rich experience spanning over half a century, emphasizing that he had not borrowed anything from other authors, but just wanted to state the results of his most successful training practice. He did not mean to be a writer or philosopher, but just wanted to describe briefly how to educate horses "with all regularity and benefit."[148] Generally, Regenthal despises any sham or punditry with respect to horses, "such reasoning stirs all blood in my veins."[149] Theoretical speculation is nothing to him, practical experience is everything. Regenthal demands orderly, quite tight attire, a rather large hat, and absolutely rejects any rough boots, because he frequently sees untidy, incorrectly equipped equestrian students. He does not like too mild a spur, for it tends to desensitize the horse. The sharper spur, though, has to be applied with care to avoid making the horse stubborn or twisting of his tail. He warns of inappropriate punishment using spurs which ruins the horse. The spurs should be applied two or three fingers' breadth behind the girth in order to work well.

Imperial Seat

Regenthal considers the "old" school-saddles monstrous and uncomfortable for horse and rider. His "own kind of saddle has been brought to this form primarily by me [Regenthal] and has become a model exported to various princely courts and other foreign countries."[150] Its construction must be done in a way that "the rider is almost forced to stay straight in the saddle, as if he stands on the ground; there is definitely no such thing as sitting to be seen."[151] This kind of seat can still be seen at the Spanish Riding School of Vienna, and each rider must observe it: as exemplified in the famous equestrian portrait of Emperor Charles VI, Regenthal's most prominent student. Hamilton painted this famous work in 1730 depicting the stallion Favori, who was certainly trained by Regenthal.[152] His type of saddle is present in many equine portraits by Johann Georg von Hamilton. For breaking in the colts, there is another type of "saddle called Pastin," consisting of "leather, canvas, and straw, without any wood or iron," so that the "Pastin Riders," called that in reference to the saddle, are less likely to be harmed when falling with a young wildling.

Regenthal disapproves of the severe "old-time" curb bits; these "inventions were all monstrous." Good horses are not educated by sophisticated bits, but by methodical riding. He considers himself a representative of a new era in equestrian art: "Nowadays we think differently, we maintain, groom, ride, and work our horses in a different way compared to the old-timers; they did not know the right way."[153] All he needs "is a curb bit with a mouthpiece in order to ride all [horses] in the most beautiful manner."[154] He deems the cavesson indispensable for making all parts of the body manoeuvrable and skilful. It is quite obvious that horse owners' mentality has not changed much during the last 300 years: "All those err and are wrong who believe the mouthpiece educates the horse and makes him obedient, resorting to this equerry now and that trainer then."[155]

Image 40 – Charles Parrocel, Airs on the ground. (Private archive.)

Image 40a – Charles Parrocel, Airs above the ground. (Private archive.)

Internationally Renowned Training Centre

In a "Remark on Some Students" Regenthal reports on the "countless number" of equestrian students from all nations whom he trained successfully, so that they could work in Paris and elsewhere as qualified trainers. Francis Stephan of Lothringen (spouse of Maria Theresia, and since 1745 Holy Roman Emperor Francis I Stephan) is said to have outperformed all others, even those who became professional **écuyers**. Regenthal trained him for six years. In contrast, he tells of another student "from a great French family, who shall remain nameless, having been recommended to me by a high noble hand,"[156] who, having achieved nothing, as much as Regenthal tried. Nevertheless, the Viennese Imperial Riding School under Regenthal's tenure was an internationally renowned training centre for Europe's noblest and best riders, with the Emperor himself watching the scene with great interest.

Regenthal repeats: "The true position of a rider must be straight, as if he stood on the ground, his armpit, knee, and heel must be in a straight, perpendicular line."[157] This results in a stable, safe position, avoiding undesirable spur contact. By the way, a "general rule is to begin the training session tracking to the right, and to end the session to the right,"[158] which Grisone and Galiberto had already established. Striking off at the canter is done using the outside leg, as still done today in the Spanish Riding School. The student must "always try to appear friendly," caress his horse often, showing no impatience, and "not becoming enraged and choleric." "For there is nothing more disagreeable than to see a rider spur and beat his horse, especially when he himself has been the cause for such evil treatment."[159] "There are many hot-tempered riders" who "beat and tyrannize their horses, so that you really pity them; I would rather like to wish such an imprudent, impatient rider barbaric incest."[160] Violence of this kind just has no place in the Austrian equestrian tradition.

Imperial Riding School: With Certainty and Love

While equestrian disciples should ride with curb bit and cavesson for some time, it is "neither decent for a great lord nor other cavaliers to use the cavesson permanently, and even less appropriate for a soldier because he needs his right hand for his weapon."[161] The curb reins are, of course, held in the left hand. Only if a horse is not fully trained, can the right hand assist the left one. The right hand with the crop is placed two fingers' width in front of and above the left one, the tip of the whip pointed toward the horse's left ear. This corresponds with the position of a lance, whereas today the whip is held vertically upright like a sword when riding solely on the curb.

> "…much is demanded of a beautiful and good rider…An **écuyer** who understands everything that belongs to a well-working riding school, has to be held in high esteem, for not only must he control the riding school, where respect, obedience, attention, diligence and all other good customs are requested, in order to educate the equestrian disciple with all precision, but he must inform him also with all sureness and love, as far as the execution is concerned: The most beautiful occasion comes naturally when the student is mounted…, the horse gives him more authority than rapier, dancing school, and grammars."[162]

A riding school is character school. With "sureness and love."

Correct and checked equipment guarantees the rider's safety. Furthermore Regenthal describes the *redopp*, the courbette of disciples riding on "jumpers," referring to mounts for schools above the ground, and riding at the "carousel." Regenthal likes to hold the whip beside the horse's eye in order to bend or direct him. He prefers unobtrusive weight-aids: "What the mind wants is also wanted by the body with the hands and the legs in a good harmony; hence they support in best co-ordination and carry out what he wants to undertake with his horse."[163] Riding begins in the head. Generally "the écuyer's good and sane reasoning is paramount," "depending on the écuyer's good judgement and experience."[164] The constant of good equestrian art: *The thinking rider.*

Patience, and by No Means, Evil Treatment

After the disciple's education, Regenthal describes the education of the horse. Together with quiet preparation it is important for him that the horse goes on the lunge in a balanced manner, so that it does not later pull on the hand to compensate for a lack of balance.

> "Time and patience are requested here, by no means evil treatment, for by impatient, hard procedure, where you quickly beat, the horse gets ruined for life."[165]

Starting the colt takes place with "steady stroking," without pressure and stress. The young horse must stand absolutely still during mounting and dismounting. In addition to the cavesson, a snaffle bit is used, the reins of which are held in the left hand. From the beginning the rider demands an erected neck, so that the horse's front becomes light, displaying high action, supported by aids of the legs and whip at the shoulders. Regenthal warns of other methods:

> "Nowadays all these abuses are finished and discarded because we have a better and safer method, namely trotting out our horses well. The trot is the true foundation of the whole equitation."[166]

For Regenthal equestrian art stands in a new era of effective and humane handling of the horse.

As the horse gains lightness, the snaffle is replaced with a curb bit instead, and is made so light "that he presents the canter himself."[167] Here, the horse must lay his weight neither on his shoulders nor on the rider's hand. At a halt from the canter, the nose must remain perpendicular. By riding on the curb alone, the horse is definitely brought to absolute obedience and can be ridden through all desired movements. Like Galiberto before him,

Regenthal, requests absolutely correct lifting, lightening education in the cavesson, which he thinks other nations use incorrectly. Especially the French come off badly:

> "The French discard it completely, do not know how to use it, may the Lord forgive them. They do not know what it is good for."[168]

Regenthal, however, likely did not know his contemporary Guériniére, who viewed the use of the cavesson with scepticism. While Guériniére only quotes **Salomon de la Broue** and The Duke of Newcastle's opinion about it, he himself seems to be little convinced of the cavesson's efficacy.[169]

Without Draw Reins

Contrary to French equitation, Regenthal principally approves of the Duke of Newcastle: "The Marquis Neucastel, who was an incomparable rider, and whom alone we owe thanks for advancing this noble equestrian art thus far."[170] Although Regenthal appreciates Newcastle's accomplishments, he contradicts the Duke's opinions in almost every respect. This extends to the cavesson, which Newcastle applies in conjunction with several draw reins excessively, so that the horses "almost cannot move." "Therefore I have completely discarded the draw reins, because they pull down the head too much, and with it bring the neck, which, after all, is an adornment, out of its beautiful position."[171] After the horse's training with the cavesson is finished, he is ridden on the curb bit, to which "now again the snaffle can be laid."[172] Its reins are used like the cavesson's. Again a sideblow against French equitation: "If the French used the snaffle bit in my manner, I would concede their rejection of the cavesson a little."[173] In this way, Regenthal regards himself as the inventor of the bridoon. Guériniére, who published "L'École de Cavalerie" in 1729 [*Ecole de Cavalerie*, Xenophon Press 1992, 2015], one year before Regenthal's death, already mentions the bridoon.[174] Chances are he became acquainted with it by one of Regenthal's disciples.

Image 41 – Shoulder-in, SRS 2003. (Photo Poscharnigg.)   Image 41a – Shoulder-in, Guérinière 1729. (Private archive.)

Shoulder-in

The same could apply to the shoulder-in movement that Regenthal calls "Head in, croup out." He uses it to enhance obedience, after the horse willingly goes forward and carries out the levade. Unlike Galiberto, who called shoulder-in "Canton or angle," developing it alongside a wall, Regenthal takes a pillar as the centre, around which he rides the air, completely in the manner of Newcastle. "This action, head in, croup out, is one of the most efficient…It teaches to bend the neck, it frees the shoulders…It helps [the horse] understand and accept the bit more and more, making the horse, in all parts of his body, so skilled and free, as no other lesson can."[175] Newcastle, too, describes it in this way and recommends it as the first lesson for trotting a colt:

> "It is not sufficient to keep the head and neck of a horse within the volte, but [one should] give an entire *plié* or bend to his whole body from the nose to the tail…From whence you may perceive the excellency of this lesson in making a horse's shoulders free and easy."[176]

As mentioned previously: To call this movement an invention by Guérinière is a popular historical mistake, but Newcastle, who described it in 1658 with extensive images can also not have been the inventor, since already in 1650, Galiberto had discussed it before him in all three basic gaits.

Pillars, the Air Redopp et al.

For the work at pillars, either single or as a pair, Regenthal recommends prudent, careful procedure to avoid accidents. Unusual for riders nowadays: Croup in (travers, haunches-in) is supported by holding the switch towards the outer eye. Further, Regenthal describes renvers voltes as a novelty for the equestran art of his time:

> "I can easily state to be one of the first who have burdened the horses with such unusual lessons, demanding almost the ultimate obedience."[177]

The *redopp*, being related to travers or renvers, must show a distinct two-beat rhythm, and both fore must hit the ground simultaneously. Similarly, both hind feet must do the same, if the movement is to be considered perfect.

Contrary to Galiberto, Regenthal asks for the levade only when the horse shows fundamental progress in his training. First the horse is tethered between two pillars, and the croup is driven to and fro with care, until he rises. "As in other lessons patience is thoroughly recommended here, for so much can be won by it, as can be ruined with untimely punishment."[178] When the horse likes to carry out the levade, courbettes can be trained, first around a pillar, and later without it. Simple courbettes are followed by those backwards and sideways, so that the hoof-prints of the courbetting horse formed a cross-shape in the footing. At that time, this was a very popular high school figure. Regenthal defines strict obedience as "Fundamental Methodus":

> "One of the most important things is that I remove all other thoughts from my horse's head and do not allow him to think anything else, than to regard only me as soon as I mount, and carry out exactly what I demand from him."[179]

The best of his stallions were taken to stand stud at the Imperial stud in Hungary then subsequently returned to the riding school, and they continued working in discipline as before.

Regenthal's ideal pirouette at the canter looks somewhat different from today's pirouette: the inner hind foot stays on the same spot, even digging a hole. The roan, Peso d' Oro was famous for this. Connoisseurs considered only Regenthal capable of showing such an "extraordinary school."[180] Nevertheless, Eisenberg also rode this horse in Luneville for two and a half years.[181] According to Regenthal the passage best suits a great monarch, "the longer the feet can be held high, the more beautiful is this air."[182] And he notes: "Superbo, whom His Majesty rode in many functions, was extraordinary in this air. He lifted his legs so high that he often touched the rider's stirrups and maintained the figure also a very long time, so that there was much admiration about it."[183]

All Blows on The Tormentor's Neck

Especially for the schools above the ground, Regenthal demands "true information," without which horses cannot be trained. "Most riders present their horses sometimes with this movement, sometimes that movement, though they have never learned them; and they also do not know in the slightest how to train them with a true foundation. And when their horses do not obey their inconsiderate demands—which is impossible for them to do—or do not present the thing they have in mind, they spur, beat, and mistreat them in a way which moves one to pity. I would like to wish such a rider all the same blows on his neck, so that he can feel them with real pain."[184] This again suits the philosophy of equestrian tradition of Austria perfectly. Like other airs above the ground, the croupade is first taught between two pillars, then without the pillars. Natural disposition, capability, and inclination are decisive. Even horses of medium strength can carry it out. A true horizontal position proves the correct execution. Other horses may prefer to show the ballotade.

> "The horse's temperament will provide much by itself…for if the disposition lacks here, as in all other movements, nothing good can ever be expected. The rider will take a lot of pains for nothing."[185]

This, of course, holds also true for the step and leap movement and the capriole. The horse must not be overburdened in any way; he should not feel the need to defend himself. The thinking rider's "reason and science" prevent problems here.

Image 42 – The Duke of Newcastle, Regenthal's respected authority. (Private archive.)

Subtle, with Minor Aids

In his "Compendium," Regenthal repeatedly uses the adjective "subtle" when he deals with fine effects. The horse should "be treated with minor aids." This reminds of Castiglione's "*sprezzatura.*" Riding must seem effortlessly light and unstrained. "The rider must remain still and straight in the saddle, aiding subtly with tongue and switch." The horse's nose must never deviate from its perpendicular position. Regenthal must have greatly impressed his contemporaries, for one of his capriole horses a good rider and "erudite cavalier" wrote an epitaph. Emperor, empress and court had often admired this Kladruber: "A well-trained horse must under any circumstances satisfy his rider."[186]

In the "Chapter on National Horses" Regenthal points out that quality depends on the individual, because among all breeds there are good and bad ones for any purpose. In conjunction with this, he describes a regrettable historic constant, namely the Austrian lack of self-confidence:

> "Almost all our German cavaliers have fallen into the most abominable habit that they value anything foreign more than our own good things, which is so much less laudable, since no other nation in the world does the same."[187]

Horses from Vienna to Madrid

As is generally known, the excellence of breeding horses in Regenthal's era mainly depended on animals of Iberian origin having come to Austria over the centuries. But then the tables started turning: as mentioned, the Emperor had sent Austrian-bred stock to Spain, an unprecedented fact. And Regenthal reports that the King of Spain had presented the Emperor with twenty-four horses, among them, unfortunately, many "defective and bad ones." The accompanying Spanish equerry admired the Austrian breeding results and the perfection they were ridden with:

> "He did not desire anything more than taking some from this school with him to Madrid and to ride them in front of his king, as they are ridden here, and he would give a finger from his hand for this."[188]

For 200 years, Iberian equitation had been the paragon of excellence. Now, this paragon had been exceeded. The torch-bearer of Spanish equestrian culture henceforth was the Viennese Riding School.

Image 43 – John Wootton, The Byerley Turk. (Private archive.)

The conviction of breeding the best horses was adamant. This can also be seen from a marginal note by Regenthal about horses that are only suitable "for making a fast run on a distance, which is not my affair."[189] Hence, Austria did not develop a breed like the English Thoroughbred. In 1683, a Turkish stallion had been captured in the Battle of Vienna, called the "Byerley Turk" after his later owner. The horse became the first progenitor of the English Thoroughbred.[190] This horse did not receive any attention in Austria at the time. His potential was not acknowledged because breeding in Austria had taken a completely different direction. The Imperial Court's eminent horse experts, like Regenthal, only valued horses suitable for equitation in the Spanish-Neapolitan style. Therefore, Regenthal regrets and criticizes that the former excellent Danish breed increasingly crossbred with Barbs and Turks. The European trend to alter the stock by crossbreeding with oriental blood caught on in Austria only in the 19th century. With respect to horses, the Casa de Austria remained especially conservative, mainly because the Spanish horse and the way to ride him had constituted the identity of the country and dynasty for centuries.

100 School Horses a Year

Regenthal recommends as a preferable stud a well-made beautiful "Spaniard, for they have the advantage above all others."[191] Yet one must beware of defects: "In order to realize this correctly, I see no better means than an efficient riding school."¹⁹² Here, the stallion's physique and character have to stand the test in order to be selected as a standing stud. This procedure is still successfully applied at today's Spanish Riding School of Vienna. Beautiful exterior is not enough. The act of mating preferably takes place in hand, in order to preserve the stallion. The stud farm should be in a rocky, mountainous region to make the foals harder and more durable:

> "Our Imperial Karst Stud is where foals are bred, and because they are raised among big cliffs, where grazing for forage is done with some adversity, they develop a level of stamina that is unique in the world. All day long, they walk on stones, thus developing unbelievably hard hooves. The flesh, too, is as hard as I ever saw among horses."¹⁹³

Effective breeding saves the Imperial Court money, for 800 horses are needed each year, which otherwise would have to be bought. Regenthal reports, that he has "one hundred or more school horses" in the Imperial Riding School a year. To a large extent, Regenthal's directives regarding breeding correspond with today's practice at the Federal Stud of Piber.

Image 44 – J. G. Hamilton, Lipizza Stud. (Private archive.)

All Horses Naturally without Vices

Bringing the foals into the stable must be done without any violence, Regenthal stresses:

> "I must remind here that, according to my opinion, all horses altogether do not have any vices by nature or birth, but that anything there is vicious has been taught to them by people…Naturally all horses are without vices, and if they have any, they have been taught by man's evil treatment…Praising and reprimanding at the right time is the only means, and one of the most beautiful and necessary sciences regarding this noble profession is that I know when and how much I shall praise or chastise my horse."[194]

And if a horse is difficult when being shod, it is obvious "that this and the like have been taught to him by a man's ignorance or lacking diligence."[195]

Regenthal: Ingenious Brevity without Complication

Regenthal's "Compendium" about the education of men and horses as well as horse breeding is a fragmentary account with ingenious brevity without complication. While reading it, one can imagine how the author confidently dictated to the scribe. Each line of the passed-down, raw version displays solid knowledge. Regenthal's method is empirical: only experience counts. He despises speculation. Despite his baroque attitude he belongs to the Age of Enlightenment. As contemporary sources prove, Regenthal was an eminent factor, a monument during his lifetime, a veritable institution. If the concept "classic" is defined as an era of ultimate cultural achievement, then Austria's equestrian art during Regenthal's tenure absolutely deserves this predicate. Regenthal's era is the apex of Austrian equestrian art in a socio-cultural environment during sweeping expansion of power and grandeur. Many of the horses Johann Georg von Hamilton depicted in his superb paintings were trained by Regenthal. Two artists met sharing their respective competencies at the highest levels.

Corner Stones of Regenthal's Work:

Regenthal already practiced shoulder-in that *was not* adopted from Guériniére. He considered himself one of the first to ride renvers voltes. He considered himself the inventor of the bridoon. He developed a new school saddle, more comfortable for horse and rider alike. He was a vehement opponent of violence against horses, completely refusing severe bits and draw reins. He promoted elegant riding by the cavalier seated completely still in the saddle, acting seemingly without effort and in unison with his horse in a centaur-like manner. He considered riding with loose and even flitting reins and ultimate collection as the acme of equitation. Guérinière called it "descente de main." How Regenthal and his disciples influenced French equitation is a matter deserving further research. He considered himself a herald of a new, enlightened era of equestrian art and humane handling of the horse. He postulated the thinking rider who discerns wrong traditions and errors with common sense and acts accordingly.

Linguistically Regenthal's "Compendium," "The Primary Directives," is a pleasure and delight for the well-versed reader. The fine diction, richly embellished with foreign words, of Latin, French, and Italian origin, lets us sense how elegant conversation was at the Imperial Riding School when conducted in German. The noble flow of language was massively different from the brittle German style in the manner of Lessing. The Viennese court's idiom is a "more European" German, befitting an international nation. In 1730, Regenthal died, and had he not left us his dictation, we would know almost as little about him as of the other Chief Riders in Vienna:

Vicenzo Rizzi (1635-52)
Giacomo del Campo
Hannibale Rocci (1679-95)
Pietro Capitolo (1695-1709)

With Regenthal's death, the era of Spanish-Italian Riders at the Imperial Riding School came to an end. Chief Equerry Count Gundaker Althan reported to the emperor in 1738 that only six of fourteen riders were fit for service. Pastin-Rider Pietro Micheleti, aged seventy, was almost blind; Franz Carl Gojo del Quasto had bloat; Joseph Antonio la Bruna, Nicolà Gonhalvo et al. were unfit to ride.[196] Regenthal's spirit lived on in his many students. Two of them became internationally renowned **écuyers**, spreading his philosophy in Europe: Eisenberg and Sind.

Friedrich Wilhelm Baron Reis von Eisenberg,

(ca. 1700-70) from Saxony-Weimar, studied under Regenthal in Vienna and acted as Chief Rider at the court of Count Daun, Viceroy of Naples. Interestingly, two hundred years earlier, riding masters had come from Italy to teach in Vienna. In the 18th century, an écuyer from Vienna taught in Naples. In 1739, he was appointed Chief Rider at the equestrian academy of the Grand Duke of Tuscany. This was the later Emperor Francis I Stephan, Regenthal's favourite riding disciple. During a stay in England in 1727, Eisenberg published "Description du manège modern dans sa perfection" [*Description of the Modern Manege in its Perfection*, Xenophon Press 2015] in London, a successful work, dedicated to Louis XV of France and, in a new edition, to George II of England. Among the subscribers was the later authority on the training of cavalry horses and a devotee of the Duke of Newcastle, the horse aficionado, Henry Herbert 10th Earl of Pembroke, who met Eisenberg in 1754 on his Grand Tour in upper Italy. Eisenberg was then Chief Equerry of the Academia di Pisa. The copperplates in his equestrian book were engraved by Bernard Picard, in all likelihood after drawings by Eisenberg. A talented painter with charm, he made a series of fifty-five gorgeous gouaches reproducing the copper engravings in his book on the Earl's order in 1755. Today they still hang at Wilton House. They are an important document of Austrian equestrian art because they depict celebrities and horses of the era. As an aside, Eisenberg later presented the Earl a self-portrait that Joshua Reynolds restored.[197]

Image 45 – Bernard Picart, Reis von Eisenberg and Le Royal. (Private archive.)

In 1747, Eisenberg published "Dictionnaire des termes du manège moderne," a "Dictionary of All Common Terms in the Manège and at Equestrian Exercises," which was integrated in his book's heavy German version of 1748:

"WELL-ESTABLISHED RIDING SCHOOL OR DESCRIPTION OF THE MOST MODERN EQUESTRIAN ART…"

A logical system dominates this equestrian oeuvre: Each air is first described with cavesson on one page, and on the opposite with the single curb bit. The images are both decorative and informative. At the beginning Eisenberg offers principal characteristics of horse breeds, of which he prefers the Andalusian. The later horses are started, (at the earliest four years of age) the longer and better they last. He advises gentle prudence, especially with spirited animals, who should not be burdened with too much training so as not to make them unwilling; "for if you want to educate a horse, you need not demand too much at one time, and treat him a little sensibly."[198] A thinking rider requests "that you do not beat the horse, but teach him using good manners."[199] Sanctions are applied in right dosage, because "the punishment must fit the crime."[200]

All aids must be released as soon as the horse reacts in order to reach the goal: a preferably immobile rider in the saddle of a sensitive mount. The horses should "be instructed with all these advantages, which are beautiful, good, and necessary with a certain tenderness and all possible economy."[201] If the horse wants to pull on the cavesson or bit, the rider reacts to this by steadily changing between give and take. When the horse obeys, "one must release the bit, since this is a show of gratitude for his obedience."[202]

The aim is a cavalier "sitting on his horse in an upright, easy, and free manner," showing "that he does not have much trouble with his mount."[203] Eisenberg lets beginners ride first without stirrups for some months. Eventually, the disciple can be seated on a "jumper" between pillars to gain courage and an independent seat. The seat conforms to Regenthal's: at ease with stretched legs. The training of the horse commences with snaffle bit and cavesson, without which the horse cannot be brought into a good form – erected neck, perpendicular nose, collection, bent – states Eisenberg, who also adamantly disapproves of hyper-flexion at the poll, "for this would cause the neck to lose its position and the horse would lose his good looks completely."[204] The walk is at the beginning: "The effect the walk should have in the *manège*, is vast and serves to gentle the wild horses' ardour."[205] Traditionally "the trot constitutes the foundation of equestrian art."[206] The aim is "that the horse trots with frankness and regularity."[207] Eisenberg describes many facets of the trot up to pirouettes in piaffe.

The air "head inwards and backside outwards" obviously corresponds to shoulder-in in the manner of Newcastle on a circle around a pillar. Described awkwardly, the graphics, depicting a sideways movement rather than a forward one, do nothing to further illuminate the execution of this exercise. Eisenberg realized the limitations of his artistic capability, yet he considered the exercise important to help even unfavourably built horses adjust their heads and necks correctly: "I recommend this movement, because it is of great importance, and those who use it will sense its effect.[208] Ridden at a canter, Eisenberg thinks this movement is one of the most difficult, but gives the horse "the greatest perfection" because it develops best flexion of the haunches.

Advanced education is carried out on circles, from which the rider turns to the inside to change the canter lead. Eisenberg recommends the change only after five strides. He finds this more beautiful and elegant, showing greater obedience and the choice of riding schools "of superior taste." He describes courbettes where the forelegs touch the ground after the bound. But he also knew the "courbette in a different way," he had only seen under Regenthal in Vienna and subsequently introduced in Naples, and considered it to be the most difficult of all exercises. "This school is the best to give the courbettes splendour and bring them to perfection."[209] Unfortunately, neither text nor images inform about their properties. Sind, also knew them under the name "true" courbettes. Regenthal's practice definitely reflects in Eisenberg's book; and the author pays his professor repeated tribute, reports of his unique horses that did matchless things and were ridden by the "highest" celebrities. Such reports become even more vivid in Eisenberg's elaborate gouache illustrations that decorate the Smoking Room of Wilton House.

Johann Baptismus von Sind:
"L'ART DU MANÉGE PRIS DANS SES VRAIS PRINCIPES"

The second prominent riding master educated by Regenthal, Johann Baptismus von Sind (1709-76) was an Austrian cavalry colonel from Moravia. He became Chief Equerry of the Elector of Cologne and was a connoisseur of Guérinière and the French equitation of his time. In 1762, he published his first riding instruction in Bonn. Another edition came in 1774, published in Vienna and Paris: "L'art du manège pris dans ces vrais principes…" ("Equestrian art according to its true principles.")

In keeping with the Age of Enlightenment, Sind strove to lift "the veil of prejudice" in his quest for useful truth. The book's first part deals with the horse as a pupil to be schooled; the second is about the horse as a "domestic" which has to be cared for in case of sickness: "The horse has intelligence; but it is limited…He has docility…It takes the right mixture of gentleness and rigour to reduce it to occasional disobedience."[210] The old timers had used brutality against the horse. Paar and Regenthal brought "lucky discoveries": "The work I publish today is only the result of lessons, strengthened by long experience…

and I have seen various abuses by many young people who wanted to make themselves a mock method opposed to the true principles. My goal today is to show the most natural, gentlest, finest ways to make a horse subtle and obedient, and to bring him into the hand, so that his attention is limited to the hand only in all movements."[211] Sind defends himself against Paty de Clam, who claimed the Germans trained their horses violently without amenity. Clam had just not seen Paar, Regenthal, Trautmannsdorf, Dietrichstein, Eisenberg and their students to be convinced of the opposite. Clam considers the Imperial horse breeding superior to the French.

Sind's method of training works approximately like Regenthal's, whose methods and goals he acquired including that a seat features a stretched leg. Colts are started with the cavesson. From the beginning, a stable position of neck and head is trained, thereby controlling the rest of the horse's body. The horse's nose is always perpendicular. Sind proceeds with gentleness and patience, rewarding any obedience, refusing injustice and roughness, applies the spurs extremely seldom, but rigorously punishes true disobedience. "My immobile seat and my discrete hand soon calm him; he becomes attentive, sensitive and obedient."[212] Thus he achieves "amenity of posture and noblesse of movement."[213] For him, collection is expressed by the utmost beauty a horse can display. Discussing work on voltes, Sind describes his ideal: "The most beautiful aspect of this lesson is to see the horse work without any visible aid or movement from the rider, who, always keeping his fair seat, allows the reins to flutter sometimes; so you might say, the horse manoeuvres by himself and observes the correctness of the changes and demi-voltes himself, without being led by the rider." Anyone who did not trust such words and did Sind "the honour of visiting his *manège*" was convinced by "precision and accuracy" of the execution.[214]

Sind refuses "head in, croup out" for, if carried out too tightly around a pillar, the shoulders become tense. According to Guérinière, he prefers shoulder-in alongside a wall and in corners, where he can collect the horse very effectively. Incidentally, Galiberto also taught this. Sind rides this on the curb only, without visible aids for spectators. Once the horse has become sufficiently subtle through the movement, he carries it out on the circle. He admonishes the upcoming Anglomania, and instead, advocates that a horse destined for campaign riding [open country] and hunting must first be schooled basically and academically if he is to go well and safely over field and stream and remain healthy for a long time. In summary, Sind states: "As far as horses are concerned, you should proceed with intelligence and discretion, so as to educate them in a way that they achieve the admiration of the spectators and do the **écuyer** credit."[215]

Interestingly in his historic work, "L'Oeuvre des Écuyers Francais" the patriotic riding master Michel Henriquet attributes Eisenberg and Sind to the French equestrian culture, though they pass down the Austrian tradition.[216] Equestrian art had become a pan-European heritage.

Image 46 – Winter Riding School, Vienna, noblest riding hall in the world. (Photo Poscharnigg.)

Winter Riding School:
Architectural Apotheosis of Austrian Equestrian Art

Though Charles VI had renounced the crown of Spain after the War of Succession, he maintained the Spanish King's coat of arms and title. Under the construction supervision of Gundaker Althan, Joseph Emanuel Fischer von Erlach designed the Winter Riding School, built from 1729 to 1735, "and the Emperor, himself made the riding school's construction a personal concern."[217] Regenthal visited the Lipizza Stud on imperial order, to work out improvements; he was most likely also consulted as the leading horse expert on the planning of the Winter Riding School. No other riding school in the world built since compares in beauty to this architectural marvel.

The Winter Riding School is the architectural apotheosis of Austrian equestrian art, then at its apex. The will to shine with architecture as did the riders and their horses led to a comprehensive work of art, where man and creature cooperate in an uplifting environment. The jewel of equestrian art of Spanish origin received an architectural frame. The riding palace's matter and light correlate with the physique and dance of horses. The centaur-like unity of man and animal takes place in a sublime space. Man and animal aspire to achieve the paramount, uplifted by the architecture's background. On the 17th Sept. 1735, the "Wienerisches Diarium" reported that the Winter Riding School was inaugurated in the presence of Regenthal's two most eminent students: Emperor Charles VI and Francis I Stephan. And "precious" stallions, educated under Regenthal's direction, were presented by an absolutely worthy successor, Adam von Weyrother, the new Chief Rider.

Adam von Weyrother (1696-1770)

acted as Chief Rider in the "City Riding School" 1735-45, at a time of change and innovation. At the dawning of an age, "he served as a Cornet with the Visconti-Cuirassiers, entered the service of the Prince Adam Franz Lichnovsky."[218] In 1724, Chief Equerry Prince Adam Franz zu Schwarzenberg ordered him from Brussels to Vienna, where he held the position of a "saddle-servant" under Regenthal for some years. As an Imperial Chief Rider he achieved nobility in 1735.

The foundation of the "Campaign Riding School" in 1752 did not take place during his time of service, but under Chief Rider Ernst Emanuel Wagner von Wagenhofen. Why Adam von Weyrother only worked at the Imperial Riding School/City Riding School, is unknown. Regardless, he taught the young nobility at the Academy of Maria Theresa and retired in 1758, although still acted as a Chief Rider for the Bishop of Olmütz. While Regenthal, a Baroque empiricist, summed up his life's equestrian experience as a great equestrian professor of emperors briefly in a concise, noble work, his student, Adam von Weyrother revealed himself as a utilitarian encyclopaedist of diligence, concerned with scientific detail and comprehensiveness. Both Christoph von Regenthal and Adam von Weyrother, are renowned celebrities at the climax and heyday of Austrian equestrian art. Three years before his death, Adam von Weyrother published his seminal work:

"L'UTILE À TOUT LE MONDE OU LE PARFAIT ÉCUYER MILITAIRE ET DE CAMPAGNE,

DIVISÉ EN QUATRE LIVRES. 1. De la connaissance du Cheval 2. De la cure des Chevaux 3. De la Ferrure. 4. Des qualités and devoirs du parfait Écuyer. ... Par le Sr. A. DE WEYROTHER, Chevalier du St. Empire Romain, ancien Officier de Cavalerie, and Écuyer Académicien... A BRUXELLES, Chez J. J. BOUCHERIE, Imprimeur-Libraire, rue de L'Hopital. Avec Privilege de SA MAJESTÉ."

"The Utility for the Whole World, Or the Perfect Equerry/Riding Master for Military and Terrain. Divided Into Four Books

1. About the Knowledge of the Horse
2. About the Horses' Cure
3. About Shoeing
4. About the Properties and Tasks of the Perfect Écuyer…

By Sir A. de Weyrother, Knight of the Holy Roman Empire, Retired Cavalry Officer, and Academic Écuyer…"

Image 47 – The Weyrother-Coat of Arms. (Dokumentationszentrum für altoesterreichische Pferderassen.)

A Lance for Academic Equestrian Art

A riding master of excellence writes here in the style of critical enlightenment, striving for universality, realizing that knowledge and abilities of a perfect écuyer are so multifaceted that they can hardly be found in one person. Adam von Weyrother appreciates "several great men." "The whole world knows them": "At the Imperial Court we had the famous Count of Paar, who died with the reputation as the greatest horseman and most virtuosic riding master."[219] As witnesses are mentioned: Adam de Weyrother; Jean Michel de Weyrother, academic écuyer in Brussels; and Francois de Weyrother, his son, Chief Rider of Her Majesty the Empress. Sind and Eisenberg, too, considered Joseph von Paar the most eminent riding master of the era beside Regenthal.

For Adam von Weyrother, after Paar follow

> "at the French court, the gentlemen Solleysel, la Guérinière and de Garsault…To help the truth to its right, I feel obliged to confess frankly, that the doctrines of these three great men still stand indefinitely above today's principles; for it is not about very sophisticated finesses, by which you can form a real écuyer and train a horse…If you really show a horse, educated according to the new rules, it will suffice to compare it to another one, trained according to the simplest and wisest principles, to find out the invalidity of the one, and the validity of the other."[220]

This proves that Adam von Weyrother does not agree to the simplistic horse breaking in the English or Prussian manner, but still cherishes the dignified training according to the Iberian tradition. He profited from the advantages and errors of the mentioned masters. Constantly he wanted to acquire useful knowledge for his country and the world. Therefore, he undertook tiring and expensive voyages to overcome national prejudices. Only in this way could one develop excellent qualities as a horseman. It can be concluded that Adam von Weyrother knew Guérinière and Garsault personally and gathered immediate information about their work. Nevertheless, from an equestrian point of view, Adam von Weyrother does not state anything that Regenthal would not have promoted.

Horse: Creature with Intelligence and Character

Adam von Weyrother requests horse-friendly training as the other authors in the Austrian tradition do: "There is not a difficult horse that cannot be won by gentleness."[221] And he adds: "Before you undertake to train a horse, you must consider that you deal with an intelligent animal, susceptible to any stimulus…You must study his character."[222]

To concede the horse psyche and individuality seems remarkable during a time when materialism emerged. In 1748, Julien de la Mettrie published his book, "The Machine Man," which first influenced philosophy in Prussia and, later, the rest of Europe. According to this volume, the horse is clearly considered a machine even more, a perception that was considered modern at the time, but proved not to be beneficial to the welfare of the animal. Many riding masters of the 19th century used the machine-metaphor, like Francois Baucher, for instance. Adam von Weyrother distanced himself from such thinking: "If the animal obeys, you always have to caress it; but this is not the same with the punishment, which should be used only with discretion and on occasion; if the horse makes an error, it is almost always the rider's and rarely the horse's fault; a complacent man will always be a bad judge in this respect and punish the horse, when he himself would be to blame."[223] Servants and ignoramuses, above all, beat horses.

Educate Horses and Form People

An écuyer must have distinct traits of character:

> "A riding master must be firm, yet gentle; intelligent without conceit, bold without carelessness, lively without turmoil; but cold-bloodedness and patience are his most excellent qualities…The term écuyer, in the whole sense of its meaning, defines a man who is able to train horses and form people. One forms people by training their ability to stay firmly in the saddle without restraint, by correcting their mistakes; by developing their natural amenity, and by teaching them to know themselves and their horse."[224]

Such a philosophy proves the level of an equestrian culture which was considered an instrument of education for the complete personality, building character with psychological finesse. The horse becomes, through the intermediary écuyer, a forming force for the human ego, a key to self-knowledge. Adam von Weyrother distinguishes different riding masters for the academy, the military and the terrain.

> "The academic riding master must be a great horseman…He must hold his position in a noble manner and combine firmness with gentleness; his behaviour must generally be above any reproach."[225]

And he must be aristocratic, so that the youth entrusted to him can respect and believe him. This explains why all non-aristocratic riding masters were bestowed nobility when they taught academically.

The military riding instructor must form men of all shapes and sizes fit for riding. In this context, Adam von Weyrother remarks: "It would be desirable that a general and equal principle unites the whole cavalry." That it was not so, obviously contributed to the inferiority of the Austrian cavalry in the conflicts with Prussia. Adam von Weyrother apparently did not have much estimation for the campagne-instructor, the one for terrain and hunting; he need not be aristocratic, just has to fulfil his tasks.

With Ease and Amenity

Generally Weyrother complains about his era's decadence, seeing equitation as an art form and intellectual process in danger:

> "It is true that nowadays good écuyers can rarely be found, but this is a deplorable misery…Today everybody calls himself a riding master; there is almost no groom who does not think he is an artist; this allowed the equestrian art fall into disrepute and abasement."

Riding takes much time with "taste and intelligence," and "the ablest riders admit they learn each day."[226]

As soon as the rider is seated in the saddle, he should praise his horse, sit upright effortlessly, the legs stretched, the stirrups not too short, for "you ought to ride with much ease and amenity, without any artificiality."[227] (This kind of seat with straight, perpendicular legs is consistent with the Austrian-Spanish tradition as defined by Regenthal, not Guérinière.) A tense or casual appearance must be avoided, but the middle between the extremes should be found in order to ride with grace. "A cavalier must ride his horse with skill and ease…, with light hand, be bold without carelessness, treating his horse without excitement and anger."[228] A good rider can be spotted by the way he rides a self-trained horse with loose curb reins, without use of the snaffle bit and without visible aids. The horse is collected, without being over-flexed at the neck. He considers hyper-flexion a serious fault, characterizing a badly trained horse.

The snaffle bit should only be used to lighten up the horse's mouth. Curb bit and bridoon are never used at the same time in order to save the mouth. Someone using the snaffle bit too much is no horseman. The cavalier rides with imperceptible movements of the hand and yields, as soon as the horse obeys: "Thus the light hand consists of giving and taking the rein with a soft movement of the hand in order to refresh the mouth and maintain its sensitivity."[229] Such a principle characterizes cultivated equitation of any era: we already know it from Galiberto and Regenthal. Guérinière, too, knew it and called it "descente de main."

The bridoon obviously is standard equipment for controlling a bolting horse in the open terrain if the curb bit has no effect. The bridoon reins is fastened to the saddle of military and campagne horses. The cavesson, still praised as indispensable by Regenthal, is used only for groundwork by Adam von Weyrother. Among the curb bits he selects the mildest, effective model. He considers the English saddle the best among many others.

Image 48 – J. E. Ridinger, Make a horse "bulletproof." (Private archive.)

Encyclopaedic Personality

As mentioned, Adam von Weyrother strives for encyclopaedic quality with his work, and indeed he treats a comprehensive spectrum of topics. Given the circumstances of the 21st century, his universality seems almost incredible. He is the écuyer who rode at the opening of the Winter Riding School in front of two emperors, both very good riders themselves thus he must have been a superb cavalier. He proves in-depth, exact knowledge of the horse in the stable and outdoors; he knows the anatomy in detail, the horse dealers' tricks, shortcomings and virtues of horses. Additionally he demonstrates his savvy as an impressively well-versed veterinarian. For a number of diseases he recommends operations or medications, the production of which he describes in detail. Some especially effective compounds, though, are kept secret and only distributed via the chemist, Caroli in Brussels' herb market, directly or by mail order. Adam von Weyrother thinks the perfect écuyer must have excellent knowledge of horse healing because veterinarians cannot be trusted. The same holds true for farriers: only a rider who knows about the matter thoroughly can judge the quality of work. He states: "If a horse is difficult to shoe, this is always the fault of the people who raised him."[230] And he offers various tricks to shoe such a horse nevertheless. Generally, his knowledge about horse-shoeing seems impressive.

Among the many interesting topics in Adam von Weyrother's work, some may be mentioned here: for safety reasons, he recommends that women sit on the horse like a man, which garnered strong resentments in his day. The instruction of how to accustom a horse to shooting in the saddle provides horsemen of the 21st century with very useful information. The voice aid to stand still is, by the way, "hou!" When hunting with hounds in English style, Adam von Weyrother most intensively warns of excessive demands from the horses and advises it is better not to arrive at the finish than to race the horse to death. He also proves to be an expert concerning the increasingly popular practice of carriage riding, demanding that the coachmen love their horses and work more than wine.

Definitely in the manner of enlightenment, Adam von Weyrother asks for critical comments. He planned further books. But all life is finite. Adam von Weyrother died in 1770. Thus his encyclopaedic horse-project was discontinued. Between the lines, it is apparent that he suffered under the profound changes of the era's equitation. As an artist in the saddle, he had a perfect command of equestrian art. But this skill, only developed by years of intensive training, received increasingly less prestige because of the Anglomania and the effective Prussian military equitation. So he decided to be useful as an expert in all respects of horsemanship, definitely in the sense of utilitarianism, and also corresponding with the ideas of Emperor Joseph II. Generally, European equitation was losing refinement and was on the way towards the more primitive. With Christoph von Regenthal, Joseph von Paar, Adam von Weyrother in Austria, and Francois Robichon de la Guérinière in France, European equestrian art was at its climax. Nothing before or after could match this quality.

Image 49 – J. E. Ridinger, "Changing to the right." (Private archive)

CAMPAIGN-RIDING AND ANGLOMANIA

Academic Equestrian Art as Jugglery

The Habsburgs' male line became extinct with the death of Charles VI in 1740.[231] Along with this came a change in equitation in general. After two and a half centuries, the realm of the Spanish horse approached its end. Military tactics changed, already aiming at what was to culminate tragically in World War I: The massive industrialized deployment of men, horses, and machines as well as their mass annihilation. The mounted combat between man and man became increasingly unimportant, and with it the proper, intricate education of horse and rider, including the Iberian horse, having been ideal for the purpose of intelligent individual combat. In the Prussian sphere of influence, equestrian art as a cultural accomplishment was disregarded and ridiculed, as a humorous tale attributed to Carl Friedrich von Münchhausen shows:

> "I hurried down the stairs, finding the horse so wild and boisterous that nobody dared approach or mount him. Dismayed and confused the most decisive riders stood there; fear and sorrow overshadowed all faces, as I sat on his back with one single leap, not only intimidating the horse by this surprise, but also bringing him to complete quietness and obedience by application of my best equestrian arts. To show this to the ladies even better and spare them any unnecessary sorrow, I forced the horse to jump with me through one of the tea-room's open windows. Now, here I rode several times at a walk, trot or canter, even jumping on the tea-table, performing the whole school well-behaved in miniature, to the ladies' complete satisfaction. My little horse performed skilfully all the way, neither breaking pots nor cups."[232]

And the Prussian Chief Equerry Ludwig Friedrich von Jagow stated: "Equestrian art is nothing but jugglery."[233] In such an environment, void of art, it was easy to make military equitation simpler and more effective. Friedrich Wilhelm von Seydlitz (1721-73) introduced the Prussian campaign-school and more effective cavalry attacks at the gallop. With such simple technique wars could be won as long as firearms were slow and of short range. Only the invention of the machine gun would finally render it pointless to gallop at an adversary in large numbers in order to overrun him, thus defying death.

Image 50 – Hyacinth de la Pegna, Prussians lay down their arms after the Battle of Maxen 1759. (HGM)

Tougher Handling of the Material

"The cavalry's altered way of the abandonment of single combat and caracolling, the united assault and the need for speed during the attack, in order to suffer as little as possible under the fire of the infantry, demanded only so much obedience from the horses that the rider always had them in hand safely, could control the speed of their gaits, force them to inevitable jumps across barriers and to ride against the bayonets and fire of the infantry…The horses, as well as the manner of riding on duty, demanded a more forceful and energetic handling, which had to be made useful for the rider with little skill as fast as possible. The time needed for a finer product was not available…Though school riding had to go along with campaign riding in a certain way, the Prussian and German riders generally did not take pride in artificial but in bold riding."[234]

1752: Viennese Campaign Riding School

In order to be successful against the Prussian enemy again, Austria had to modify her cavalry tactics according to the innovations. The bold mass-attack of a riders' storm was on the agenda. Hence even in the era of Maria Theresa a "Campaign Riding School" was introduced in 1752. Contrary to other countries, this did not mean the end of the "K. k. City Riding School," which had the name "Spanish Riding School" since about 1800. Both together were called "K. k. Court Riding Schools."[235]

The symbiosis of both schools, their mutual influence, and the use of synergies was the reason for the continued high equestrian quality in the Danube Monarchy. Nevertheless, heavy cavalry became the weapon deciding battles, riding down the enemy's infantry using great impact. Restricted range and little accuracy of the firearms at the time limited the losses. Hussars and other light cavalry overtook the pursuit. Hence Maria Theresa's General Regulations of 1769 read:

> "Since the winning of a battle mostly depends on the cavalry's first attack at the right time, it is of importance…to attack the enemy with the sabre in hand at the right time; this must be done not only with one part, but with the whole wing of both parts at the same time, so that the hind part can immediately support the front part, should they be driven back. After fighting the enemy back, the cavalry should not chase him too long, but soon rearrange the eventual disorder of squadrons, in order to take new advantage; but the Hussars and other troops for this purpose overtake the pursuit of the beaten enemy's cavalry."[236]

Maria Theresa reigned 1740-80, enjoyed the Spanish equestrian tradition of her family, and was said to be a good rider. "Contrary to his mother, Joseph II felt strong admiration for Frederic II of Prussia."[237] Accordingly, the Emperor liked Seydlitz' cavalry style. Joseph II, Emperor 1765-90, promoted a strictly utilitarian point of view, so that an abolition of the Spanish Riding School could have been expected. But the respect toward the great equestrian background of the Casa de Austria may have outweighed the reform impetus here. Moreover the cost did not play a big role, since Charles VI, in wise foresight, had created a fund for the maintenance of the Spanish Riding School, the yield of which secured the financial demand of the institute.[238] So while Joseph II may have preferred the uniform coat to the Spanish court attire, the Spanish equestrian art remained a rock in turbulent waters.

Image 51 – Anomymus 1765, Maria Theresa on horseback. (Private archive.)

Oriental Blood

While the normal soldier's horse in the modern Prussian-style cavalry could be quite coarse, Europe's aristocratic officers increasingly preferred horses "of the blood," or oriental blood. These horses offered a feeling of speed already at the walk and were, at the gallop, clearly superior to the Karsters, Andalusians, and Neapolitans. The Iberians went more upward, whereas the orientals went more forward. Just as 250 years before the Iberian horse had conquered the continent, now the oriental horses had their turn. For the English Thoroughbred, the stud book was closed in 1793. With the weakening of the Turkish Empire and the strengthening of European, above all British colonialism, more Arabs, Turks and Barbs came to Europe, matching the orientalising fashion in painting, music, and attire.

They became the horses for the equestrian élite who knew how to handle them. These were horses with fine nerves, many of them not really apt for fighting at the frontlines, because hysterical if hurt; dangerous for stupid riders due to being intolerant of violent treatment. All depictions of the time show that these horses were very rarely ridden on the curb alone, but almost always on a Pelham or curb bit with a bridoon. Spirited Thoroughbreds can be stopped more easily with a snaffle bit. With a sensitive, elegant Thoroughbred an officer could nicely parade in front of his troop. Among the captured oriental horses, breeding selection had been carried out according to military principles. English Thoroughbreds were selected for their speed, a very good, but not necessarily military criterion of selection.

Image 52 – Martin Ferdinand Quadal 1788, Joseph II and generals at Minkendorf 1786. (HGM)

Liberation from the Restriction of High School

But this did not stop the widely spread Anglomania. It mainly consisted of riding on somewhat lively horses, so-called hunters that were docile and submissive enough to jump over all barriers without taking care of their health. These horses were no longer carefully trained; they were just to be used. In England, hunters, so-called Meltonians, had a doubtful reputation because of their "reckless riding"; they were considered a "real gang," riding according to principles like "Better spoil a race than not gain any advantage," or "Never ride slower than approximately 16 miles an hour."[239]

Equestrian youth, did not necessarily consider this barbaric, decadent or vulgar, but instead as liberation from the rigid restrictions the High School had imposed in the manner of Regenthal or Guérinière. Do not learn much, just ride ahead, posting instead of sitting, galloping with a forward seat instead of correct canter, just staying in the saddle instead of acquiring an elegant, upright position, riding on the forehand instead of collection. This revolt against the frame of rational equestrian rules corresponds to the "Sturm und Drang" period, a youth-movement since 1750 that wanted to have rational rule exchanged for the unleashing of strong sentiments, freedom, heart, desire, and overwhelming feelings. "The young wild ones" insisted on the freedom of the "original genius." In literature, William Shakespeare, who created his dramas ingeniously without rules, became these youths' idol: Anglomania in equitation.

These military and cultural tendencies in 18th century Europe led to a renunciation of High School, a development massively enhanced by the French Revolution of 1789, and effective long into the 19th century. Fine equitation in the sense of High School, though, was continuously maintained in Spain and Portugal until the Napoleonic Wars almost completely annihilated these countries' horse breeding and equestrian art. As mentioned, Austria wisely maintained the High School and campaign school together – for the benefit of equitation and horses. Modern military riding was traditionally part of Austrian equestrian art, as Galiberto had already proven.

Image 53 – Joh. Christian Brand, Cavalryman 1765-70. (HGM)

Image 54 – "A general." (Dokumentationszentrum fuer altoesterreichische Pferderassen.)

Paris: High School Politically Incorrect

By the French Revolution of 1789, High School riding in France became politically incorrect because it was identified with the old, hated regime of the absolute, exploitative kings. Equestrian High School was simply considered anti-republican. Napoleon and his wars accelerated the decline of classical equitation, massively reducing the continent's horse population, especially on the Iberian Peninsula. With intricate actions of rescue, Austria managed to save her best breeding stock from the French soldateska [band of soldiers].

French cavalry did not exactly prove as torchbearer of fine equitation, as the Comte d'Aure reports: "With thoughts more at war than equestrian art, the young French officers only desired to leave school. The riders remained confident and took their position according to their nature as well as they just could. With his cavalry Napoleon had been able to work miracles; but our officers rode their horses slovenly, reins flopping, legs stretched forward."[240] The French Revolution had annihilated the High School of Versailles whose most prominent representative was Guérinière. The High School was forced out of France's consciousness; a real amnesia took place. The brothers d'Abzac as well as some surviving riders from the great stables of Versailles had heroically kept their positions to protect the horses from revolutionary riots, risking their lives, though unfortunately in vain, for they could save the precious mounts, but not French equestrian art. A cloak of oblivion spread over the nation's classical-scientific equitation. In France, the reservations against the High School of Versailles reached far into the 20th century, as écuyer Philippe Karl reported from personal, painful experience.[241]

Image 55 – Philipp v. Stubenrauch, "K. k. Austrian Generals." (Private archive.)

Vienna: High School Alive

The Casa de Austria traditionally insisted on High School, for it had never been seen cut off from military equitation. And even in the sanctuary of equestrian art, the Winter Riding School, the famous inscription reminds that the sublime hall also must serve for military training. The Spanish Riding School's Chief Riders of the 18th and 19th centuries always had to deal with campaign riding and cavalry, which meant the Spanish-Austrian tradition was maintained in practical equitation. On the one hand, traditionally trained horses schooled new generations of riders, while on the other hand the Chief Riders passed on the heritage. They, in turn, educated cavalry officers who passed on their knowledge to the mounted troops. Furthermore, the contact with everyday military riding prevented the riders of the Spanish Riding School from becoming alienated from practice, avoiding decadent *l'art pour l'art*. Thus it was a closed circle: The High School passed on its scientific principles to the military; the contact with the military preserved the High School from artifice.

Vienna Adopts Guérinière

In France, the High School of Versailles and its best proponent, Guérinière, had disappeared from public conscience. But in Austria Guérinière was appreciated. As can be seen from Adam von Weyrother's book of 1767, observing Guérinière's work in person, but finding the Count of Paar superior as the representative of Austria's equestrian art. Both of his grandsons Gottlieb (1771-1828) and Maximilian von Weyrother (1783-1833) acted as Chief Riders at the Spanish Riding School, but also as military riders. "In the Imperial Spanish Riding School's library there is a copy of **École de Cavalerie** with notes of possession by both Weyrothers and handwritten remarks by Gottlieb."[242]

Technically, the Viennese Spanish Riding School had no need to resort to Guérinière, for anything he taught was available in Vienna, and even better, as contemporaries judged. The weak point of Austrian equestrian art was the lack of written tradition. Austrian equestrian art was always considered something practical that needed no written documents. Who knows, maybe the "written text" of such a fundamental matter was not trusted. According to the Viennese saying "Everything written is a poison." Until the 20th century there is no detailed, written regulation for the training at the Spanish Riding School. What we had so far seen about Austrian equestrian art in writing were historic lucky strikes: The Neapolitan Galiberto wrote in Italian translated into German; Regenthal quickly dictated the summary of his equestrian life, being published only at the end of the 20th century; Adam von Weyrother left us an incomplete hippological encyclopaedia in French.

So, if the Spanish Riding School's Chief Riders wanted something about the theory of academic equitation in writing, almost nothing was there: Galiberto seemed too practical for the time, not scientific enough, old-fashioned and mostly forgotten; Regenthal's dictation lay somewhere in oblivion, almost nobody knew about it; Adam von Weyrother's incomplete encyclopaedic project was of little use for practical everyday riding. Generally the Chief Riders of the 19th and 20th centuries obviously knew nothing about their predecessors' testaments.

From outside the Austrian equitation, the Duke of Newcastle would have been a choice, but his book, though logical and clear, had come of age and was not suiting the Austrian school. Francois Robichon de la Guérinière's (1688-1751) "L'École de Cavalerie" (1729), however, seemed attractive, for the explanation according to the era's scientific standard was there, generally suiting the Austrian tradition. Written in French, the time's leading cultural language, it was, seen from the Austrian point of view, politically correct, because it was not republican. To acknowledge Guérinière also meant to be against the French Revolution. In 1817, there was a German translation. The Viennese Spanish Riding School's Chief Riders could rely on an eminent, clearly structured book about scientific equitation.

Image 56 – Joh. Jarosch, Spanish Riding School after 1800. (Private archive.)

Symbiosis: Campaign Riding and Spanish Riding School

Nevertheless, High School riding remained a side issue even in Austria, and especially during the first half of the 19th century. More popular were campaign equitation and English steeple-chase-riding. "The aim of campaign riding is the training of a horse useful in war. These horses must have enough speed and endurance, in conjunction with the ability to carry a certain weight…: the campaign horse ought to be in such equilibrium that an equal amount of power both at the forehand and the hindquarters can be developed."[243] For indeed there were more important issues than cherishing High School. "It is generally known that Austria had a famous (and expensive) cavalry…But this wonderful and trained cavalry was completely unable to manoeuvre and work in large masses…, contrary to the French Cavalry that had trained this."[244] This was yet one more reason why Napoleon could inflict heavy losses on Austria. In 1805, Austria was defeated at Ulm and Austerlitz.

Therefore reforms of the army became necessary, like the foundation of the k. k. Central-Armee-Equitations-Institut, which was discontinued in 1823, relocated to Salzburg, and established in Vienna in 1850. It had to "educate riding instructors for the cavalry regiments to achieve a regular and equal training of men and horses in the whole army, and to furnish the infantry's staff officers with ridden horses at low prices."[245] The brothers Weyrother were in charge both of this institute and the Viennese Spanish Riding School, the elder Gottfried being followed by Max. The personal union in the management of both institutes guaranteed an interaction between campaign equitation and High School, between the practical and the academic. However, it also resulted in tension between ideal and reality: The years' long education of the High School horse on the one hand, on the other hand the fastest possible training of the military horse. High School equitation survived in Dresden until 1848; and when Hannover became a Prussian province in 1866, it died there, too, surviving only in Vienna.[246] Despite all internal contradictions, Austria's cultural performance should be acknowledged, affording the luxury of cultivating High School as the sole remaining nation in Europe, even in a tempestuous epoch. The time's equestrian art and artistic equitation could almost only be spotted in circuses.

Image 57 – Julius v. Blaas 1871, Emperor Francis I in Vienna 1814. (HGM)

MECHANISTICS AND EQUESTRIAN PRACTICE: MAXIMILIAN VON WEYROTHER

"THE MOST SUITABLE CURB BIT"

Maximilian Ritter von Weyrother "is known to have acted as a Chief Rider at the k. k. Militär-Equitations-Institut in Wiener Neustadt from 1818 until July 1st 1831, where he quit of his own volition, getting an 'indefinite' position at the Emperor's court upon proposal by Field Marshall Radetzky."[247] In 1825, he became Chief Rider at the City Riding School, and Chief Rider of the Campaign Riding School, and in 1831, Inspector of both schools. After Regenthal, he was the first Chief Rider who gained some international recognition. In 1814, he published in "Vienna, at his own expense. In commission with Schaumburg and Company" his 75-pages booklet "Instructions How to Find the Most Suitable Curb Bit Given the Circumstances. With a Simple View of the Principles of Bridling."[248] The book saw its third edition in 1855 along with a translation into French. In the history of Austrian equitation, it is the first equestrian book printed in Vienna in original German language.

Equestrian Art According to Mechanics

Shortness, simplicity, and clarity contributed to its success. It was dedicated to the Chief Equerry, the Count of Trautmanndorff-Weinsberg, with Max von Weyrother's intention "to bring equestrian art to its former splendour," thus documenting that equitation had already seen better times. He considered the literature concerning bridling unsatisfactory and wanted "define bridling, as the entire equestrian art, using mechanic aspects."[249] This was deemed fancy and modern, for riders increasingly felt the machines' competition and thought to accommodate their art to the industrial age. For Max von Weyrother the principles of bridling are the laws of the lever, explaining the curb bit's effect of leverage using physical terminology. He demands softly acting chin chains, so that the horse does not star-gaze but yields to the pressure of the bit, "getting more sensation in the mouth than on the chin."[250] "The double chain is the best."[251]

Image 58 – Ludwig Koch gave this courbette's rider Max Weyrother's face. (Dokumentationszentrum für altoesterreichische Pferderassen.)

He reports the current thoughts about curb bits: "Generally there is the opinion that the shanks in front of the line make the horse flex more at the poll, and that the shanks behind the line raise the head more, and finally the shanks on the line bring the horse into a good position." He contradicts these views, "for the lifting or lowering depends completely on the position of the hand."[252] He recommends not choosing the mouthpiece's position according to the canine teeth but exactly opposite the curb-groove. In order to fit the horse with the right curb bit, the width of the mouth and then the height of the rear jaw are measured with a ruler. These measurements determine everything else: The length of the chin chain "must be one and a half times the mouthpiece's width."[253] The measured height of the jaw indicates the height of the upper shank. "This is the only correct height which gives the curb bit its correct action; it prevents both the rising of the chin chain and the falling through the curb."[254]

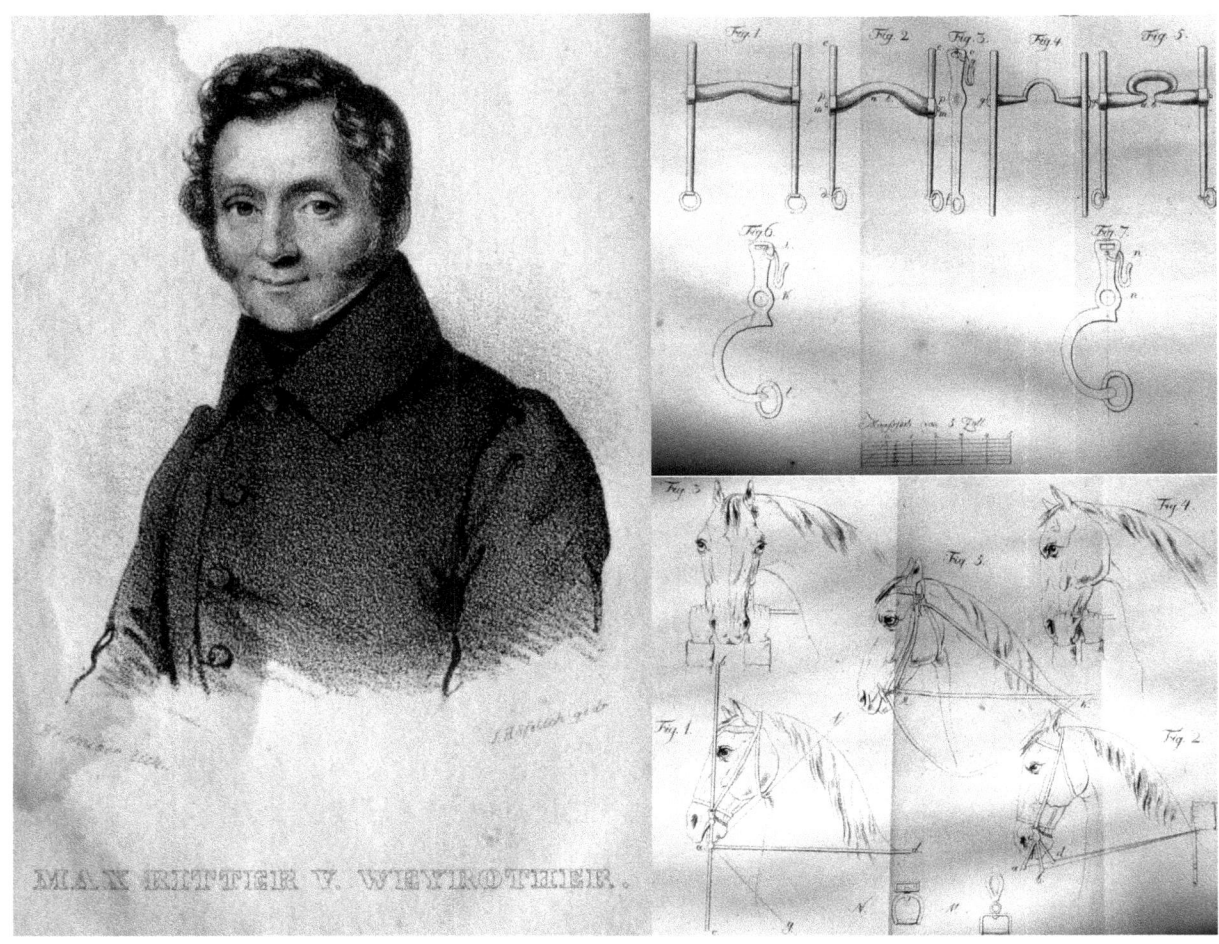

Image 59 – Max Weyrother, his curb bits and draw reins. (Private archive.)

Thinking Rider and Fine Guidance

"The lower shank must at least be twice as long as the upper shank."[255] "The greater length of the lower shank makes the curb bit relatively stronger but acting softer, because the reins' pull cannot act as fast on the curb bit as by a shorter, lower shank, for the force of the pull must travel through a longer distance. Hence, I found it very suitable to take the width of the mouthpiece as the lower shank's length."[256] "By the measures described here, each form of mouthpiece can be fitted for the horse."[257] He accepts jointed curb mouthpieces only as transitional bits from the snaffle, since they are not suitable for precise riding because of their uncertain and not-straight action. "How much they disturb correct and fine guidance must be clear to every thinking rider."[258] Like all authors of Austrian equestrian tradition, Max von Weyrother postulates the thinking rider. The following sensible definition suits this tradition: "Accepting the bridle is the attentive reception of each impression effected by the rider's hand through the curb bit in the horse's mouth.[259]

102

Contrary to Regenthal, who discarded all draw reins and other side reins, Max von Weyrother sees the trainer forced to use effort-saving "lifting and draw reins" for lack of time, though correct education "would, of course, be achieved better by the patient confidence of the green horse."[260] He sees the draw reins as a last preparation for the curb bit "and especially suitable for the wonderful air *l'épaule en dedans*."[261] Verbatim this means "the shoulder to the inside," commonly translated as "shoulder-in." Max von Weyrother uses Guérinière's French term in the original. Galiberto called this movement "canton or angle," Regenthal "head in, croup out," and Newcastle or Ridinger also knew it. It is unlikely that it was not practiced at the Viennese city riding school, being already part of the general equestrian knowledge. French expression was in vogue, hence Max von Weyrother used the French term.

Vienna Conducts Horses Better than Men

Altogether the author's booklet succeeded with clarity, conciseness and comprehensibility. Such simplicity and savvy also appealed to the French, where an officer translated the oeuvre: Max de Weyrother: *De l'embouchure du cheval*…Paris: Anselin 1828. A reviewer of the "Revue encyclopédique" deems the book valuable, since many accidents are caused by incorrectly bridled horses: "M. Weyrother's guidelines…are…a sensible application of the principles of mechanics and physiology, supported by the experience which the author proved as the head of the Imperial Institute of Equitation in Vienna and the Royal School of Madrid. The art to conduct horses is, as generally known, understood a little better in these two capitals than the ability to rule people; and the riding masters there deserve much more confidence than the statesmen."[262] The reviewer may be forgiven historic incorrectness for his humorous side blow to Metternich's policy of repression. Another French critic calls the booklet a "merit" and "enrichment for the French cavalry."[263]

"FRAGMENTS FROM THE BEQUEATHED WRITINGS"

Max von Weyrother died in 1833, leaving only fragments, thus his students and devotees published: "Fragments from the Bequeathed Writings of the Imperial Royal Austrian Chief Rider Max Ritter von Weyrother. Collected by Some of His Friends. With the Author's Portrait. Wien: Heubner 1836."[264] In the foreword to the 98-page-booklet, Max von Weyrother's friends state that he endeavoured "to achieve a more sensible and educated way of treating this useful animal" and his work "leaves permanent benefit in the army." These friends reveal themselves not exactly as followers of classical equestrian art, for they regret that "equitation started to deteriorate because of the old-fashioned principles of the so-called school-riding. Its students did not find satisfaction in practical life, calling this kind of education a pedantry which had become an unnecessary thing and game outside the four walls of a riding school…Due to convenience, obstinacy, and lack of exercise many instructors ignored the public's interest to use the docile horse also for purposes other than only side-passing, dancing, courbettes, jumping…But Max von Weyrother soon realized this." Such general low regard of High School was characteristic of the era from the French Revolution until the middle of the 19th century. Nevertheless, High School must have been further cultivated in the background.

Image 60 – Joseph Heicke 1852, Field Marshal-Lieutenant Schlick and adjutant, 1848. (HGM)

"… that the Rider Remains Effortless"

As a man of practical experience, Max von Weyrother finds "the simplest method is always the best for every student."[265] He intends to describe the horse's natural gaits and to plan dressage on the "foundation of experience and mechanical laws."[266] He calls the riding instructor "handler" of man and animal.[267] What a regrettable difference to his grandfather Adam. Basic knowledge of physics, anatomy, and statics are the fundamentals of his equestrian treatise, and this determines seat, position, and aids. He demands perpendicular hips and wants to sees the knees "slightly forward." This resembles the style of Guérinière and campaign riding. Thus Regenthal's "standing seat" is passé. The thighs should not be turned too much, but only touch the saddle in a way "that the thigh stays without any constraint of the muscles."[268] The back should remain flat, the head firm but not stiff; cramping the fingers is to be avoided: "This position has to be gained by the rider, and it will be easier for him to do, the more he finds his posture without constraint."[269] "It cannot be observed to much that the rider remain effortless."[270] This repeated call for effortless riding, also in the cavalry, is a hallmark of the Austrian equestrian tradition.

No Permanent Pull

When studying Max von Weyrother's description of the reins' effect on the hindquarters and comparing it to Gustav Steinbrecht's "Gymnasium of the Horse" [Xenophon Press, 1995], one realizes the scope of this short equestrian treatise.[271] Even the beginner handles the reins with one hand on the curb only, in a manner first described by Newcastle.[272] The cessation of the aids when the horse has obeyed corresponds to reasonable riding in all epochs: We saw it demanded by Galiberto, Regenthal, Adam von Weyrother and Guérinière who called it "descente de main." Max von Weyrother: "But this pull, like any other, may not continue, but must subside as soon as the horse steps forward with his hind legs"[273], "otherwise his mouth easily gets hard, losing all obedience to the rein."[274] Likewise the leg aids: "The skilled rider's continued aids are not supposed to be used so visibly; he uses them more delicately, applying them only stronger when the horse's jump abates."[275] Max von Weyrother's complete treatise profits from its simple, clear description in the style of a military manual for beginners; and he does not want "to confuse the student by constantly yelling at him."[276] The sitting trot is the only option even for novices; the rising trot (or English trot, as it was called then) is mentioned nowhere.[277]

In order to teach the horse haunches-in, Max von Weyrother recommends preparatory shoulder-in, which he calls "shoulder-inward." "Thus it is inevitably necessary that the horse which should perform the travers movement, is prepared. The best method for this is the movement shoulder-inward, where the horse is made used to the double leg aid and is taught the movement of the shoulder and the transverse leg."[278] The chapter "The Canter" explains the exact footfall. Striking off at the canter is effected with the outside leg, the inner one hanging near the horse. At a fast gallop, the rider allows the horse more stretching "but without letting him go on a loose rein."[279] Maybe a side blow to Anglomania.

With Friendly Patience

During the "Training of the Green, Unworked Horse," Max von Weyrother stresses various points: "Trust and obedience are the indispensable requests the trained horse must meet." But they can be hindered with incorrect treatment: "All insubordinations of a horse are due to fear of man, or due to the horse's lack of understanding that which is demanded of him, or due to the inability to perform what is required too much, too early and perhaps, too often." Therefore it is highly important how the green horse, afraid of man, but also the trained horse, is treated in the stable: "Especially every observant rider's experience proves that rude or cruel treatment in the stable can make even the otherwise most willing horse unwilling for any work." Once the horse is mistreated in the stable, even the greatest master cannot ride fully efficiently. "This becomes all the more relevant with young, very sensitive, spiritual [sic] horses afraid of people, especially of higher blood or noble breed." Thus Max von Weyrother demands affectionate handling according to the manner of Austrian equestrian tradition: "No other animal gets so used to man's voice and no other recognizes him so soon in his intentions as the horse." "Quiet, fearless attitude in conjunction with friendly patience always remain…the unconditional requests for the groom as well as the handler. This ground training in the stable must necessarily precede proper dressage."[280]

"…Well-Calculated Strictness…"

In crass contradiction to this horse-friendly attitude we find Max von Weyrother's instruction about "Taming of a Horse Uncorrectable by Kindness." Since Grisone, European equestrian literature has not seen such brutality: "Should all efforts of kindness be in vain, well-calculated severity must be applied. In the same place where the horse resists, the punishment must be applied with lashes of the whip, hunger, and thirst. The horse is held in the place where he showed malice, gets punished regularly using two school whips without touching the legs until he shows pain, is then immediately led back to the stable, tied reversely, and not fed. In the afternoon he comes back to the arena, where he receives his half-portion of oats and some water. Only after the horse has accomplished his lesson in the arena, is he fed again properly in the stable. After two or three repetitions of this cure, the horse will not be disobedient again."[281] What a decline in comparison to Regenthal's or Adam von Weyrother's humane treatment. Leopold von Heydebrand reports that "because of the fast training which seemed to be appropriate for military horses during the wars, crudeness in the horses' treatment became usual."[282] Max von Weyrother could also not evade this completely.

Degree of Learned Skill

Max von Weyrother states the aim of any horse training in a simple way: "The supreme purpose of equitation concerning the horse's training can be no other than, first, to make the horse skilled to obey the rider and, second, make him willing to obey assiduously even when exerting all power and effort." "The common cavalryman's horse, just as the school horse, must be able and willing to go, and go skilfully...The degree of the learned skill is the only discerning feature of the various trained horses."[283] Such insight distinguishes him from his epoch's trend to see campaign riding as something completely different from High School. Thus Max von Weyrother was ahead of his time since only in the course of the 19th century did the idea prevail that campaign school is a necessary preliminary stage to High School.

Regularity in the Austrian Cavalry

In the Appendix to the "Fragments" there is "written information for the directors of the Imperial-Royal Military-Equitation-Institute at the time."[284] The institute, states Max von Weyrother did not have success so far due to the lack of trained school horses. They would have to be able to master all three basic gaits in the arena "in all tours," the travers, the lead change, and jump over ditches and obstacles. That way the officers-in-training could get the right riding feel resulting in "regularity of equestrian art in the Austrian Cavalry."[285] Adam von Weyrother had already demanded such regularity in 1767, but half a century later it apparently still left much to be desired.

Image 61 – K. k. Feldzeugmeister 1851. (Private archive.)

High School Crowns Campaign Riding

It is Max von Weyrother's achievement that he could save the art of High School through a period when equitation clearly was prone to barbarity. High School may have been overshadowed by campaign riding, yet it was not abandoned entirely, but was seen as the crown of equestrian training. He took Guérinière's ideas as a theoretical basis whose doctrines resembled the previous practice of academic equestrian art at the Spanish Riding School of Vienna. Here, movements such as shoulder-in or the principle of the cessation of aids after their success already had been in use in the 17th century, long before Guérinière. From Max von Weyrother's scarce written documents we learn only few facts concerning High School. Generally, his philosophy seamlessly fits into the tradition of Austrian equestrian art: The thinking rider, the largely humane treatment of the horse, the emphasis of effortless riding, even for the cavalryman.

On the other hand, Max von Weyrother proves himself a true child of his time: The use of the draw rein and crass brutality in order to quickly train a cheap cavalry horse. Not even the seasoned trooper, Galiberto, who daily experienced the cruelties of the Thirty Years War recommended such methods which were obviously standard in 19th century training programs. Horse and rider were "handled" by "handlers" for their military duties according to mechanistic ideas. In the spirit of the age of materialism, man became a machine, and the horse had to accept being treated as one too. So, did machines ride machines?

Overall, Max von Weyrother must have been an impressive, formative personality. Gottlieb Wilhelm Ludwig von Biel, a pioneer of the European Thoroughbred, published in 1830 "Something about Noble Horses" in Dresden, reporting: "I came to Vienna, saw the equitation of the Spanish Riding School there and felt that the principles of equestrian art were handled differently from other arenas I had visited. Only Max Ritter von Weyrother's instructions revealed the idea of true equestrian art for me."[286]

Weyrother Formative for Louis Seeger

With his mechanical approach, Max von Weyrother intensely influenced his renowned student, Louis Seeger (1794-1865) [*System of the Art of Riding*, Xenophon Press 2016] who pays him high tribute in his "System of the Art of Riding" (1844) because through him he gained "knowledge of the horse's gait-mechanism."[287] Seeger, a pronounced mechanistic author, founded Germany's first private riding school in Berlin and became a highly respected authority there. From the teaching of Max von Weyrother, Seeger took over an important principle: "But these three manners of equitation, namely riding a horse in natural posture, in balance, and in the High School, must be considered as a harmonious whole."[288] Such "classification of the schools into progressive stages" regained academic High School its position as the university of horse training.[289]

It was no longer despised as an outdated game of old-fashioned pedants. Its preliminary stages were the basic school of "natural," formless riding, and then the secondary school, the campaign riding. Seeger intends "to unite the often separated followers of equestrian art who are only antagonistic because of their views concerning the combination of various riding styles." A major issue of the era was the predominance of quantity over quality, as Seeger knew: "The need for large amount of cavalry masses does not allow for a special selection of horses."[290] The epoch's military principles required "to put the cavalryman in rank and file quickly, no matter how much the horse must suffer, and much sooner the same gets ruined. Without these circumstances such rash training is condemnable."[291] A dilemma of the time: Riding masters like Max von Weyrother or Seeger felt that the modern fast training methods were evil; but War's destructive force demanded its cannon-fodder. And riding instructors needed workplaces.

Seeger obviously borrowed a great many passages from Max von Weyrother, creating a book which Weyrother, who passed away too early, probably would have written in a similar way. Seeger's merit in this historic context cannot be estimated too highly, for integrating the old masters' principles in modern diction into a scientific structure demanded courage, knowledge, and skill. And in Max von Weyrother's spirit he succeeded in harmonizing traditional academic equitation with contemporary campaign riding, and he was acknowledged for this. Moreover, he strongly influenced Gustav Steinbrecht. Thus Max von Weyrother's influence was far-reaching.

Seeger Warns of Francois Baucher

Austrian equestrian art had "adopted" Guérinière, since, due to the practice of oral tradition, hardly any Austrian systematic literature existed and even then, was only accessible with difficulty. But equitation always eagerly desires a theoretical basis for "intellectual" riding. In France, Guérinière was deemed politically incorrect, and so a genius who was thought to have invented the equestrian art anew, prevailed. Many people believed in François Baucher (1796-1873). He wrote his first book, "Méthode d'équitation basée sur de nouveau principes." The first edition came out in 1837, the last, the 13th (!) in 1867.[292] His enemies often criticized his performances in the circus. But where else could he have presented his art? To this day, Baucher's methods produce fine horses if riders know to apply them wisely. On the other hand, lots of horses were deprived of their natural desire to go forward by unintelligent users. Baucher's ideology never caught on in Austria, but in the rest of Europe it did, even in Germany, where his ideas were tested for the cavalry. Louis Seeger massively attacked Baucher: "But everything of his system ends up in depriving the horse of his power to defend himself by weakening his natural instinct to move forward."[293]

Max von Weyrother's friends saw "the most justifying proofs of his art in the many and beautiful riders educated by him and his instruction."[294] Among them is, besides Seeger, also Borries von Oeynhausen (1812-75), instructor and Vice-Commander at the Imperial-Royal Central Institute of Equitation, who wrote books "that clearly show Weyrother's influence."[295]

Image 62 – Cavalry exercises. (Private archive.)

RIDER'S SPIRIT AND EXERCISE MANUAL FOR THE AUSTRIAN CAVALRY

2nd Half of the 19th Century

With the end of the Napoleonic Wars in 1815 Austria and Germany faced the problem of having only a few good horses available, with mostly young and weak horses that had to be treated rather considerately. Therefore, campaign riding was mainly occupied with dressage in the arena, neglecting jumping and brisk galloping over terrain.[296] This was an intolerable circumstance in view of the development of increasingly better firearms that shot faster, wider, and more precisely. The principles of Anglomania and racing had to be applied even more. Leopold von Heydebrand describes the change of cavalry riding in the second half of the 19th century:

Image 63 – Ludwig Koch, Colonel Rodakowsky, Battle of Custozza 1866. (HGM)

Image 64 – Alexander v. Bensa, K. k. hussars and Prussian cuirassiers in the Battle of Koeniggraetz 1866. (HGM)

Flesh and Blood against Rapid Fire

"In former times, the cavalry had to undertake long marches for any deployment of the army, thus conditioning the horses as necessary. During an attack, the riders could get within relatively close proximity of the enemy without suffering under his fire; as long as the firearms' range was less developed, they just had to cover a short distance at the fastest gait. But nowadays even the cavalry is transported by rail, so the horses have to be trained before; furthermore they need more speed and endurance since the precision arms' range is very wide. So the riders can only somewhat reduce their losses during the attack by covering the route with speed. For these simple reasons contemporary equitation must concentrate on the training of the horses' skill suitable for the purposes of the new times. Therefore the message is: The fastest possible training, aiming at speed, endurance, and safe managing of obstacles."[297]

This meant that the principle of a cavalry's mass attack in Prussian style still prevailed, but the speed had increased. The cavalryman and his horse, two creatures of flesh and blood, galloped in a race against the deadly, inventive spirit of the weapons industry. In 1865, a US "Gatling Gun" was patented, and was able to shoot 200 times per minute. And in 1885, the Maxim-machine gun was presented, firing up to 600 times a minute. The recoil of one shot was used to eject the empty cartridge case, compress the spring, plus load the new cartridge. In addition there were cartridge belts and water cooling.[298] These were black clouds on the cavalry's horizon. As late as World War I (1914-18), dashing mass attacks were merely brainless mass-suicides.

1866: 6000 Soldiers and 6000 Horses Dead

The Battle of Koeniggraetz, where Austria was ruinously defeated by the Prussians, became a turning point for the Austrian cavalry. For many years, the cavalry had suffered under cost-cutting policies. Moreover, the Prussians used breech loader rifles for the first time in Europe. These could be loaded faster and while lying on the ground. These "needle guns" may have prompted the saying "The Prussians do not shoot that fast." The significance of hand-to-hand combat was lessened by the increasing atomization of firearms. Troop transport by rail also became a novelty. Telegraphs and tele-printers began replacing the traditional dispatch rider. A last Austrian cavalry attack turned out to be useless. Austria had to leave 6000 soldiers and 6000 horses dead on the battle field.[299]

Cavalry Reformer Leopold Wilhelm von Edelsheim-Gyulai

Austria had lost the 2nd Italian Independence War where Colonel Leopold Wilhelm von Edelsheim-Gyulai distinguished himself in such a decisive attack that he got involved in the adaptation of the exercise manual. His incursion deep into the French front line caused "the admiration of the whole military world."[300] He had assessed the situation correctly and educated his men accordingly, having "already trained his regiment in Italy especially for distance and terrain riding, fording and taking obstacles." "His completely new handling and training method" became the foundation of the "later Exercise Manual for the Imperial and Royal Cavalry."[301] Edelsheim-Gyulai emphasized individual riding. The cavalryman should be able to operate on his own, independent of the division, as a scout, dispatch and chaining rider. What seems self-evident was not easy in reality, for the horses were trained almost exclusively in closed formation; although they "knew exactly all signals and commands they were not entirely obedient …Edelsheim corrected this issue with natural and simple dressage methods very successfully, and also understood how to develop the mobility and manoeuvrability of closed divisions from the squadron up to the troop division in a new manner. His main attention was the fast transition into a front of attack from all formations and directions, insisting draconically on tight closeness during the approach and attack. This requirement was considered the main principle of Edelsheim's system."[302]

Image 65 – Eduard Kaiser 1859, Leopold W. v. Edelsheim. (Wikipedia, public domain)

"EXERCISE MANUAL FOR THE IMPERIAL and ROYAL CAVALRY"

The reforms of the new exercise manual for the Austrian cavalry were incorporated in 1862, but did not bring the desired effect quickly. For large states can only be manoeuvred like big ships: gradually. Edelsheim-Gyulai (1826-93) "deserves the distinction of encouraging the Austrian cavalry to a new, spirited riding."³⁰³ He is the "father" of the Exercise Manual for the Imperial and Royal Cavalry which was valid – with slight alterations – until 1918 and even after.[304] Podhajsky states that it "corresponds almost completely to Weyrother, Seeger, and Oeynhausen's work."[305] In 1869, Edelsheim-Gyulai became General Cavalry Inspector and General of the Cavalry in 1874.[306] Indeed this cavalry manual is a monument of superior equestrian culture. It shows "rider and horse the basic means for warfare."[307] The preface indicates the unexpected: the scope the regiment affords may not be reduced, "any deviation from simplicity and natural state, any schematizing and pedantry must be avoided." What a difference to today's administrative excesses and pseudo-science.

"…With a True Disposition and Brave Heart…"

The "general regulations" offer something ingenious: the cavalryman must "be inspired by a real rider's spirit, should he live up to his profession. Only a man of loyal disposition and brave heart; who trusts in his strong arm and his horse, which he loves and cherishes more than himself; who under all circumstances is capable of a bold decision, immediately followed by fast action – has rider's spirit. Such a man does not know difficulties, the attack is his element."[308] Obedience may not impair independent decision, but the rider should "always understand the orders' meanings so that he knows how to act according to their purpose." Practice is more important than theory: "Exercises only intended to please the eye have to be avoided as a useless game." And the soldier is considered a living individual: "Under no circumstances may he be forced to mechanical memorization."[309]

Rejection of Drilling

There was a clear rejection of drilling in terms of mechanistic materialism. Despite its empirical and practical orientation, the "Exercise Manual" is characterized by humanistic philosophy in the tradition of Hegel, and later Wilhelm Dilthey or Wilhelm Wundt, understanding man as thinking and intending subject, influenced by psychology and romanticism. Horse and rider are living creatures, thus needing psychological empathy in order to achieve good results: "It must never be forgotten that every individual can only come into his own if he is used according to his abilities."[310] This military manual mirrors the scientific discourse of the era. The cultivated treatment of the horse promoted paved the way for scientific research of the horse's psyche. In 1912, the physician, psychologist, and First Lieutenant of Cavalry Dr Stefan von Maday published his distinguished and painstakingly documented book "Psychology of the Horse and Training."[311] These are a few of the reasons why even today, in the 21st century, connoisseurs tear up when they hear about the "Exercise Manual" which they discuss with enthusiasm and respect. There was a club www.reitergeistofmiddletennessee.com with members in 13 US states and a monthly newsletter "Reitergeist" (rider's spirit). The "Exercise Manual" contains, above all, the cavalryman's training on foot and horseback; equestrian training in the riding school and the "large rectangle" (100 x 200 paces); negotiating cross-country obstacles; use of weapons, training in rank and file; training reconnaissance and security services; the recruits' training on horseback; handling of the colts.

The Hand: "Steady, Light, and Soft"

In the quest for the features of Austrian equestrian art several points seem remarkable. In all equestrian treatises discussed so far, a light hand is important: "The contact is correct when the horse always wants a soft support of the jaw by the bit."[312] A good hand remains the major principle; "it should be steady, light, and soft."[313] Furthermore, we continue to discover the cessation of the aids once they work, the *descente de main*: "When the horse has reacted to the increased effect of the rein, this stronger effect should be discontinued immediately, though the rein's effect must not be stopped completely. If this timely yielding is neglected, the horse's mouth becomes dull."[314] "The mouth should be kept fresh by the hand's steady contact and yielding."[315] "The instructor should often guide the recruit's hand to make it soft and steady."[316]

The head's perpendicular position with the horse's nose on the height of the hip is considered ideal, but: "For the military horse, the head position is the best when he can walk most comfortably for himself and the rider, in the position which he can endure longest and, even if handled firmly, can be kept obedient."[317] Auxiliary reins may only play a side role: "The draw rein only serves to prevent the horse from avoiding a position that he already can take and must not be used to force him into a position." "Generally a light bit is advisable," i.e. a curb in the manner of Max von Weyrother.[318]

The reins are managed on the curb bit exclusively by turning the left hand. Two-handed riding is done 3:1. The rider's hips should be perpendicular; the thighs touch the saddle without pressure, "with the knees slightly forward." The rider should not tighten his muscles strongly, and should keep the thighs relaxed. "The toes always seem to be slightly turned away from the horse when the legs hang naturally."[319] The stirrup leather length allows four fingers between the rider's crotch and the saddle. "During the entire training the correct seat has to be continuously demanded and observed under all circumstances."[320] This combination of directives has culminated in the well-known elegance of the imperial and royal cavalry.

Image 66 – Ludwig Koch, Cavalry exercises. (Dokumentationszentrum für altoesterreichische Pferderassen.)

Never Punish out of Anger or Mood

"The principle is never to be tempted to interfere stronger than absolutely necessary." Blows on the head can easily hurt the eyes and are strictly forbidden. "The whip should only be used as the last resort…The horse's fear of his handler and fleeing from the whip prove its incorrect use."[321] Generally, the manual demands careful handling of the horse and mild aids. The trainers must "avoid the rude use of the whip." For trot and canter during lunging, the whip is just lifted and only touches the horse if necessary. The lunge line is "vibrated softly until" the horse slows down.[322]

By working on two tracks the horse should be taught increased obedience and necessary flexibility in all his joints with the most possible care. Side steps may only be exercised with horses well in hand and willing to move forward off the leg aids. For the cavalry horse the following exercises suffice: "shoulder-in, half-pass, haunches-in, and the full-pass." "These side steps may only be executed at the walk."[323] Recruits only train them briefly since young riders may acquire seat problems by training side steps too much.[324]

Striking off at the canter is done as follows: "the inside leg stays in touch with the girth, the outside one is put on slightly stronger behind it, and the horse is driven forward by both legs."³²⁵ "Outside the arena and the large rectangle the rider must always use the rising trot in order to facilitate the movement of the back for the horse and to achieve more endurance. While riding in the arena and the large rectangle, riders may only post when they are taught or if exercises using the sabre are carried out."³²⁶

Cross Country Riding Necessary

High importance is attached to terrain riding: "as often as circumstances allow, there should be cross-country riding without special order, led by the platoon commander."³²⁷ Obstacles have to be negotiated: "jumping over ditches with or without water; over obstacles, over ditches and barriers at the same time; passing of wide ditches with or without water; climbing down steep descents; finally passing through slightly swampy areas…The cavalry horse must always navigate the obstacles in a composed manner, and without causing disorder or delay in the convoy. He should not jump obstacles higher than necessary."³²⁸ Descending steep hills is carried out in the "old manner;" the rider must lean back with his torso. Some of the troop should be able to swim on horseback. The manual offers in-depth practical instruction for swimming.

Fighting on Horseback

"Fighting on horseback always has a practical purpose, namely to prepare the rider for the attack and hand-to-hand combat." During training, "every rider must try to land a blow or stab, stop his horse quickly, turn, and heartily repeat the attack immediately in the same manner. Fast, nimble turning and a fresh attack of the enemy is important. The one who succeeds earlier will have a big advantage in the following skirmish." "On horseback, riders generally only shoot with the revolver; the rifle is used on horseback only rarely in the terrain if the rider is single, at a standstill, and when there is no time to dismount. Shooting the revolver while riding is unreliable and is only allowed in the skirmish when the sabre has broken or when chasing the enemy."³²⁹

Thrashing Impact of the Riders' Attack

This applies to the "attack in closed order": "the attack is decisive and hence, the most important movement of the cavalry. The major conditions for a successful cavalry-attack are speed and surprise during the advance, vehemence, and full power during the impact." The attack normally starts 1000 paces in front of the enemy. "During the attack on infantry and artillery, it is of utmost importance to only be exposed to the effective fire for the shortest possible time; thus, even at the risk of having less power available for later moments, the

Image 67 – Cavalry-steeple-chase. (Dokumentationszentrum fuer altoesterreichische Pferderassen.

range where the enemy's projectiles are devastating must be traversed at a gallop in order to come to the skirmish as soon as possible. Having approached the enemy within about 100 paces, the order "Double march!" must be given, repeated by all officers. The sabres are taken for the attack, whereupon everyone bears down on the enemy shouting "Hurrah!" at the horses' fastest speed. The platoon shall be closed as much as possible in the middle, and every rider must chase ahead with the firm decision to break through the enemy's lines. The platoon commander must try to break into the enemy's lines. Going into a fast gallop too early should be avoided since the distance between riders decreases, making the complete thrashing impact of the closed riders' attack less effective." "During the skirmish the rider should deliver as many blows or stabs as possible. Blows should be directed to the opponent's head, face, neck, or rein hand, stabs towards the chest or side." "Each man must know that he who holds the ground is the winner, and the one who leaves the place is the loser." Fleeing enemies "must be pursued at highest speed whereby each rider must seek to unmount as many enemy riders as possible."[330]

Mounted Recruits' Training

"The mounted recruits' training must be undertaken thoroughly without any haste; it is divided into three periods:" 1st, stabilization of the seat (for about three months); 2nd, riding with the snaffle bit; 3rd, riding with the curb. Proceeding from one period to the other does not happen automatically, but only after the skill is acquired, considering that everyone progresses at their own rate. Equestrian training is an "important service" and only "well-ridden horses" may be used for it. "The young soldiers should be taught the value of the horse, that it has to be kept healthy and strong, and that it must become willing and obedient by reasonable, friendly treatment."[331]

Image 68 – Fritz Schoenpflug, Bottled rider's spirit. (Private archive.)

Image 68a – Fritz Schoenpflug, Another cavalryman. (Private archive.)

Starting Colts in Four Periods

So that the colts become trained: "a cavalry horse should have stamina and unconditional obedience." "Exercise according to age and strength makes imperfect horses useful, whereas wrong treatment against nature spoils even good ones. Too little exercise makes horses lax…Exaggerated demands…wear down the feet and cause lung diseases." Colts that are asked too much, too early will become ill later even under normal strain. Too much short canter, sharp turns, artificial movements, etc. damage the joints. "Rude and violent training has the same effects; it makes the horses unwilling, afraid of people, and very often evil and stubborn."[332]

Starting colts happens in four periods: The 1st period is only for strengthening. "The length of the periods cannot be predetermined for it depends on age, strength, and quality of the colts, as well as the maintenance and treatment they receive. But the colt's training can be completed six months after the beginning of the 2nd period if done correctly, and if the actual training (2nd period) has not been started too early. No horse must be used for militarily until it has five years of age. The requirements should be increased gradually. Premature procedure damages the horses and sets back the training." Like the recruits, the horses advance to the higher period according to their development and success, meaning not all horses advance automatically. "That would delay or rush the training of individual horses." "The colts' training must always be carried out in the manner of an individual training."[333] Some colts may be used for their service earlier, some later.

Curriculum of the four periods:

1st period: The colt learns to carry the rider quietly in a relaxed manner.

2nd period: The horses are ridden straight, first without, later with a certain amount of collection and contact. When the horses react to the contact of the reins, shoulder-in can be ridden, then rein-back, half-pass, and extended trot. Shooting the revolver is first done on the ground, later in the saddle, with oats as a reward. Getting used to weapons and drums, pikes, and flags is also always supported by rewarding with oats. Jumping still happens without rider. Twice a week there are cross-country rides.

3rd period: Should "make the horses skilful, fast, and agile," the neck more flexible, the mouth fresher. Haunches-in is practised and striking off at the canter from a walk, and practising a fast gallop and jumping with the rider. All of this is done with the snaffle bit. Remounts with unfavourable confirmation may "in exceptional cases" be treated with draw reins in order to achieve faster results.

4th period: Getting used to curb bits and the sabre. Exercise movements in rank and file.

Source of Hippological Wisdom

This manual is a source of hippological wisdom: "Before every demand, the rider must first make the horse understand what he wants from him with great patience and as distinctly as possible." Almost always, the horse has not understood or has not been sufficiently prepared if he does not obey the aids. "In both cases, severe interference or punishment would be completely inappropriate." As soon as the horse shows willingness, even only to the slightest degree, he is rewarded. "This is the best way to make a horse willing and to keep him in a good mood. If the rider would continue his requirements recklessly, he would cause fatigue, disgust, and finally resistances." "Generally no horse is evil by nature. Rude treatment in the stable often paralyses any efforts of the handler in the arena, whereas gentle treatment even improves horses that were previously wicked." "Every cavalry officer should aim to become a good colt-handler. He can only achieve this if he is a good rider and horseman."[334]

This philosophy of gentleness especially pays off for the "treatment of horses afraid of people," that would prefer no contact with humans because of brutality and faults during their breeding or training: "this requires great care, special calmness, and much patience. Such colts must be given grooms who surpass others in that love for the animal, diligence, good will, and patience. The general principle is that the groom deals with the horse in a comfortable manner. Whenever he approaches the horse, he first must address it with a friendly, soft voice, coming near it so that it can see him before he moves closer. Frequent offering of feed from the hand is the best way of getting a shy horse accustomed to people."[335]

Codex of Military, Chivalric Elite

If today, at the beginning of the 21st century, all young horses were trained according to such a manual, they could lead a better life. Though, legions of vets, osteopaths, charlatans, and braggarts would have less business, and breeders would have to supply less "material." The "Exercise Manual" is a document of superb horse culture in a quality that generally does not exist today. Considering today's equestrian sport, the majority of horses are in an era of disgraceful barbarism. This manual was also a beacon in the 19th century. Whereas Francois Baucher, for instance, offered an ostensibly strictly "scientific" time table and system for the military training of horse and rider, the Austrian cavalry manual proceeded humanely and gently.[336] Man and horse were developed according to their abilities without being squeezed into a pattern. Schematic programs are even explicitly forbidden. And while in other countries cavalrymen just rode "somehow," Austria consequently attached importance to a correct but effortless seat, a good, soft hand, and the cessation of aids after their effect. The previous tradition gathered from historic documents is carried on and adapted to the new circumstances. The spirit of Spanish-Neapolitan-Austrian equitation lives on in this cavalry manual. Until its end, the Imperial and Royal Cavalry did not consider itself a producer of cannon fodder, but an institution for the cultivation of a military, chivalric elite.

Heroism without Tactical Purpose

While noblesse in the treatment of horses and the goal of equestrian elegance and serenity were paramount, the military purpose of cavalry attacks with sabres in the era's wars was questionable. Shooting rifles on horseback was to be done only in exceptional circumstances and the revolver was only a substitute for the sword. In Koeniggraetz, the Austrian cavalry had proven more heroism than tactical appropriateness. If the Emperor's military leaders in the war theatres had been as considerate deploying the Austrian cavalry as the cavalrymen training horse and rider, there would have been fewer unnecessary deaths. Romantic heroism and knightly ethos increasingly became a philosophy that ignored reality. Until the collapse of the Danube Monarchy, the splendour of the cavalry's equestrian spirit outshone the shadows of reality. And today enthusiasts conjure up the reincarnation of riding in the tradition of the Imperial and Royal Exercise Manual.

Image 69 –Ludwig Koch, Halt from a canter and salute. (Dokumentationszentrum fuer altoesterreichische Pferderassen.)

MATHÄUS VON NIEDERMAIER AND THE VIGOUR OF HIGH SCHOOL

Advisor for All Other Types of Riding

In the first half of the 19th century, devotees of Anglomania and campaign riding thought dressage would only unnecessarily harm the horses' natural desire to go forward. But over the course of time, there was a certain harmonization as Heydebrand reported in 1898: "Today's campaign riding consists of a union of principles of school, racing, and hunting equitation. Therefore all sensible riders and soldiers consider the four branches of equestrian art fully equal and practice them as far as possible."[337] In this context High School serves as an "advisor for all other equestrian disciplines."

"The thinking and skilled rider learns from High School, the lessons which he can use to improve or completely correct any weaknesses and ineptitudes of his horse destined for other purposes." "This task elevates school riding to become the basis of any riding; I would like to say, it is the spirit or philosophy infusing and illuminating the entirety."[338] Thus High School had been honoured again, though brisk forward riding was no longer neglected. Hunting and racing equitation were enthusiastically practised among officers and encouraged officially by prizes.

While other nations had given up High School, it persisted in the Danube Monarchy: "In Austria, too, the funds for maintaining the 'Spanish School' were not granted by the Reichstag, but by the Emperor who has a great liking for any kind of riding, and is himself a very good and dashing rider. He retained the institute, paying from his own purse, the costs exceeding the interest of a fund endowed by Emperor Charles VI at the foundation of the Spanish School."[339] Politicians regarded the sanctuary of High School as a useless, expensive anachronism.

50 Years with the Spanish Riding School

No one guaranteed the continuation of the Austrian-Spanish equestrian tradition by active work with men and horses in an adverse environment as long and sustainably as Mathäus von Niedermaier. (Also known as Mathias Niedermeier, Niedermayer, or Matthäus

Image 70 – Moritz Ledeli, Spanish Riding School 1886. (Private archive.)

Niedermeyer.) He lived from 1813-96, serving the Emperor from 1832-87, apart from seven years, for about half a century; he became Chief Rider in 1865, and First Chief Rider of the Spanish Riding School in 1884.[340] The uncertainty of the correct spelling of his name indicates he is one of Austria's forgotten geniuses. He must have known and ridden horses that were trained and active in the era of Max von Weyrother, absorbed the old personnel's savvy, and therefore linking the practices of baroque and modern ages. Horses educated by him were ridden well into the 20th century! Imagine: Niedermaier learned from riders who had their apprenticeship in the 18th century, and he learned from the horses trained by these riders; their time plus the time when he himself taught horses and riders; the time when he left his legacy in the form of trained stallions, encompassed 100 years!

He must have been a paramount horseman: "As a visitor to the Spanish Riding School doubted the exact determination of cadence in the piaffe and passage, Niedermeyer had a metronome brought from the nearby Burgtheater and asked the guest to let the instrument beat arbitrarily, sometimes faster, sometimes slower. Niedermeyer's stallion 'Pluto Betalka' piaffed exactly according to the respective rhythm. After this proof of supreme obedience, the visitor intended to make a compliment, calling in admiration: 'Mr Chief Rider, this was like in a circus!' Niedermeyer, obviously hardly pleased with this praise, had a fully filled glass of water put on his grey horse's croup, piaffing the stallion without even spilling a drop of water. Then he said: 'See, this is elasticity and

Image 71 – Joseph Heicke, Lipizzaner of the Spanish Riding School during Niedermaier's tenure, capriole. (Private archive.)

softness! Try to see this in a circus!'"[341] At the Viennese court, Niedermaier's metronome performance was nothing novel; Baron von Sind reports from the era of Charles VI that the passage had to be ridden exactly to the music's time as the ballet master demanded.[342]

A more appreciative visitor was the French General Alexis Francois l'Hotte, "one of the 19th century's finest riders," to whom Niedermaier presented "his bay precision-jumper 'Pluto-Perletta' in 1884."[343] In his "Questions Équestres" of 1895, L'Hotte highly acknowledges the Viennese Spanish Riding School, its cultivation of Guérinière, and the Lipizzaner which he regards as "old Spanish," thus classifying it clearly superior to the Spanish horse of his epoch.[344]

"TRAINING OF THE GREEN HORSE, TREATMENT IN THE RIDING SCHOOL"

We would know next to nothing about the excellence of Mathäus von Niedermaier if there were not a manuscript of 26 sheets with about 100 pages. It is in a room of the Viennese Stallburg, a few feet above the home of the Spanish Riding School's Lipizzaners. Its title is the "Training of the Green Horse, Treatment in the Riding School." The manuscript's preliminary cover shows the year 1885. It is a document of finest equestrian culture from a first-class expert, who knew every detail, and wrote meticulously. He seems to be a polite, assiduous civil servant, explaining most complicatedly and in detail, discussing in endlessly long, interlaced sentences. Linguistic gesture and style appear old-fashioned for the year 1885. It is clear that a conservative person, even for the era's standard, wrote the text. Until recently, no one had published Niedermaier's manuscript as a printed book; unfortunately this befits the usual tradition of Austrian equestrian art. We still can view the exquisiteness of Niedermaier's work in a famous painting of 1890 by Julius von Blaas: "Morning Work in the Winter Riding School." The depicted horses must have been trained in Niedermaier's era and they display a maximum upright neck, nose almost perpendicular, best freedom of shoulder, and active hindquarters. The artist presents them full of verve and noble, joyful brilliance.

Ideal: Free Enthusiastic Horse

In his manuscript, Niedermaier describes how to achieve this. Especially at the beginning, he borrows many things verbatim from Max von Weyrother, above all his principles and the mechanistic approach to balance the horse. Niedermaier's ideal, as Xenophon's, is the free, uninhibited horse that "collects himself with induced enthusiasm in all his beauty." He has an erected and yet rounded neck and moves in the best possible balance. "From this ideal position that art tries to take the horse to, there are many deviations we can reduce."[345] Since the rider sitting on the horse disturbs its natural balance, it has to be reinstalled at least approximately.

Starting with Care and Love

The colt is started with a cavesson on the lunge line, which Niedermaier still calls "corda" (Italian "rope"), in order to learn confidence and obedience. "After several lessons, during which the horse has always been treated with care and love, he comes to know the circle and becomes more trusting."[346] "Here the horse is praised and given some oats as a reward."[347] Friendly contact and "gentle talking" are the standard procedure.[348] Since "the intended good gait should be acquired," the trainer tries to "drive the colt more and more into the rein, respecting his conformation and ability," "encouraging [him] gently."[349] The aim is that the horse bears more and more weight on the hindquarters in order to alleviate and erect his forehand so that he "does not drag but actively moves his hindquarters" and "after every exercise the future rider must approach the horse, caress him, give oats, and get to know him."[350] The basic training is executed intricately with much labour and devotion.

Nothing is left to chance during the first mounting: The handler holds the "corda," the whip-handler prevents the horse from moving sideways or backwards, "two very reliable

Image 72 – Joseph Heicke, Lipizzaner of the Spanish Riding School during Niedermaier's tenure, canter. (Private archive.)

men" hold each cavesson rein while another aide supports the right stirrup.[351] Cross your heart: which trainer of our days does not dream of such staffing? Starting must "be done gently without demanding too much," for the remount should not have any reason to defend himself.[352] The rider does not take the reins too short, has the arms bent so as not to lose his position in case of resistance. He holds the crop toward the left ear of the horse. The little fingers are directed upward toward the breast.

Work to Bring Out the Forehand And Make Shoulders Free

In addition to the cavesson, Niedermaier advises to use a snaffle bit, because the green horse walks with stiff hind legs and needs to be erected in order to gain balance. Using a curb bit causes the mouth to become dull; "this is prevented by lifting with a snaffle bit" which impacts the lips. Lifting the horse, he "is exercised more in the forehand and the shoulder is made free…This has to be done gradually in the beginning and increased with time."[353] Only under time pressure should the colt be started with the mildest of curb bits and fine hands. Horses with weak hindquarters should not be required to show more erection of the neck than they can perform, since the "general rule for the increasing demands on the horse" is that it may only "be increased as much as he is able to do because hastened training does not result in a balanced walk and good posture."[354]

To avoid the horse leaning on the bit, lifting the poll is not done with both reins at the same time, and the whip handler drives subtly without causing haste. By erecting the poll and driving, the horse is gradually brought to his ideal posture and can lift his shoulders in a "free movement." If this works well, bending can commence: First at a standstill, then at the walk, the head is taken to the rider's knee through interrupted contact in the style of *descente de main*. Rein-back supports bending the hindquarters and equally narrowing all angles.[355]

Fresh and Resolute Walk

In the "large rectangle" the horse learns a "fresh" and "resolute" walk and trot, "acquiring a determined and lively gait" without dragging the hindquarters behind him.[356] Thus, he is taught increasing contact with the bit: "The correct concept of contact leads us to true knowledge of a well-trained horse and a good hand…in order to educate man and horse… the horse's mouth must correspond in harmony to that of his entire body."[357] During continued training, the horse is not only stopped but brought to a collected halt, followed by a half-halt through rein and leg, causing the mount to collect even more. Then comes the *arrêt*, leading to immobility of the horse that takes his haunches completely under himself supporting the rider's weight. For this the forehand must be erect, the bent hocks placed underneath with both hips "placed forward" on a straight line.[358]

As a Thinking Rider to Higher Perfection

Niedermaier dislikes leg-yielding and the exercise "head in, croup out" according to him, these exercises only lead to a "bad *l'epaule en dedans*" which is "very harmful for the horse"[359] "The thinking handler" must take care to use several flexing exercises to avoid bringing the horse on his shoulders. Shoulder–in, on the other hand, brings the horse on his hocks and into a beautiful posture; therefore, it is the foundation of all movements.[360] The flexion must go through the entire body, with the forehand only moved in so far that the rider "sees the arch of the inside eye."[361] The movement is especially suitable for "the trainer who, as a thinking rider, wants to lead his own horse to higher perfection."[362] Niedermaier devotes much of his manuscript to the shoulder-in, discussing it in verbose detail.

Niedermaier discerns different kinds of canter in two, three or four "moments," deeming the last the most perfect, though only very strong horses can execute it correctly, for "the canter in four moments must be heard at equal rhythm and regularly set hoof beats, only then it is the most perfect."[363] Striking off at the canter is initially effectuated mainly

Image 73 – Joseph Heicke, Lipizzaner of the Spanish Riding School during Niedermaier's tenure, renvers. (Private archive.)

from a collected trot, "the rider properly holding his horse with the outside rein, using both reins"[364] At first, the horse may strike off somewhat crookedly. If he strikes off on the wrong lead, the "rider must not punish or even mistreat the horse." The more "the horse is worried or confused, the less he will understand the aid."[365] During the canter, the aids are continued "proportionally" without tiring the horse by overusing the gait; otherwise he cannot place his haunches underneath and may easily lose the pleasure to work, "and without this, no horse does his movements as well as he could if he went with good will."[366] According to the horse's abilities, the trainer increases the requirements for the canter.

Thorough Equitation Instead of Rhetoric

Successful training of the horse will allow him to "be shoulder free," bear head and neck in self-carriage, react to reins and legs, and walk in balance so that he can become accustomed to the curb bit "according to the principles of bridling." If the horse does not collect in accordance with his conformation, "the rider must use his professional experience to drive the horse into the curb with all patience and regularity…which often takes more time and experience than some superficial riders with rhetoric and disrespect for thorough equitation deem necessary."[367] Here, the Imperial Chief Rider clearly rejects the then popular "hurry-up" training methods of Anglomania.

Image 74 – Julius v. Blaas 1890, Morning work in the Winter Riding School. (Private archive.)

Not the Slightest Movement of the Hand

Riding on the curb bit requires a hand that "is light, soft, and steady." A "skilled" rider's hand ought to be so quiet "that at each varied movement and position not the slightest motion of the hand is visible."[368] The reins can first be held 2:2, but on a trained horse definitely 3:1. The curb reins can be adjusted by turning the hand as previously described by Newcastle. The rider must "be armed with all patience to accustom the horse to the curb bit, repeating intermittently the previous training."[369] Riding on the curb advances to a collected halt from the canter. If the horse is well "in hand" and strong, he can learn the flying lead change. "In order to attain this important, purpose-proving ability in equitation with one's mount" Niedermaier refers to the Exercise Manual.[370]

Inexhaustible Patience

In contrast to previous meticulousness, Niedermaier's manuscript offers fewer and fewer detailed instructions toward the end, and definitely ends as a fragment. As for "planning the reprises," he stays taciturn, only stating that finished lessons should be repeated only as often so that they cause no harm, making the horse suitable for any military service. The procedure must always be individual. Less able horses must train the exercises that they cannot perform well, but otherwise have to be spared. Concerning "exercise with remounts outdoors," Niedermaier refers to the Manual, nevertheless giving some instruction for jumping, "feeding the horse oats, caressing him" until the horse quietly understands what is wanted of him. "Force and punishment" work badly, making the horse timidly rush or dodge the obstacle. As always, you have to contend with little in the beginning "if you do not want to make the horse stubborn, powerless or defective."[371] Similar is his recommendation for carefully accustoming horses to horrors such as the noise of weapons: "An inexhaustible patience…consistent treatment and never punishment."[372] Quiet desensitization is of utmost importance for Niedermaier, also for the benefit of "the Supreme Service." This indicates that Niedermaier had to make horses bombproof for the Emperor. And he deems it unsightly if even military horses cause disturbances because they were not patiently accustomed to frightening things. He considers the riding school to be the best place for this.

Insight into Historic Training Practice

With some precaution we could say that the manuscript by Chief Rider Mathäus von Niedermaier gives us detailed insight into the training practise in use at the Spanish Riding School of Vienna since the 18th century until Holbein's era. Though Niedermaier often refers to the Exercise Manual in his 12 lessons for the "Dressage of the Colt," he absolutely reflects the baroque tradition of courtly-academic equitation on a paramount level. Like no other author of Austrian equestrian art before or after him, he described in detail the initial training of the remount and the gaits. If he had written about the complete training of a High School Horse up to the capriole, we would have one of the most comprehensive works of hippological literature. Niedermaier's methods conform to the previous Austrian equestrian tradition, constituting an academic island amidst military and hunting equitation of the 19th century. The high importance of humane treatment of the horse was and still is reached by only few riders.

Image 75 – Joseph Heicke, Radautzer stallion of the Spanish Riding School during Niedermaier's tenure, croupade. (Private archive.)

SOVEREIGN RIDING: FRANCIS JOSEPH I AND ELISABETH

Spirited Campaign Rider

Emperor Francis Joseph I (1830-1916) acknowledged the Spanish Riding School as a source of identity for dynasty and nation, though he himself only rode a levade on a Lipizzaner at the Hungarian coronation, otherwise as an audacious campaign rider he preferred English Thoroughbreds and hunters. He did not shrink back from risky terrain and obstacles, and rode attacks in manoeuvres. After fording the Elbe River during a hunt in 1874, a very steep, sandy escarpment had to be managed. All riders led their hunters by the hand. Prince Windisch-Graetz tried to ride, but his mount somersaulted back into the river. Only the Emperor negotiated the obstacle gracefully on horseback: "His Majesty, who rode Goldney, did not dismount but rode out with extraordinary bravery despite great danger."[373]

The Emperor's posture on horseback can be considered the epitome of perfection, effortless equestrian elegance, an imposing example for every cavalryman. The long-term Emperor's commitment for High School complies with his will to preserve, and is a sign of reverence to the Spanish tradition of his family. Like his cavalrymen, he probably rode the attack unswervingly and with courage, but the order led him and them to doom.

Obsession in the Side Saddle

Francis Joseph took less time for hunting than his wife and cousin who sometimes would have liked to have him by her side: "But it would be dangerous, for you would not let yourself trammel by Captain Middleton, and you would dash over anything where they look if it is not too deep or wide."[374] Empress Elisabeth of Austria-Hungary (1837-98) was cherished as the supreme female rider of her era, and her father had already said, "If we were not princes we would have become riding artists!"[375] She practiced most intensive riding – apart from travels and cures – as a flight from inner chaos, from nervous boredom and mental emptiness, from politics, court intrigues, representational duties, her mother-in-law, the Viennese high aristocracy, and the gaping crowd. In the morning she rode hunts, in the afternoon demanding dressage, receiving lessons at the Spanish Riding School of Vienna: "Elisabeth devoted herself to this art with body and soul."[376] With obsession she took part

Image 76 – Ludwig Koch, Emperor Francis Joseph I, Spring parade. (Dokumentationszentrum fuer altoesterreichische Pferderassen.)

Image 77 – J. C. Charleton, Empress Elisabeth, steeplechase. (Private archive.)

Image 78 – Wilhelm Richter 1876, Empress Elisabeth, circus lesson. (Private archive.)

in English or Irish fox and stag hunts amidst 150 riders of whom often only 20 reached the goal, so selective was the matter. Crowds of spectators came in special trains. "During the hunts minor accidents happen around her continuously."[377]

The overwhelmingly beautiful Empress Elisabeth – she rode even the most dangerous obstacles rapidly in side saddle – was always ahead and did not even get discouraged by serious "bumps." Reports confirm "that there was not a lady and only a few gentlemen in England, who could ride like Her Majesty."[378] The Emperor paid the bill for such distraction, an Ireland-excursion costing 158,337 Gulden and 48 Kreuzer. In 1875, the circus of Ernst Jakob Renz stayed in Vienna with fabulous dressage which so much excited the Empress that she took lessons from Renz's daughter Elise. "A small, round *manège* is added to the Imperial mews and four real circus horses are acquired, able to do various tricks, like the famous 'Avolo' that gets down on both his knees with the Empress in the saddle."[379] In the summer resort of Ischl, these horses were also honoured, "way back in the garden where nobody can see it" a little dressage and jumping school was established.[380]

Image 79 – William II, Francis Joseph I, Manoeuvre in Hungary, Komorn 1896. Photo Heinrich Sanden, Vienna. (Private archive.)

The fact that Imperial Chief Rider Johann Meixner (1865-1917) prepared the Emperor's mounts together with the cavalrymen for manoeuvres and parades reveals how closely cavalry and High School equitation were interwoven in Austria.[381] It can be taken for granted that the horses which Emperor Francis Joseph rode in military functions and hunts were not only perfectly trained according to the cavalry manual, but also in High School to put the finishing touches on them, meaning Meixner could train horses for campaign riding as well as academic equitation in supreme quality. Francis Joseph I himself appears on horseback in almost all depictions, including photos, with an excellent seat even in old age. His horses display the best muscling and posture achieved through expert training. In comparison, the horses of Prussian Emperor William II show a striking discrepancy. In contrast to Meixner's mounts, the horses that Paul Plinzner trained for his emperor using rollkur in all photographs cut a rather sad figure: in front rolled under and camped out behind. One emperor had better equitation; the other had the better army.

Image 80 – Empress Elisabeth, Portrait as a young lady. (Private archive.)

CAVALRY AND SPANISH RIDING SCHOOL: HOLBEIN and MEIXNER

Johann Meixner: Playful Ease

We know quite a bit about Johann Meixner, with the Spanish Riding School of Vienna 1885-1916, because of Gustav Rau who honoured him intricately in his essay "In Remembrance of Chief Rider Meixner." "A riding master is someone able to train a school horse according to traditional academic equitation and contribute to the development of classical equitation."[382] Among them "Meixner is today (1913) doubtlessly the most important; a born rider with decades of training continually leading to the perfection of equestrian technique…Additionally there is Meixner's gorgeous posture on horseback, his exemplary seat…As Vienna wants to keep the old classical school, Meixner can be deemed classical, concerning seat, posture, and guidance…The rider's body is never seen in any unsightly motion, not for even a moment, you never observe any harsh aid. Everything occurs with playful ease. Here we have the utmost harmony of rider and horse; playfully, Meixner controls any movement…Meixner applied, in order to break resistance, tough aids sometimes; though his horses, once ready, were very soft…In the last years before the war, Meixner worked his horses much at a great trot, displaying the maintenance of impulsion as rebuttal to opinions that Vienna rode too much in shortened gaits…There is nothing heavy, dragging; everything is life and action… Meixner's own experience has proven previous masters' knowledge."[383]

Rau was enthusiastic about the verve of Meixner's horses in all gaits and movements: "Neapolitano Bona's passage is high, solemnly hovering; every step is exactly controlled, the horse freed from gravity…Favory Ancona's passage displays great solemn beauty…, activation, rendering of power, and control of a mechanism by supreme equestrian feel."[384] Regarding the work in-hand, with Meixner holding the snaffle rein "with his ring finger," Rau says: "It is the maximum of fine aids to be seen."[385] Even equestrian genius, Meixner did not entirely avoid circus-like effects: He loved to canter tightest voltes around spectators.[386]

Image 81 – Ludwig Koch, Chief Rider Johann Meixner, Levade.
(Dokumentationszentrum fuer altoesterreichische Pferderassen.)

1914: 1st Interview at the Spanish Riding School

James Fillis proudly stated he was no "penman" but a "horseman."[387] Similarly Meixner may have reacted to Rau's request to document his knowledge in writing. Nevertheless, he was ready for an interview "about equestrian art and his way to work horses" in 1914.[388] He requires the "rider to sit perpendicular to the tailbone. Shoulder, hip, and heel must be in a vertical line, the thigh should be placed slightly forward; the whole leg is stretched… The most important aids are executed with the seat…Meixner has been riding without stirrups for 23 years…Meixner rode horses on the snaffle bit until they were almost entirely schooled…Many horses are only defeated after a fight; some easier, some harder… Horses that constantly chew and bite are never in the hand. Starting a colt successfully requires no forcing, but making a program for routine procedure. A young horse must be ridden through a daily agenda…Young horses must not be demanded to have their noses immediately perpendicular to the ground. Over-flexing is even worse. Then neck and head must be lifted somewhat by the snaffle bit…Working horses should only be ridden in moderate posture. Rein-back should only be trained very sparingly."[389] This contrasts to Niedermaier, Meixner's predecessor, who thought rein-back to be an appropriate means for bending the haunches.

Images 82, 82a, 82b – Moritz Ledeli, Spanish Riding School, Piaffe, Passage, and Canter. (Heydebrand, op. cit.)

As today's riders of the Viennese Spanish Riding School, Meixner attaches great importance to exact riding in the corners. When training remounts, "it should be tried to ride little with the legs but a lot with weight. In this way, you put more impulsion into the horses…The spurs ought to be used as little as possible. The impulsion must come from the seat."[390] "Good work at the walk must never be forgotten…But the highest responsiveness is only gained using the school trot. The work in this gait shows the whole of equestrian finesse, the tuning and correspondence between the rider's hand and legs…At first, the canter should not be ridden too short, but more ahead."[391] Striking off at the canter is effectuated by the outside leg: "By forcing with the outside leg, every horse strikes off…at the same time the inside rein gives an *arrêt*."[392]

"In the work on two tracks, both reins and both legs must always be active. This is the only way to maintain the same verve as in riding on a straight line…Only completely trained horses can perform a pirouette at the canter…It is imperative that the horses can perform the canter in renvers and also travers through the corners before the pirouette. Only then, is the flexion of the haunches perfect. Especially difficult is the canter pirouette in renvers… The Passage must only be started when the horse shows a really good school trot. You shorten the tempo trying to maintain the ease of the movement without letting the horse become tight…Meixner refused any work in hand, only perhaps using it as preparation for piaffe and school jumps. A rider with a good hand, states Meixner, does everything in the saddle. If you reward a horse after a successful school jump, he will repeat the jump anytime it is required …The capriole is the most difficult school jump. Only extraordinary horses with particular mettle correctly strike with their hind legs…The *redopp* is a two-beat canter; front legs united and rear legs united, jumping alternately between front and back. Thus, it is actually not a canter and is an unnatural gait. It is easiest to ride in a renvers volte…Everyone who can handle draw reins must not get used to riding with them always. You ought to ride with draw reins only for a short time…Young horses should only be worked with draw reins for a few minutes…The rider can work strong horses in the saddle from the beginning."[393] Lipizzaners, that often come to the Imperial Riding School in a weak state, are worked "on the lunging line in campaign manner" for up to three quarters of a year.

Images 83, 83a, 83b – Moritz Ledeli, Pirouette at a canter, Terre-à-terre, Pesade. (Heydebrand, op. cit.)

Cavalryman Director of the Imperial Riding School: Franz von Holbein

Meixner became famous not only for his superb equitation, but also his collaboration with another celebrity: Field Marshall-Lieutenant Franz von Holbein-Holbeinsberg (1832-1910), son of the Burgtheater's director, Franz Ignaz von Holbein, and late descendant of Hans Holbein the Younger, King's Painter to Henry VIII. He attended the Viennese Zentralequitationsintitut, became dragoon commander, "Chairman of the Remount Assent-Commission Nr. 1," and was an award-winning rider. "In 1873, he took part in the first race of the Campaign Riders Society in Pressburg. This society had been specially founded to promote the skills of officers and horses in the Imperial and Royal Army with a prominent competition. The first time, Holbein was only fourth, but three years later he finished first, receiving a prize by Emperor Francis Joseph I and a commendation by Empress Elisabeth, who was present during the race."[394] "Excellence Holbein" was a popular character in the Viennese society and was even portrayed by Gustav Klimt. In 1898, Holbein was entrusted with the general management of the Spanish Riding School by Supreme Equerry Rudolf von Liechtenstein.

Franz von Holbein and Johann Meixner: "DIRECTIVES

FOR THE IMPLEMENTATION OF THE METHODIC PROCEDURE OF TRAINING RIDER AND HORSE AT THE IMPERIAL AND ROYAL SPANISH COURT RIDING SCHOOL."[395] Also in 1898, Holbein wrote – in collaboration with Johann Meixner - the first and so far, last, official, principally still valid written manual for the training at the Riding School. The team consisting of cavalry officer and Chief Rider, both in charge of the management of Europe's last institution to preserve academic

Images 84, 84a, 84b – Moritz Ledeli, Mezair., Courbette, and Ballotade. (Heydebrand, op. cit.)

equestrian art, proves the final symbiosis of two thus far seemingly contrary spheres of riding.

Equestrian Art without Pedantry

The foreword states that, in times of mass cavalry and hasty training, an institute must be preserved "and tasked to practice equestrian art in supreme perfection" so that "without obsolete pedantry" "the profound meaning of High School and its truth can be once again acknowledged and spread." For only its principles can assure that horse and rider will be trained as fast as possible. High School then becomes the basis of information for campaign riding, "indirectly also contributing to the country's increased military strength." Every rider of the School must "pursue and try to reach these aims with all his intellectual talents and physical power."[396] "The purpose of the Imperial and Royal Spanish Court Riding School" is "to preserve equestrian art in its supreme perfection" and, it being the foundation for every modern manner of riding, "to always assert its validity anew." Furthermore, it must educate school-riders and horses, select stock for breeding, and teach.[397]

Three Kinds of Riding

Method and equestrian system at the School seem simple and sophisticated: "The higher equestrian art may never be regarded only as High School alone, for it involves all three kinds of equitation, such as: First: Riding the horse in his natural posture without collection on straight lines, the so-called riding straight ahead; Second: Riding the collected horse perfectly balanced in all gaits and turns: the campaign riding; Third: Riding the horse in artificially erected posture with increased flexion of the haunches and regularity and skill in all common, extraordinary, and artificial gaits and jumps, eavesdropped from nature herself…this kind of riding is called 'The High School'. The first kind of riding can be thought of and practiced on its own, but the second kind of riding is already a result of the first.

Image 85 – Levade in the pillars. Spanish Riding School. (Private achive.)

The third kind of riding is simply unthinkable without the two above-mentioned ways, especially without previous campaign school. This school encourages the horse's desire to go, educates his natural talents in posture and gaits, and strengthens all the horse's body, therefore making his ligaments, sinews, and joints flexible. Thus it increases skill and endurance of the mount, awakes his intellect and understanding… therefore being the only correct preparation for High School which has to be seen as a unity involving all three kinds of riding. Hence the perfect, methodically trained school horse in principle must… also be useable in fast gaits and be an entirely useful campaign horse anytime."[398]

School Horse: Always a Useful Campaign Horse

Unfortunately, this important dogma definitely fell into oblivion in the equitation of the 20th and 21st centuries. How many sport horses today can be used outside a riding school without danger? Neurotic sport horses of almost all disciplines would benefit if they had brisk cross country rides now and then, something most competitive riders turn their noses up at. Such equitation mainly suits the equestrian pariahs, the recreational riders. What decadence in comparison to the principles of Holbein and Meixner.

To Art Its Freedom

These principles require the Spanish Riding School's Riders' methodical work and understanding of the purpose of each lesson with precise knowledge about the level of dressage of each ridden horse. As all authors of Austrian equestrian tradition before them, they emphasize that riding is not only a physical but also an intellectual act, for "the rider need not only ride but also think, because only a thinking rider will reach the goal he has set in a relatively short time, treating the horse with utmost care."[399] With caution, thinking riders are "not given any distinct regulations," considering "that one-sidedness and schematic affect may damage any art."[400] Even if a military person drafts these "directives" he elegantly concedes to art its freedom.

The cavalry manual also refuses any schematics. The books by Guérinière, Max von Weyrother, Louis Seeger, Borries von Oeynhausen, and the Imperial and Royal Exercise Manual serve as a guidelines according to which students and other pupils must be strictly trained. Unfortunately, Holbein and Meixner do not have any knowledge of Adam von Weyrother, Regenthal, or even Galiberto, who might have suited their program. But they require "riders to stay informed about older or recently published works on equestrian art."[401]

Form and Custom at the Spanish Riding School

Two short pages treat "the form and custom at the Spanish Riding School." It is very important "that no rider, as long as he is on horseback, takes the liberty to remark or even backtalk." This may only happen after dismounting. "Riding must always start on the right hand," a principle valid in European riding at least since Grisone. And of course every rider must salute the painting of Charles VI. The rules of the arena must be observed, there must not be any "arbitrary riding around," "therefore each rider may only ride on the prescribed lines, circles and turns."[402]

As far as "various gaits and tours, turns, and figures ridden in the Imperial and Royal Spanish Riding School" ahare concerned, there are "ordinary, extraordinary, and artificial" ones. Ordinary gaits are walk, trot, canter, and jumping. Extraordinary ones are the passage, school halt, pirouette, levade, courbette, ballotade, and capriole. Artificial ones are "school posture, school walk, school trot, school canter, piaffe, work on two tracks, and all gaits ridden in counter position." The sketches attached to the "Directives" serve as a basis for performances and school quadrilles. "So-called circus-tricks during functions must strictly be avoided since they are beneath the institute's dignity."[403] This is basically correct, as the only preserved traditional institution had to distinguish itself from cheap circus riding. On the other hand, this discredited the epoch's geniuses Francois Baucher or James Fillis who almost only could perform in circuses. Circuses were for all representatives of equestrian art, who were not members of the Viennese Riding School, the only place to present academic equitation, but also for fancy riders, riding artists, charlatans, and dazzlers.

Nature without Art, But Never Art without Nature

There is an appendix to the "Directives," equally as long as they themselves, discussing some points of the School's work in detail. "The old masters' principles" are honoured here, without which Guérinière, Weyrother, Seeger, Oeynhausen would not have been able to develop their doctrines. Obviously, the authors did not have any knowledge of "the old masters." Apparently, there is an idea that there must have been something prior to Guérinière, e.g. Xenophon, knights' tournaments, and martial equitation. The conclusion: "Only when artificiality in school riding became rampant, a sharp separation between school riding and campaign riding happened, one that brought a disadvantage to both kinds of riding." Riders are encouraged to harmonize the two kinds without neglecting the campaign school as a necessary basis because "only after this, may there be a transition to art, such as High School, for you can conceive nature without art, but never art without nature."[404]

Remarkable that the authors of the "Directives" recognized that mere oral tradition of equestrian knowledge fostered false concepts and views which had to be corrected using "simplicity and truth." For example, "Work in the pillars and on the long line must not become a torture, which can be the result of unreasonable work." The method must be taught to every rider and "must not be a monopoly for some individuals surrounded by impenetrable mysticism!" Holbein and Meixner consider lunging a necessary basic task; the training in the pillars, however, as "the most important work for High School," making the horse supple, more beautiful, and stronger, encouraging collection, increasing his "intellect," controlling his temperament. Moreover, the "thinking rider" discovers the aptness for airs above the ground. "After finishing campaign school," young horses come into the pillars "without force and fight."[405]

Arcanum Shoulder-in

Most of the Directives' appendix is devoted to the discussion of shoulder-in. Holbein and Meixner (erroneously) call it an invention of Guérinière, finding it "virtually epoch-making" and an "Arcanum."[406] The started colt may already begin with it. The advantages

Image 86 – Shoulder-in, Spanish Riding School in Graz 2005. (Photo Poscharnigg.)

of this household remedy at the Spanish Riding School: correct flexing of the neck between the first and second vertebra; control of spine and haunches; collection, suppleness, and obedience for other movements; freer, more ground-covering trot with the outside leg; more energetic, higher canter; easier learning of other work on two tracks; the horse carrying himself without laying on the rider's hand.

Young riders should, after having been trained on experienced horses, soon start colts in order to give the aids more surely and exactly. Due to military draft, "trainees and *eleves*" of the Imperial Riding School will get the opportunity for terrain riding, establishing "a close contact between campaign and High School" equitation. To promote this even more, "k. and k. officers of the army are ordered to the k. and k. Spanish Court Riding School for higher education."

Renaissance of High School

Anglomania had a "refreshing influence on equitation on the whole continent," having "continuously maintained a fresh rider's spirit," but "may not be misunderstood and exaggerated." High School, on the other hand, must "finally be freed from the spell of mysticism by simplicity and truth, commencing a renaissance away from the numerous erroneous and medieval concepts." By collaborating with campaign riding, academic equestrian art thus hoped for an innovative new start, to build a bridge between tradition and modernism to find a place for the old art in the present. It would have been interesting to know which of the riders' ideas Holbein and Meixner thought to be "erroneous" or "medieval."

Conservatory for True, Noble Equestrian Art

Considering the Spanish Riding School's future, it should be free from restrictive, meaningless traditions: "But the k. and k. Spanish Court Riding School must – keeping closely in accord with the old masters' golden rules, be free from holding on to customs lacking both flexibility and sense, free from methods contradicting nature, and should distinguish itself clearly from pseudo artists on horseback, remaining a conservatory of true, noble equestrian art!"[407]

This sounds somehow like the motto of the Vienna Secessionist Movement [in art], "To time its art, to art its freedom," and indeed equestrian art had to find its place in concert with the era's other arts. Equestrian art could not work in an avant-garde manner like painting or music because it works with living animals. Radical innovations, if you consider the "systems" of Baucher or Fillis as such, may threaten the horses' health, whereas traditional classical methods allow horses to live long, and useful lives without being exploited and worn out prematurely. Therefore, music could seemingly be reinvented, for example by giving up tonality, as prominent composers of the epoch did, Arnold Schönberg, Alban Berg, Anton Webern and al.

Visual arts could distance themselves more and more from nature and toward impressionism, expressionism, cubism etc., thus becoming increasingly abstract. Horses as a medium of art, however, do not allow revolutionary experiments since the animals' nature remains unchanged. Holbein and Meixner did the right thing, mainly saving the Riding School from artificiality and denaturalization by unconditionally making cavalry riding the basis of High School, which had incidentally always been the case in the history of Austrian equestrian art. The excellence of the Viennese Court Riding School was ever-founded on martial equitation, though of Iberian style, useful only in skirmishes in the war theatres of

Image 87 – Ludwig Koch, Capriole. (Dokumentationszentrum fuer altoesterreichische Pferderassen.)

the ending 18th century. And in the course of the 19th century, the connection to cavalry remained intact through the influence of Gottlieb and Maximilian Weyrother.

Holbein's "Program for the Summer-Work at the k. k. Spanish School in the Year 1899"

The previous starting remounts in the style of old classical academic tradition rather than that of campaign, as Chief Rider Mathäus von Niedermaier did it, must have been a mighty thorn in Holbein's side. Obviously he saw important need for modernization and issued a letter of intent for the Chief Equerry in 1899, "Program for the Summer-Work at the k. k. Spanish School in the Year 1899." This beautiful manuscript is sewn in two sheets with the official seal of the Chief Equerry. (Stallburg, Archive of the Lipizaner Museum.)[408] It discusses the starting of colts in 1898-99 plus training the

Image 88 – Lipizzaners, dominantly grey since Holbein. (Photo Poscharnigg, 1998.)

stallions 1892-97. The young remounts are lunged, started, and then "ridden daily, if possible in the open riding school, in groups at a walk and trot for at least an hour."[409] Niedermaier would certainly have strongly objected to this procedure. At the age of four and a half, "the proper dressage starts in the most caring manner."[410] The old remounts are under the supervision of Holbein himself until their completed sixth year "to strictly further their training methodically so that they form a completely ready campaign school group in 1899," whereupon they are dressed for High School.[411] It is apparent that only a limited circle of people, among them Scholar Herold, is engaged in the young stallions' training. Perhaps riders of the baroque breed like Niedermaier resented the spirit of cavalry in the Spanish Riding School.

Holbein's Memorandum

Franz von Holbein also wrote a "Memorandum," "The Court Studs and Their Tasks." Here he describes what is required of a horse in the industrial age: "Horse breeding generally has been changing for some time; many inventions of the modern times…have greatly reduced the demand for utility horses."[412] The desire to ride far and the savvy to do so have disappeared in the younger generation. For longer distances, the railway is used, for shorter trips the hackney carriage. Race horses are only bred for the winning and "what happens to the animal afterward is completely unimportant."[413] They only run on good turf, whereas the working horse has to go on poor ground under heavy loads "securely and with good humour."[414]

The breeder must "patiently wait for the full development of the young animals without judging too early."[415] Especially for Lipizzaners, Holbein refuses any experiments, "otherwise the type would disappear within a few generations forever."[416] "In close connection to the stud is the Spanish School in Vienna, being the reservoir for the six lines which otherwise could not be maintained…; care must be taken that in this institute there are always some apt sons and heirs of every line…just like the foreign blood for the stud, the circus rider would be a destructive poison for the school."[417] Concerning the Lipizzaners, Holbein knows that "these horses take longer to develop and train than others…, these young animals change so much in their developing years that you do not know later why you had one castrated and the other kept as a stallion."[418] Apart from a few exceptions, Holbein excluded all non-greys from breeding, "more so since the greys in Lippiza are generally better than the other colours;" and "20 or 30 grey equipages in line surely look nobler than mixed colours."[419] This questionable but far reaching decision benefitted the colour white, but not necessarily the quality of a mount. Julius von Blaas' famous painting, "Morning Work in the Winter Riding School," contains four greys, and four other colours. A xylography of 1886, by Moritz Ledeli, equally shows eight stallions in the Winter Riding School, only four of which are greys. And an engraving of 1812 depicts only one grey among four horses. Hamilton's stud painting shows all colours and piebalds. In all probability, great talents for High School disappeared with the aggressive breeding policy for uniformly white coach horses. The "Directives" by Holbein and Meixner are the last important written document on Austrian equestrian art before World War I (1914-18).

Images 89, 89a – Moritz Ledeli, Croupade, Capriole. (Heydebrand, op. cit.)

DOOM OF THE AUSTRO-HUNGARIAN CAVALRY

Denial of Reality and Madder Red Breeches

Before World War I, the Austro-Hungarian cavalry lived under an illusion of tradition, self-importance, and power, having been more or less unchanged for decades: "Not only externally, but also internally the cavalry has kept quite the same character, the traditional cherishing of equestrian customs and exercises, the cult of the proud rider's spirit, the conservative idea of battle and deployment, only accepting the mounted skirmish, reserve toward other weaponry, the idealization of careless bravado."[420]

The reform of the army in 1867-69 had brought an end to the difference between light and heavy cavalry, though the three troop types: dragoons, hussars, and ulans were maintained according to tradition. In 1869, Archduke Albrecht stated with realistic foresight: "Cavalry has become an auxiliary force and, as painful as this knowledge of course is, the era of its magnificent mass impact is over."[421] Surely no cavalryman wanted to believe this, especially renowned riders like Colonel Arthur von Pongracz who still claimed in 1914: "Ever a fearless cavalry will shake even the firmest infantry and override a shaken and battle-weary one, gaining absolute victory."[422] And "since despite the introduction of firearms to the entire cavalry, their use and therefore the fight on foot were only considered as something unusual," dim, unobtrusive colours were still not deemed important.[423] Regardless, a rider is always visible from a distance. Because the Austrian volunteer corps for Mexico was disintegrated in 1867, large quantities of smart, madder red breeches were available. This colour was thought to make the fabric more durable, and hence it became the choice for the whole cavalry. "That is how the cavalry got the red trousers, its hallmark for 50 years."[424] Vanity prevailed over usefulness. Riders could jauntily indulge in traditions of patriarchal esprit de corps. This thinking was encouraged by public figures like the heir to the throne Francis Ferdinand, "who, far from modern knowledge, indulged in antiquated views about the cavalry's strategic value or equestrian mass attacks."[425] The elite weapon, bursting with self-confidence, remained in romantic dreams that denied the reality, for since "1866, the Austrian-Hungarian cavalry did not have opportunity to fight a coequal enemy." The price would have to be paid in 1914: "The cavalry did not have a rider or officer who had ever ridden an attack. Our mounted weapon faced something completely unknown, uncertain."[426]

Image 90 – Alois Pfund, Cavalryman 1916. (Archive Weiss.)

Good Horses, Bad Saddles

Since there was no longer a difference between heavy and light cavalry, there was demand of a uniform type of horse. Local breeding stock had to be improved by cross-breeding. Arabs were a preferred choice because of their short backs and hard hooves. Oriental expeditions acquired additional suitable stallions. Up until 1914, breeding results had been satisfactory "and the reasons for the dramatic equine losses of our cavalry may not be sought in the horses' minor quality."[427]

Was it sheer stupidity, corruption, or negligence? Just one and a half months after the beginning of war, only a fraction of the Austro-Hungarian cavalry horses were considered fit for service. The rest were terribly injured by the M.1883, a saddle with a rigid tree. Additionally, the horses were severely overloaded with almost 300 pounds. Improvements were under way, but the change to the saddle "Miederbock System Wilhelmi-Kybast" which adapted better to the back with its leather side fenders, progressed very slowly. The white saddle pad, visible from afar, was replaced with a greyish brown one; the uniform became less obtrusive and more practical. The units

Image 91 – Cavalryman riding a courbette. (Dokumentationsarchiv fuer altoesterreichische Pferderassen.)

received more machine guns, the weaponry was improved. The remount training lacked in personnel, "so rational training, as would have been the new system's purpose, was practically non-existent."[428]

Firefight Only in Utmost Emergency

"In order to promote the knowledge and interest for shooting and fighting on foot, cavalry courses were initially introduced at the army shooting school…The firefight always remained unknown territory, only treaded hesitatingly in utmost emergency."[429] Australian cavalrymen, for instance, did not make a fuss: One of four riders on foot held the horses while the others shot. Playing the noble knight in historic fashion turned out to be inconvenient on the battle ground: "Wherever our riders met Russian cavalry, the latter dodged the mounted skirmish and alit for a firefight, skilfully making use of our preference for the mounted fight by apparently attacking in small divisions, but returning and luring the pursuers into a prepared fire ambush by riders on foot and additional infantry…As a consequence to failed equestrian tactics at the beginning of the war, the army command decided to transform the cavalry divisions more effectively by reducing the number of riders." "Cavalry-riflemen divisions" were formed, "becoming nothing else but horseless riders."[430] In the winter of 1916-17, there was an urgent lack of horses, and in the summer 1917, "the entire cavalry," apart from some exceptions, "was sent into battle on foot, since Austro-Hungarian cavalry had ceased to be one of the three main military branches."[431] "What had become of the riders' dreamed romance? Riders without horses and horses reduced to skeletons. For man and creature, war had become an endless ordeal; the ideals of a charging youth enthralled in equestrian battles were sinking in the swampy fire trenches of Volhynia."[432]

Image 92 – From chivalric pride… (Photo M. Seebauer, Vienna, Archive Weiss.)

Image 93 - …to gas masks for horse and rider. (Wikipedia, public domain.)

Horses Defeated by Murderous War Machinery

If cavalrymen complacently considered academic equestrian art at the Spanish Riding School an outdated game, they soon had to accept that classical cavalry had also become an anachronism in view of +the reality of war. This also rang true outside the Danube-Monarchy, and was only unwillingly admitted. "It was not easy to discontinue the elite troop which was in the hearts of the state rulers as well as the officers and men…The smartly dressed cavalryman thought himself more than an artilleryman or infantry."[433] But the horse as a weapon had lost in the competitive war against the murderous machinery of war, and was obviously not going to accomplish anything of importance anymore. Thus, the representative "War Family Register of the City of Vienna" of 1917 depicted dogs, eagles, snakes, but not a single horse, only cannons, tanks, battle ships, airplanes etc.[434] At the beginning of the war, Austria-Hungary still had 34,000 cavalrymen.

This eye witness report by the Russian Colonel Tichotzki from the first weeks of war documented the most sublime absurdity and bitter tragedy of traditional cavalry attacks despite pluck and bravery: "The Hungarian hussars, in developed line, in their colourful uniforms were an unforgettable sight…Not a shot was to be heard from the Russian positions. The shooters quietly waited until the enemy came into effective firing range…

Suddenly a murderous fire of rifles and machine guns started at the Russian Lieutenant Colonel's command…Men and horses were mowed down, the lines confused, order ended…The landscape in front of us was empty again, and only the wounded and dead hussars reminded in a bloody episode of war here!"[435]

Loss of the Knightly World View

World War I cost Austria-Hungary 1.5 million dead soldiers. In this vast massacre, eight million horses died altogether, so there was a shortage toward the end, and the loss of horses was considered more severe than the death of men. On the western front, cavalry troops experienced massive losses during traditional deployment. "The situation in the vast territories of the eastern front was distinctly different; both sides deployed their cavalry troops intensively in the mobile warfare of 1914-1915, above all for armed reconnaissance and the securing of terrain. But also in the east, the era of traditional battle cavalry had inevitably come to an end as early as 1914. The cavalry lost its position as a military main branch. In the war's latter years, all powers strongly reduced their equestrian troops. Previous cavalrymen were often deployed as police forces in behind the front, or they transferred to different branches of the army, for instance the large logistic system of the artillery with its many horses. Many cavalry officers were taken over by the aeronautic forces."[436] One of them was renowned rider Sigmund Josipovich. One can only imagine the enormous emotional load such a revolution meant for the Austro-Hungarian cavalrymen educated in the traditional rider's spirit: Not only the monarchy collapsed, but also their world view, their self-esteem. "World War I and its battles of material led to a pronounced change in mentality. Before World War I, the general concept of war was still characterized by open field battles where the soldier bravely, knightly, heroically should face the enemy. This image could not be preserved due to requirements and experiences in trench warfare. So, during and after the war this ideal image of the soldier shifted to complete desensitization, lack of emotion, and endless endurance."[437] The last great cavalry attack took place in 1917, when the Australian 4th Light Horse Brigade with 12,000 riders, and the English 5th Mounted Brigade, led by General Edmund Allenby, conquered Beerscheba against the Turks, an enemy not up to the era's military standard.[438]

Joyfully Trimmed to a Small State's Size

In 1918, Austria lost World War I and the victorious powers enjoyed trimming it to the size of a small state, with just as many inhabitants as a modern city. The equestrian art specific to Austria could live on in the Spanish Riding School which was saved from doom. Otherwise it became extinct with the old cavalrymen and horses. From the 21st century's view, it seems easy to reproach the epoch's horsemen with denial of reality. But

Image 94 – Dragoons in Graz 1935. (Archive Weiss.)

also after the Austro-Hungarian cavalry had ceased to exist, there were again enthusiasts in the whole territory of the Danube-Monarchy cherishing the radiance of this equestrian culture, desiring its revival. Both then, and now this was, and is more a matter of heart than of rational thoughts.

Melancholy and Nostalgia

"It was really an impressive image of awesome beauty, delighting the hearts of laymen and experts alike, whenever and wherever our riders appeared – alone or in a throng – in their shiny and colourful uniforms, inseparably one with their sleek, light horses, always carefully groomed, correctly saddled, bridled, and packed. Of all cavalries, the Austro-Hungarian had the most efficient and thorough equestrian training and the best riding style; nowhere else was the duty carried out in such painstaking detail, and nowhere else were there such exemplary, severe rules and customs."[439] "An Austrian-Hungarian cavalry will never be again. We must bid farewell to it forever!"[440]

Such 'most thorough equestrian training" and 'best riding style" are the result of centuries of equestrian culture of Spanish origin, which never ceased to work. This equestrian culture became something specifically Austrian. Perhaps the Austrian cavalryman's obvious desire for representation is due to the Spanish equestrian flaunting and boasting in conjunction with simultaneous nonchalance, making the control of the horse seem effortless. The continued connection between cavalry officers and the Spanish School shows its effect. This equestrian pride likely contributed to the refusal to battle on foot, since a true cavalier could only imagine fighting in the saddle. At the same time, an interesting parallel occurred some thousand miles westward in California, finally dominated by U.S. "gringos," where

Image 95 – International cavalry enthusiasts in Lang, Styria 2012. (Photo Poscharnigg.)

most of the old vaqueros, also practicing equitation in the Spanish tradition, became unemployed by modern cattle management because they proudly only wanted tasks they could accomplish on horseback.[441]

Inglorious Remaining Life

Before 1938, Austria had more than one thousand cavalry horses.[442] Not only because of the difficult domestic political and economic situation, their deployment generally was not at all glorious since "clean-up operations" were targeted against their own people. Thus the 5th squadron, successor of the k. and k. Dragoon Regiment Nr. 5, attacked workers who had barricaded themselves around a market building in Graz. Galloping cavalry shot out street lamps to make way for the following infantry.[443]

A sad decline from the noble riders' spirit in glamorous days of yore was followed by annexation by the German army. Alois Podhajsky reported on the difficulties that awaited Austrian cavalrymen in the new surroundings: "I remember this command with mixed emotions, feeling like the hen in a strange hen house, being attacked from all sides in some way. The Austrian mentality was wrongly estimated. Frequently, our preference for handling things smoothly without much fuss was interpreted as weakness."[444] After the intrusion of German troops into Austria and the annexation to Nazi-Germany in 1938, Cavalry General Perfall inspected the Military Riding and Driving Instructor Institute in Schlosshof and the Dragoon Regiment Nr. 1 in Stockerau. He appeared very dissatisfied with the standard of training; hence, Austrian cavalrymen "had to bury many customs and views as obsolete."[445] Only Podhajsky knew how "to promote the Austrian equestrian tradition" with his division by disciplined, energetic riding ahead.[446] But this did not prevent the Austrian cavalry style, already weakened by the Danube-Monarchy's doom, from finally disappearing after the annexation. The rest was "only infinite mourning," and during World War II the question still arose "whence the visible melancholy of many former officers of the Austro-Hungarian army came."[447]

FINAL HABITAT OF AUSTRIAN EQUESTRIAN ART: THE SPANISH RIDING SCHOOL

Mauritius Herold

Back in 1918, the Spanish Riding School of Vienna was in utmost danger. Many people then temporarily regarded anything imperial as evil, so the ironically modestly paid personnel dared not even lead the Lipizzaners from the Stallburg across the street into the Winter Riding School for fear of attacks. Chief Rider Mauritius (Moritz) Herold (1873-1962) fought like a lion for the life of this cultural jewel, for which he worked 1896-1925, running it from 1916. His "broom fund" to acquire means for the Riding School's daily operation became legendary.

"Memorandum about Development, Use, and Future of the Spanish Riding School"

As an important argument for the School's continuation, he mentions its military usefulness. He reports on the permanent flow of equestrian knowledge from the Spanish Riding School to the cavalry in his "Memorandum about Development, Use, and Future of the Spanish Riding School" of 1918. "Since 'High School' means equestrian art in its highest perfection, the Spanish Riding School was considered an equestrian academy, and, for a long time, officers from Austria and abroad were specially ordered here and admitted to a riding course of usually about one year. Each year, the Austro-Hungarian Army and the Honved-Cavalry also sent one particularly qualified officer, who had to have already graduated from the Military Riding Instructor Institute, to the Spanish Riding School. These graduates were redeployed as riding instructors at the military institutes on their return. This procedure certainly contributed to the Austro-Hungarian cavalry excelling as an equestrian troop. It probably was not chance that at the international equestrian competition of Turin in 1903 the four first prizes went to four Austro-Hungarians."[448] Herold clearly realized that the organic existence of the School did not allow any interruption because of the oral-practical tradition; "for if the Spanish School is discontinued once, it cannot be restarted again because riders and horses are needed for this. It takes a rider 10-15 years for a promising education; work and training of rider and horse are actually

Image 96 – Chief Rider Mauritius Herold, Piaffe. (Dokumentationszenrum fuer altoesterreichische Pferderassen.)

infinite, and it would not be modest to speak about highest perfection since even a mere standstill of training nearly equates to regression."[449]

Herold: "The Development of a School Horse According to the Usual Method at the Viennese Spanish Riding School"

Despite heavy opposition, the Spanish Riding School was maintained as the last habitat of Austrian equestrian art. Herold relentlessly promoted the School in public, and in 1923, he explained for the first time how "The Development of a School Horse According to the Usual Method at the Viennese Spanish Riding School" works.[450] A premiere: for the first time in the Spanish Riding School's history a Chief Rider published a short document about the work at this institute. For Europe's contemporary horse world, the Spanish Riding School of Vienna was a fossil, watched distrustfully and disparagingly; cavalrymen who had not learned anything from World War I thought the same. During the emperors' era the School deemed public relations work unnecessary, opening its doors to the public only twice a week. The republic's era demanded more openness. Mauritius Herold took this into account in his steadfast fight for classical equestrian art: "It is not anything mystic, as some may believe, but it is a very natural thing, based solely on the highly developed feel of the rider. This developed emotional potential virtually connects man to the horse's psyche…For the horse is a creature endowed with a mind and will…; just as a human, he wants to make his work easier." Herold concludes, "Therefore I claim that riding, strictly

Image 97 – School quadrille, Spanish Riding School. (Private archive.)

speaking, and especially High School equitation, is a permanent struggle with the horse which nevertheless happens in such fine form that the spectator does not perceive anything but always gets the impression of complete harmony between rider and horse."[451]

Touchstone Quadrille

The basic training outlined by Herold completely matches the description in the manuscript "Dressage of the Green Horse, Treatment in the Riding School" by Chief Rider Mathäus von Niedermaier, from 1885. There is nothing to be seen of Holbein's methods. "With regard to laymen," Herold explains two-tracking quite exactly. "By continuous exercising on two tracks, the horse gradually acquires the necessary skill to be taught further movements, such as pirouettes, *redopp, terre à terre* etc."[452] The passage, at the Spanish Riding School called "Spanish step," is usually developed from piaffe. The fully trained stallion is bridled with a curb bit and can also work in the quadrille. Herold considered this the proper "touchstone of the horse's degree of obedience." "With a horse not truly in hand, it would be completely impossible" to ride the school quadrille and its fast-changing manoeuvres exactly in harmony with the partners. Herold underlines, "standing still means going back,"[453] for the rider must continuously maintain and perfect the fully trained horse's standard.

Cultivated Nature

Airs above the ground cannot be reached by all horses, "there must be certain conditions given by nature, such as temperament and preferably, a faultless, strong build. Work in the pillars is the key to airs above the ground."[454] Here the horse learns piaffe and to take weight off the forelegs. "Depending on the horse's temperament and potential, moments occur under increased demand when the horse is balanced on his engaged hind-legs, and the fore-legs drawn up, or he pushes himself from the ground by his hind-legs showing an elevated forehand." Herold describes the levade, which he does not distinguish from the pesade, then the croupade, ballotade, capriole, and courbette. The mezair is not mentioned. "The phases of High School mentioned here are not at all 'artificial' gaits, but generally natural gaits, cultivated by human influence, and adapted to the human will and sense of beauty." Therefore, "High School, when practiced methodically and according to the old masters' traditional experience, does not demand unnatural things from the horse, but instead, is a cultural achievement renowned and honoured by all hippologists."[455] This final remark in Herold's essay is, of course, meant to thwart critics who would have loved to abolish the Spanish Riding School of Vienna.

Image 98 – Spanish Riding School between the World Wars. (Dokumentationszentrum fuer altoesterreichische Pferderassen.)

HOPEFUL RETROSPECTIONS: KOCH, JOSIPOVICH AND DREYHAUSEN

Ludwig Koch: "EQUESTRIAN ART IN PICTURES"

Five years after the end of World War I, in 1923, a unique way of depicting the Austrian way of riding was published by the Viennese Campagnereiter-Gesellschaft: "Equestrian Art in Pictures," by Ludwig Koch. The publication of such a beautiful book with fine colour prints was entirely unexpected given the difficult Austrian economic environment where vast numbers of people suffered bitter poverty. There was even a second edition in 1928.

Truer than Photography

Ludwig Koch (1866-1934)[456] made it his life's task to depict the horse and its gaits even more realistic than in photography. He rejected the past's horse-related art because of its incorrect and often arbitrary depiction of the gaits. A special thorn in his side was Johann Elias Ridinger, who created highly decorative but anatomically incorrect images. The new technologies of film and photo made it possible to see the single phases of the canter. This doubtlessly resulted in depictions conforming to reality. Nevertheless, they did not satisfy Koch because the photographs often showed incorrectly moving horses. If these were used in schoolbooks as examples for riders and trainers, they caused confusion and led to the pursuit of inaccurate objectives. Koch's answer was a kind of "spiritual realism": The knowing, able artist is able to select the images of horses that were "true" and exemplary from the many less-than-perfect ones. He portrayed the movements in realistic works of art. Art representing ideal and reality at the same time: "For the serious, thinking artist there could be no question which way to go, embellishment at the cost of truth, or remaining true, even at beauty's cost!"[457] Koch studied all spheres of equitation available: Campaign riding, army steeple chase, Spanish Riding School, gallop and trot races, circus riding, Hungarian herdsmen riding, even Arabian and western riding, "but our mounted troops' style, especially of our Austro-Hungarian cavalry, always points the way for me!"

Image 99 – Ludwig Koch gave this croupade's rider young Josipovich's face. (Dokumentationszentrum fuer altoesterreichische Pferderassen.)

Image 99a – Ludwig Koch, Proof of obedience. (Dokumentationszentrum fuer altoesterreichische Pferderassen.)

This virtually monomaniac life-long passion for the subject horse resulted in a wealth of graphics and paintings along with "Equestrian Art in Pictures" with its hundreds of pen and ink drawings and over 70 colour prints. Koch's work stands-up to even the most excellent horse-related artists of all epochs and countries.

Pointing beyond Themselves

In his theory of motion, Koch does not assume one centre of gravity, "but as unusual as it may seem, there are two centres of gravity in reciprocation."[458] In thoughtful detail, Koch describes the three main basic gaits: walk, trot, and canter, first verbally and then by ingenious, sparse pen and ink drawings, showing each phase of the gaits in both correct and faulty execution. Koch's skill is amazing as he depicts reality with a few fast strokes. In contrast to many prominent artists, he does not dodge difficult details yet omits things not immediately necessary to the illustration. These graphics radiate something spiritual and definite, pointing beyond themselves, always the hallmark of great art.

Image 100 – Ludwig Koch, School trot.
(Dokumentationszentrum fuer altoesterreichische Pferderassen.)

Image 100a – Ludwig Koch, Half-pass at the trot.
(Dokumentationszentrum fuer altoesterreichische Pferderassen.)

Action Never Forced and Heavy

Koch draws correct action preferably with Austrian cavalrymen and riders of the Spanish School, whereas riders of incorrectly-going mounts usually wear civilian clothing, such as tail coats, top hats, and monocles, presenting their alleged equestrian skills in parvenu-manner. For Koch, true equestrian art proves "a powerful, swinging unity, produced by the rider in most beautiful evolvement and joyous desire to go."[459] In addition to the basic gaits, Koch describes work on two tracks, piaffe, passage, pirouettes, jumping, transitions, parades, and airs above the ground. The horse's balance and action of the back are Koch's special interests; he warns of artificial erection of the neck out of the withers and forced bend at the poll since these cannot result in genuine collection. The verve is characterized truly by the legs' soft, round, and energetic movement; all joints have the same proportion of the movement. The action is effortless, never forced and heavy."[460]

Images 101 and 101a– Ludwig Koch, Pirouette at the canter, Renvers at the canter.
(Dokumentationszentrum fuer altoesterreichische Pferderassen.)

Surest Way to Keep the Horse on the Forehand

Koch particularly refuses hyper-flexion and riding forward-downward in Plinzner's style: "But if actually a deep forehand is discussed in some equestrian literature as a means to arch up the back, this is the surest way to keep the horses on the forehand and to deny them a balance to the rear. Plinzner's theory, according to which the working of the hindquarters requires a deep forehand as a compensation of weight, forgets that the forehand is already heavier itself than the hindquarters and therefore, a deeper forehand increases its weight, forcing horses completely on the forehand. Is this an equestrian ideal to aim for?"[461]

Verve from Highest Equilibration

Koch hardly dreamed that those harmful methods would become standard in modern dressage sport of the 21st century, being "enhanced" by "rollkur," a.k.a. "low, deep, round," a seemingly indispensable preparation for top competition success. The old classical ideal, as described by Koch, was not to prevail: "A truly straightened horse ridden with impulsion has his lines directed forward and raised. One can discern the horse's condition from the position and seat of the rider…Impulsion is the ultimate control of the body, produced by highest equilibration, i.e. the supreme level of physical training."[462]

Sigmund von Josipovich: Excesses of Modern Outbidding

Koch's book contains a hippological jewel, "General Considerations" by Sigmund von Josipovich: "Our Images and Equestrian Art in Conjunction with Practical Riding." Josipovich calls Koch's pictures an "immortalization of the highly developed equestrian art in the ancient monarchy."[463] He is concerned with developments in [then] modern riding, which use unnatural methods and hurried training, both of which can harm the horse. He considers the Spanish Riding School the last and world's best sanctuary of classical equestrian art, successful in keeping it pure, despite "hazardous modernization" or the "introduction of overt riding tricks" elsewhere. It ever maintains the time-honoured principles and prevents "the excesses of the modern desire to outbid from ousting the good and honest ways."[464] Such desire for the good, honest, true, and beautiful is understandable in an era of questioning values. where "anything is available on the market," "commercial merchandise and works of art, the honour of women, and the conviction of men" as Felix Dörmann appropriately described the time in his novel, "Jazz."[465]

Monument of Mastery Working in Silence

Josipovich regrets the lack of written or visual documents about the Spanish Riding School's training methods. But Koch's images, for him, reveal "a monument that modest, selfless mastery working in silence has erected for itself."[466] "The horses' swinging, elastic gait and the rider's pliant, elegant seat in harmony with it," characterizes the Austro-Hungarian school, "putting the feel of swing above form, yet choosing form individually."[467] "Complete harmony of rider and horse must be obvious; both should give the spectator the impression that their effort, is not worth mentioning."[468] All of these qualities are required of the Austrian equestrian art ever since its Spanish-Neapolitan beginnings, proving historic continuity.

Gustav von Dreyhausen: "PRINCIPLES OF EQUESTRIAN ART"

Sigmund von Josipovich was an important mentor at the "k. and k. Militär-Reitlehrer-Institut." One of his most devoted students was Gustav von Dreyhausen. His "Principles of Equestrian Art" was published in 1936 by the Austrian Racing and Campaign Riders Society, a preserver of the cultural treasure. This book, very tightly printed on obviously wood-containing paper, is testimony for the cultural will to enshrine the precious past even in economically difficult times. It is an attempt to document and remember Austrian-Hungarian equitation or "the Viennese school's system," namely "utmost impulsion in conjunction with utmost softness and perfect form."[469]

Crossing T's and Dotting I's

In his book, Josipovich comments on the text in footnotes, sometimes rather wittily: "He who, as a calligrapher, forgets the dot on the i, makes the same mistake as the riding artist, who, while he has brought the horse from behind forward into the hand, forgets to give the last sign with his hand, the short *arrêt*. If anyone thinks this means the same as erecting by the hand, he is an arrogant braggart or does not understand much about the matter, repeating something he has heard of without understanding it. What a pity!"[470] Dreyhausen, an honest seeker of truth, preferably refers to Seeger, Max von Weyrother, the k. and k. Exercise-Manual, and the H. Dv. 12, German Riding Manual of 1912 [Xenophon Press, 2014]. He tends to get carried away in detailed, exuberant theorizing though without falling into vanity: "I would like to state that I do not think I bring anything new."[471] He strives to recommend to the German equitation of his time the impulsion and looseness of the traditional Viennese school in order to be able to rise to global leadership. Both Dreyhausen and Josipovich refuse the popular riding "forward-downward": "Let us remark that the expression 'He seeks the reins downward' is, in my opinion, not true, for the horse seeks the rein forward but not downward; furthermore this expression has caused much mischief."[472]

Go Ahead and Carry Both of Us Yourself

Altogether, Dreyhausen's philosophy corresponds with classical Austrian equestrian art: "The ridden horse's ideal state would be the horse that can be ridden with an almost entirely passive hand and only leg and seat aids, with the hand only quietly indicating movement and tempo, and commanding the degree of collection and lift: It no longer reacts to aids, but rather to 'signs'."[473] Hence his principle: " 'Go ahead and carry both of us yourself', from natural riding up to the heights of art, and all equitation is just an execution of this highest principle, endless in its multitude and variety, and applied to different cases and situations."[474]

Image 102 – Ludwig Koch 1907, Officers' competition.
(Private archive.)

ALOIS PODHAJSKY: SURVIVED BARBARY OF WAR AND NEW HEYDAY

Sink into the Grave with the Old Equestrian Culture

In the autumn 1933, Master Ludwig Koch embraced a dressage rider to congratulate him enthusiastically. This rider had represented traditional Austrian equestrian art in an international competition most honourably, riding Fourth Level single-handed on the curb only. Koch really wanted to make a painting of the rider, but sickness and death prevented it. The rider's name was Alois Podhajsky. This eminent character would help the doomed Austrian equestrian art gain worldwide recognition once again, creating new direction.

The Spanish Riding School of Vienna as the last domain of Austrian equestrian art had fortunately survived the Danube-Monarchy's demise thanks to good fortune and the help of excellent people, especially Chief Rider Herold. On international tours, it mainly garnered attention and admiration. Furthermore, the connection to military riding remained since specially gifted cavalry officers were ordered there to pass on their acquired knowledge to the troops. Nevertheless, between 1918 and 1939, many people considered the Spanish Riding School a "rotten branch."[475] Furthermore, it was generally accepted that dressage and jumping had no connection to each other. And the Riding School did little to educate riders for the future. The low pay scale further added to the lack of appeal for the job. A program leaflet of the time between the wars shows how few riders were active for an entire presentation: Three Chief Riders – Zrust, Polak, and Lindenbauer – and four Riders – Neumayer, Cerha, Resch, and Lippert. And when Podhajsky became director of the Riding School in 1939, his personnel consisted of these men and one more apprentice. These three Chief Riders "were living under the erroneous assumption they were the last to convey classical equestrian art, and that this ancient equestrian culture would sink into the grave with them. Thus, they paid little attention to the education of riders during the past decades."[476] Hence, the danger arose that "convenience was called tradition" and that little enthusiasm for reform existed because future prospects were dim.

Image 103 – Alois Podhajsky and Nero, Piaffe 1936. (Dokumentationszentrum fuer altoesterreichische Pferderassen.)

Directed by a Single Hand in Elegant Obedience

Alois Podhajsky (1898-1973) was born a "soldier's child" in then-Austrian Mostar, and had been a dragoon in World War I since 1916. So he received an equestrian education in the spirit of the k. and k. Exercise Manual. After a severe war injury, he spent two years at the Military Riding and Driving Institute in Schlosshof and became an excellent trainer and bold jumping and hunting rider. A severe fall resulted in a mare's blow, which broke a lumbar vertebra, whereupon Podhajsky concentrated on dressage after his recovery.

By his diligence and genius he gained spectacular national and international success, and was subsequently commanded to the Spanish Riding School of Vienna for two years. In 1936, he placed "only" third in the Olympic Games in Berlin because German judges had strategically relegated him extremely far back. Regardless, international experts were enthusiastic about Podhajsky's style, praising his "beautiful and supple seat" and "quiet and

Image 104 – Podhajsky, Levade, Spanish Riding School 1934. (Dokumentationszentrum fuer altoesterreichische Pferderassen.)

invisible aids," "the whole old tradition of Austrian equitation had come alive again."[477] His "lighter, let us call it, more elegant control of the horse, namely a naturally, freer movement," "being, as it were, an intermediate combination of French and German style of riding" was acknowledged. Critics admired how Podhajsky's "horse performed everything his rider demanded, in elegant obedience with beautiful, natural posture on a light rein, and merely controlled by one hand."[478] Podhajsky severely criticized the new practice in dressage riding: showing a horse you have not entirely trained yourself. In old Austria, it would have been unthinkable that someone "swings himself into the saddle in order to eventually get celebrated as a winner."[479]

A Life for the Lipizzaners

As a commander of the Viennese Spanish Riding School, Podhajsky achieved great things even during World War II (1939-45). Despite the war, he succeeded in recruiting talented riders fit for military service to the School so that the old Chief Riders could pass on

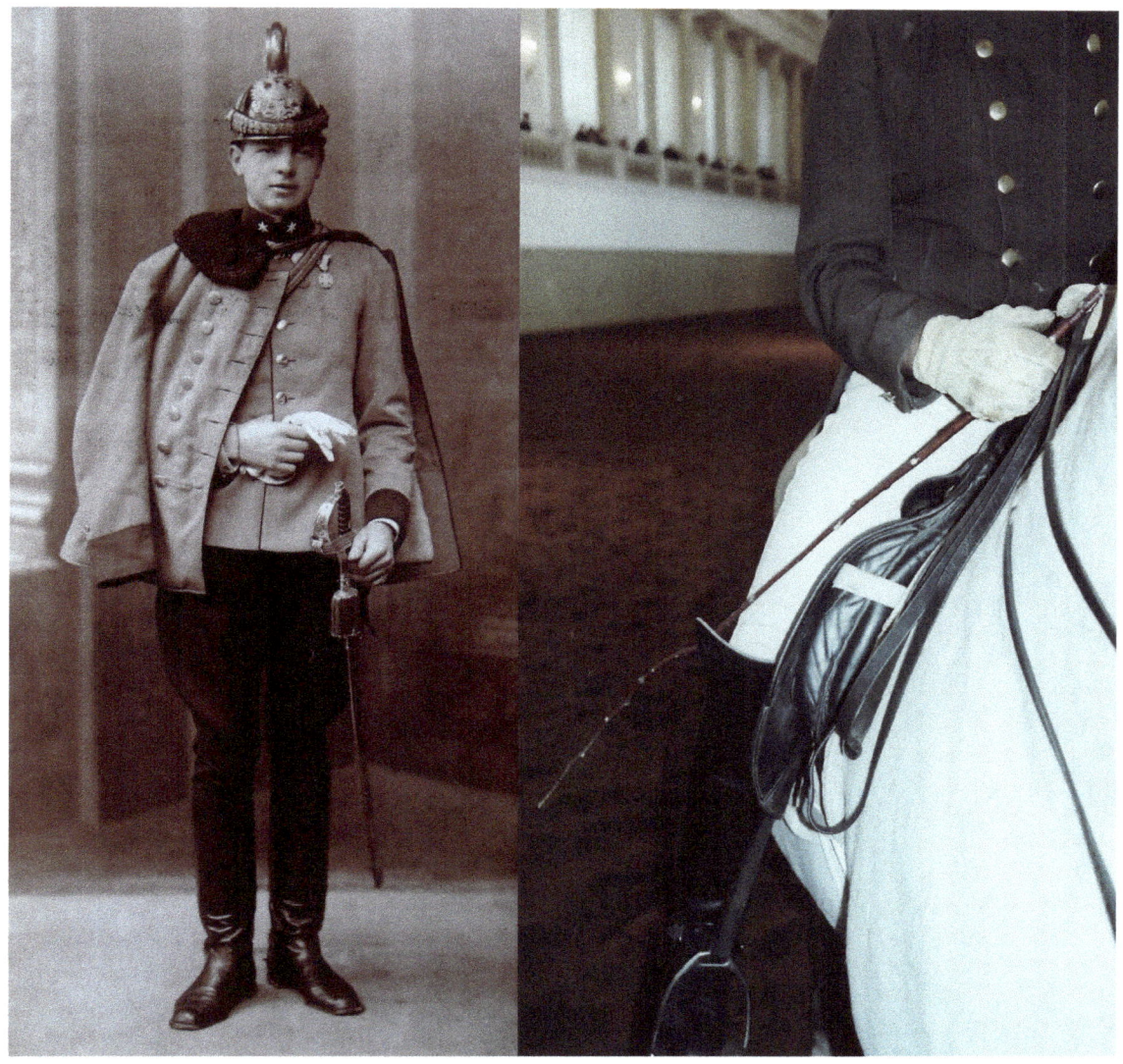

Image 106 – Podhajsky as a young cavalryman. (Dokumentationszentrum fuer altoesterreichische Pferderassen.)

Image 105 – Podhajsky demanded tradition even in details – Birch riding crop. (Photo Poscharnigg 2003.)

their knowledge which otherwise would have perished. Thus, a quadrille of 12 riders was performed in 1942. It may not have been easy for Podhajsky to convince the old Chief Riders. He reminded them of the School's glamorous era under Max von Weyrother and Mathäus von Niedermaier, referred to the "Directives" by Holbein and Meixner as a last resort and demanded improvement concerning walk and extended trot.[480] In this way, he succeeded in passing on the spiritual heritage of Austrian equestrian art beyond the old Chief Riders' deaths, effectively surviving the Second World War, and Austria's occupation by the allies. But spiritual survival alone would have been useless. Podhajsky, having become a larger-than-life character through the tragic events of war, saved the Spanish Riding School of Vienna and the Lipizzaner breed as a final physical foundation of Austrian equestrian art from ultimate annihilation by the barbarity of war. His amazing achievements are well-documented in writing, photography, and even films. He also toured Europe and the U.S.A. with the Riding School, attaining international renown for the institute. He was identified with the School and was treated as an esteemed celebrity. I was told that people stepped from the sidewalk for him instinctively, so strong was his radiance. In 1964, though, he was overtaken by a tragic yet common fate: his retirement. During that year's December 13 farewell gala, he rode a "Pas de trois," "All Gaits and Tours of High School," the "School-Quadrille," and showed "Work in Hand." (Cf. SRS's program.)

Image 107 – Photo in Podhajsky's pay book. (Dokumentationszentrum fuer altoesterreichische Pferderassen.)

Alois Podhajsky: "CLASSICAL EQUESTRIAN ART. RIDING INSTRUCTION FROM THE BEGINNINGS TO PERFECTION."

As expected, he did not stop working for the Spanish Riding School in his retirement, thus publishing the first comprehensive description of the Lipizzaners' training in their history of several centuries: "Classical Equestrian Art. Riding Instruction from the Beginnings to Perfection."

During his discussions with the old Chief Riders Zrust, Polak, and Lindenbauer, Podhajsky found the Spanish Riding School lacking a clear, detailed manual, and already began taking notes of those conversations.[481] One of his main concerns was to maintain the School's high equestrian level without any changes and to preserve the traditions without any concessions. Thus, Podhajsky undertook the creation of the first manual for the Imperial Riding School, which encompassed the entire training scale, and was also published in a book. Regenthal's unpublished "Compendium" was encompassing, but lacked detail. Podhajsky did not know it because it had fallen into oblivion. The "Directives" by Holbein and Meixner are only cursory. Herold described dressage only in a short essay.

Image 107a – The US-Army saved the Lipizzaners: Podhajsky presented the Spanish Riding School to General George S. Patton during its exile in St. Martin, Upper Austria, on May 7, 1945. He asked the General for the School's protection and for the rescue of 247 Lipizzaners brought to Czechoslovakia by the Nazis. These horses ran risk of being turned into sausage by the advancing hungry Soviet troops. Colonel Charles H. Reed and the 2nd Cavalry Division carried out this risky operation. Without the bravery of these men, Austrian equestrian art would be extinct today. (Dokumentationszentrum fuer altoesterreichische Pferderassen.)

Therefore, Podhajsky's book is a milestone of utmost importance in Austrian equestrian art's history. Here, each rider can catch up on traditionally correct procedures. Podhajsky knew the work of Guérinière, the 19th century literature, and Niedermaier's manuscript. If Regenthal had published his work as a book in his era, there would not have been the historic misconception that persisted for over 200 years that Austrian equestrian art has its roots in France, based on Pluvinel and Guérinière. But this was not the case, as historical research has proven. Seen in this light, Podhajsky's treatise come 200 years late. Only the lack of printed tradition caused horsemen to take what was available as a book: Guérinière.

As Man and Rider Always Ahead

Podhajsky's equestrian treatise not only offers information to the topic itself but lets us partake in the deep wisdom of a man whose life was marked by bitter setbacks and great triumphs. Almost every page contains philosophy which links riding to life's problems and joys. It is the knowledge of a man who pursued his aims despite seemingly unconquerable

Image 108 – Spanish Riding School, Quadrille, Stud Piber 1998. (Photo Poscharnigg.)

obstacles and massive health problems. He always pushed forward both as a man and as a rider. Equestrian treatises inspired by philosophical wisdom are extremely rare in the history of this genre of literature. Rarely can we sense the author's individuality from each line in a work of non-fiction. Modern dressage sport would be better off if Podhajsky's doctrines were considered.

Légèreté the Austrian Way

The first part of Podhajsky's equestrian treatise provides an overview of classical equitation since Xenophon, but understandably lacks in coverage of Austrian equitation before 1800. He believes theoretical principles must prove their practicality in order to achieve an artistic level. More than any other art, riding is connected with fundamental wisdom, since the horse teaches man self-discipline, consequences of actions, and empathy for a living creature. According to Podhajsky, the most important authors for the Spanish Riding School are Max von Weyrother, Louis Seeger, and Oeynhausen. They prove that the art of dressage will always stay the same because of natural laws.[482]

Image 109 – Spanish Riding School, Piaffe 2003. (Photo Poscharnigg.)

The second part deals with concepts of equestrian art aiming at educating a glamorous, obedient, pleasant horse that is a joy to ride. The author defines terms such as lesson, reprise, gaits, parades, *arrêts*, balance, contact, head position, straightening etc. As far as half-*arrêts* are concerned, he demands that they cease as soon as the desired response is achieved. This method results in a lighter contact, a *légèretè* the Austrian way, as it were. He especially refuses to bring the horse's nose behind the vertical which results in impeded walking and encourages restraint. Like Regenthal, he warns of shortening the horse's neck by forced pulling on the reins. The rider's aids are a communication between two creatures, where the rider is best advised to act like an exactly observing psychologist in order to draw conclusions from slightest indications.[483]

One of Podhajsky's particular concerns is the immediate, consequent ceasing of the aids once they work, completely in accordance with Austrian equestrian tradition since Grisone, Galiberto, Regenthal, Guérinière and al.: "Nothing is more harmful and impeding to training than permanently knocking legs…The leg's pressure must cease as soon as the horse has done the rider's will."[484] This also applies to the use of spurs: "The use of the spurs is the last resort of driving aids, and reserves should not be spent – neither in equitation nor elsewhere in life."[485] This also holds true for the use of the rein: "Never must a rein's pull become pulling."[486] Generally the harmony of the aids must be based on energetic forward riding, without which no success can be achieved.

Image 110 – Spanish Riding School, Graz 2005, Courbette ridden. (Photo Poscharnigg.)

The Thinking Rider

The thinking rider punishes only if absolutely necessary, and after cool consideration: the bigger the rider's incompetence and ambition, the rougher the treatment of the mount. In case of particular misbehaviour, there should be one single, strong smack with the switch just behind the rider's leg, but not several light lashes: "All half-truths remain ineffective and are more or less useless – in equitation as in life."[487] Like all other aids, punishment must cease as soon as it worked. Praising is more important since horses usually strive to please the rider. Patting the horse's neck must not be done hard and loud, but "the horse's neck should be patted in a tender, caressing manner."[488] Podhajsky draws conclusions to the rider's character from the way he praises or punishes, which has striking similarities to Regenthal whom Podhajsky did not know.

Image 111 – Work on the Long Rein, Spanish Riding School, Graz 2005. (Photo Poscharnigg.)

The third part discusses the horse's training according to the principle that thoroughness must never be given up to save time. "By its especially methodical and purposeful duration of training, the Spanish Riding School plays the role of an equestrian university."[489] The horse is required to meet the highest expectations without making him joyless, suffer mentally or physically, the aim being to achieve trust, obedience, and swinging gaits for a long, healthy, happy equine life. The correctness of any equestrian training is proven by the fact that the horse looks better and moves more beautifully. From serious riders Podhajsky demands prolific practical experience in the training of remounts, for if they only ride "horses trained by others, they hardly get the opportunity to understand the deeper meaning of classical equestrian art."[490] The sensitive, thinking rider will achieve faster and better results by proceeding according to the horse's individuality. The principle is: Any standstill means regression.

The Righteous Rider

The remount training takes up two thirds of the complete education, but forms the indisputable basis for the High School. This is not a problem for the "righteous rider."[491] Unerringly, he works on his horse's training and does not let himself become carried away

Images 112 and 112a – Capriole in Hand, Pesade in Hand, Spanish Riding School, Graz 2005. (Photos Poscharnigg.)

with actions that contradict classical doctrines. The reward is the feeling of increased melting together with his horse. "The spectator becomes captivated by the music in the horse's balanced motion. The entire body of the horse will shine in full beauty of the developing muscles."[492] To achieve this, the horse must never be worked backward from the front, but needs to develop a desire to move forward from the hindquarters. Everything has to be done with calm and ease: "It is known that one can do as little with an excited horse as with an excited person."[493]

Proceeding methodically, the thinking rider works without haste, yet wastes no time. Podhajsky warns of reckless training which only leads "to general trivialization, to distorted forms of motion" and the horse's untimely decline: "Nature cannot be violated."[494] The rider should always be a good psychologist. A spirited horse must be made even more obedient: "Then such a horse in all his beauty will evoke the wonderful impression of controlled power in all his movements."[495] The rider must also control himself carefully in order not to destroy long work with inconsiderate action. – Podhajsky preferred shoulder-in on four tracks, as did Guérinière.[496]

From Craftsmanship to Art

After the horse has finished the remount training, the thinking rider aims for perfection. Everything demanded thus far receives fine polishing. Armed with knowledge, experience, and empathy, the rider who has advanced to become "an individual trainer, has graduated from craftsmanship to art."[497] Flying lead changes are only demanded after sufficient strengthening of the horse, and they should not be trained too often. Canter pirouettes require "impulsion, balance, skill, and looseness." They give "deep insight into the training and attained degree of the horse's ride-ability."[498] Ideally, the hindquarters make a circle the size of a platter.

Rarity of Adorable Piaffes

Piaffe and passage are the crowning achievements of long, systematic training. Podhajsky states that the desire for quick results almost exclusively produces distorted versions of either. "A correct passage that elicits the expert spectator's enthusiasm, but even more so, a correct piaffe has become a rarity nowadays and will soon only be viewable in old paintings and photographs."[499] To train piaffe, the rider requires impulsion and, if need be, an assistant to maintain it with a whip or crop. With these he may only encourage the horse but not touch him. The helper should only touch rarely and then, only near the girth. Podhajsky strictly opposes touching the hind legs as a method of circus riding that leads to the horse's lifting his hind legs higher than the forelegs, "resulting in a more or less controlled treading on the spot."[500]

In the final training stage, the school horse should be bridled with a curb bit. All movements and exercises should also be possible with a snaffle bit. Excessive demands and overtiring are always to be avoided. "Therefore the stallions' daily work time is limited to 45 minutes at the Spanish Riding School."[501] Despite recurring setbacks, the training's overall development must always aim upward and forward. Horses may never be afraid of rider or whip; violence is the proof of "false and rough training deviating from the classical idea. Not even accomplishments that lack complete harmony can refute this statement."[502]

Any Equitation's Deeper Meaning

The fourth part deals with the rider's education which requires:

"1. The intellectual understanding of any equitation's deeper meaning
2. Attaining the right feel.
3. Acquiring the physical skill for practical execution of riding."[503]

To make horse and rider meld into one harmonious being, a correct seat must be achieved, best by lunging without stirrups, 30-45 minutes per day for six to twelve months, depending on the rider's talent. Only then does the student get his four-legged teacher, the lesson horse, to learn the aids necessary to communicate with. The riding instructor must perfectly master his subject "inspired by a consistency that does not allow for moody fluctuations." He knows the lesson horse and its peculiarities exactly, having even trained, or at least ridden it himself. A good teacher will never want to correct all of his pupil's weaknesses at once. This would only lead to confusion and stiffness: "Especially riding demands, should it develop into an art, both partners' entire ease."[504] By no means may there be yelling. The teacher forms the student as a sculptor his work.

Supreme Perfection: Single-Handed on the Curb Only

The advanced student is allowed to get used to spurs before he is allowed to handle the curb bit. The reins are held "3:1," with the switch in the right hand.[505] For a short time he can ride single-handed. "Single-handed rein control on the curb only is the supreme perfection that classical equestrian art aims for."[506] The pupil rides increasingly on his own, supported by his teacher's necessary corrections. "In this way, the student is educated to become a thinking rider – which is the final aim of instruction."[507] As a reward for good work, the student may ride High School movements, but of course not to "satisfy the young rider's vanity."[508] Each lesson should end with a successful reprise so that instructor, student, and horse finish their work with a positive impression.

Podhajsky finds it hardly possible to give a definite length of time for the education of a rider. "Usually the greatest riders are those who learned that they will never finish learning."[509] The ability to ride a fully trained school horse in a way that it presents its complete skill takes about two to four years of education. To train a horse from green remount up to High School takes four to six years at the Spanish Riding School. This may seem long, but utmost perfection requires time. More important than any time limit is the principle that "the rider first must control himself in order to be able to control the creature entrusted to him. Therein is the deeper meaning of riding as a means of education."[510]

Draw Reins: Not Made for Forcing

Podhajsky devotes the fifth part to saddling and bridling at the Spanish Riding School. A minor point is that the curb bit headstall does not have a throat latch at this institution. Side reins are only used on a horse without rider, or if the rider does not give rein aids. Draw reins may only be utilized in conjunction with a snaffle bit and only "by very skilled riders" "to maintain a horse's already learned position to facilitate the teaching of difficult airs. But never may they be used to enforce a horse's head position."[511] Modern sport and recreational mounts would be better off if their riders adhered to these guidelines.

The sixth part deals with the Spanish Riding School whose heretofore oral tradition Podhajsky wishes to document in writing to prevent interruption of the tradition during crises. "Tradition must not only be a matter of words, it should also be supported by action."[512] The Riding School survived wars, revolutions, the Danube Monarchy's demise, and World War II as a "top-tier institute of art and culture…If it continues to adhere to its old tradition, strictly maintaining its great masters' traditions, it will always stimulate the general equestrian standard." Hence Podhajsky describes, closely following Holbein and Meixner, the "customs" at the Spanish Riding School, its riding arena rules including permitted tours, turns, and figures.[513]

In the Pillars and Airs above the Ground

Despite its traditionally high importance, Podhajsky mentions work in the pillars on just five pages, for: "It should not be ignored that this work received decreasing attention during the last half century, degenerating from a means to an end toward an end in itself to be able to also show it during performances according to tradition."[514] The even more difficult topic of airs above the ground is discussed briefly on just ten pages. A pity, because these airs would require more intensive, detailed descriptions, so that they could be reconstructed should the Spanish Riding School not offer them in classical perfection anymore during a crisis or decline. On airs above the ground, Podhajsky remarks in 1965: "Today they are preserved in classical purity only at the Spanish Riding School."[515]

Codification after 400 Years

Alois Podhajsky's "Classical Equestrian Art. Riding Instruction from the Beginning to Perfection" of 1965 is the first comprehensive and detailed, written description of Austrian equestrian art after 400 years of a principally oral tradition. Various new editions underline the constant significance of the oeuvre. In his "Epilogue," Podhajsky wants his book "to always be a valuable study book and manual for general sports equitation, especially for dressage riding."[516] It remains to be seen if this wish will be granted… Only a more refined audience in search of equestrian truth and of classical riding's hidden treasures of harmony with the horse appreciates such literature.

Image 113 – First Chief Rider Klaus Krzisch and Siglavy Mantua 1, Piber 2005. (Photo Poscharnigg.) This Lipizzaner stallion performed the most strenuous great solo "All Airs and Tours of High School" until the age of 27 (!) years together with his rider, single-handed, on the curb only, proof of the supreme quality of Austrian equestrian art. This photo was taken during his last performance in Europe before a final tour in the USA.

AUSTRIAN EQUESTRIAN ART: RADIANT SOURCE OF IDENTITY

Proud in the Levade

The half century after Podhajsky's equestrian treatise saw a variety of books dealing with the Spanish Riding School of Vienna, and excellent Chief Riders published the knowledge and ability they acquired at this institute. Austrian equestrian art and the Spanish Riding School as its final refuge have sufficient documentation as never before in history. Its invincible radiance unfolded during the School's performances all over the world, proving to the 20th century its sublime quality as a living monument of paramount equestrian culture.

And what no one would have dreamed of after the Danube Monarchy's doom: The Spanish Riding School became a national symbol of a free, new Austria after World War II. It became a source of identity for a republic working its way out of bomb debris up to a state that could match any other country with respect to wealth, culture, and social balance. Therefore banknotes, stamps, and coins showed the proud and calm classical rider on his Lipizzaner in the levade.

Austria's politicians loved to show their important international guests the Spanish Riding School and the Piber Stud farm. The Lipizzaners and their riders have done more for the country's renown than cohorts of the best paid diplomats and statesmen, for the equestrian art has represented something that almost all politicians lack: authenticity, originality, and integrity. Classical equestrian art cannot be obtained by fraud or by being faked; politics can. Tourism and the souvenir industry took possession of the stately Lipizzaners and their riders: The business blossoms.

Charles de Kunffy: California, USA

The 20th century brought – besides a restriction to the Spanish Riding School above all - a surprising dissemination of Austrian equestrian art even to foreign continents. After 1918, Hungary, then independent of Austria, did not want to do without its own national centre for the formerly common equestrian culture. The Equestrian Academy of Orkenytabor developed into a jewel in a historically challenging environment, especially under the supervision of the renowned Zsigmond Josipovich. Orkenytabor always retained its

Image 114 – The European hard currency Austrian Schilling presents the cultural treasure Spanish Riding School.

connection to Vienna.[517] Josipovich educated Jenö Reznek, the trainer of Charles de Kunffy who built a reputation, has given clinics, written books that promote the finest equestrian art of Austro-Hungarian tradition.

Karl Mikolka: Brazil and USA

Another notable that spread Austrian equestrian art beyond the Atlantic deserves mention. Karl Mikolka, born in Vienna 1935, started as an eleve at the Spanish Riding School of Vienna in 1955, was a student of the eminent Alfred Cerha, and became Chief Rider in 1967. 1968-72, he was the dressage trainer for the Confederacao Brasileira de Hipismo in Rio de Janeiro and Sao Paolo. In 1974, he was involved in founding the United States Dressage Federation and became a dressage judge. An American Spanish Riding School would almost have been founded, but the owner of the designated 400 Lipizzaners died. Through his profound work concerning dressage, he found more and more devotees, and in 2003 Mikolka was inducted into the USDF Hall of Fame. His goal in life is to convince as many riders as possible of the Austrian equestrian art's principles and to discourage them from the modern notion of short-cut training.[518]

Franz Mairinger: Australia

Franz Mairinger (1915-78) from Vienna, joined the Austrian Cavalry in 1935, succeeded as a show jumper, and was invited to the Spanish Riding School by Podhajsky in 1939. He became a Rider in 1942. In 1952, he immigrated to Adelaide, Australia, where he worked

Image 115 – Stamps to celebrate the Spanish Riding School's 400th anniversary in 1972.

as a farmhand and trained Thoroughbreds. In 1954, he became trainer of the Equestrian Federation of Australia, founded in 1952. Australia, previously completely disregarded in the international equestrian world, subsequently won medals, even an Olympic gold. The "Australian Dictionary of Biography" opined that Mairinger had the ability to join "European competence and technique with the Australian riders' raw talent" "to train them for show jumping, the Grand Prix level dressage, and eventing."[519] His book, "Horses are Made to be Horses," proves his experience, wisdom, and humour.[520]

Álvaro Domecq: Spain – Austria – Spain

In 1973, Álavaro Domecq Romero founded the Fundación Real Escuela Andaluz del Arte Ecuestre in Jerez de la Frontera after having studied under the supervision of Colonel Handler at the Spanish Riding School of Vienna for a year; he also enjoyed the 400-years celebration while there.[521] The habitus of Domecq's Royal Andalusian School of Equestrian Art strongly resembles its Viennese paragon, and its program "Cómo bailan los Caballos Andaluces" obviously borrows from the historic original. This institute aims to cultivate various traditional dressage forms and of the Andalusian horse.[522] In 1995, the Austrian

SRS was to receive the Spanish Golden Horse, a high-ranking award. On this occasion, the Viennese Chief Riders, Johann Riegler and Arthur Kottas-Heldenberg rode – without having rehearsed - a Pas de Deux on Spanish horses they had chosen shortly before in Jerez de la Frontera. The performance succeeded optimally as if the Andalusians had been Lipizzaners.[523] One of the rare and fair coincidences in history is that Iberian equestrian art preserved in Austria and developed further to something specifically Austrian, found its way back to its country of origin after several centuries. It was obviously about to fall into oblivion there in its purely classical form.

Portugal

As in Spain, Portugal's classical equitation also survived its way into the 20th century, mainly through the uninterrupted practice of traditional bullfighting on horseback. In 1979, the "Escola Portuguesa de Arte Equestre," based in the park of Queluz Castle, was founded to restore the tradition of the Real Picaria, the original Portuguese Royal riding academy. The Real Picaria was previously located in the Royal Riding School of Belém, now today's National Coach Museum. The Portuguese School of Equestrian Art particularly emphasizes its ties to Austrian equestrian art: "The splendid Portuguese tradition…received a great impulse in the 18th century…under the influence of Queen Maria Ana de Austria and the future Prince José I."[524] "Moreover, the School cultivates the 'High School' of baroque equestrian art, following the technique and orientations of Vienna's Spanish Riding School, the only renaissance equestrian academy continually existing since its foundation."[525]

Image 116 – Spanish Riding School in Graz 2005, Detail. (Photo Poscharnigg.)

SUMMARY:

PLAYFUL PROOF THAT RIDING IS AN ART

1551: Grisone and the Neapolitan-Iberian Style of Mounted Combat

On our way through almost 500 years, we have discovered from the often only sparsely available documents the specific features that comprised the Austrian equestrian art, and we found surprising historical continuity. The consistent foundation of all was martial equitation in the Spanish-Neapolitan tradition, as first described in FEDERICO GRISONE's book of 1551 "GLI ORDINI DI CAVALCARE" (The Equestrian Rules). Since the conquest of Naples by the Spanish in 1496, this most successful style of mounted military combat was the standard of the Casa de Austria until the 18th century. A true cavalier had to ride in a manner that even the most difficult tasks appeared easy, elegant, and effortless. All Austrian treatises on equitation from the 17th to the 20th century upheld these standards for equestrian art and for the cavalry. Effortless elegance, full of impulsion was always the hallmark of Austrian riding. With pride in their hearts, cavalrymen galloped toward the murderous machinegun fire that was to annihilate them forever.

Manoeuvres plus exercises of High School – pirouette, piaffe, passage, levade, capriole etc. – served not only as means of one-on-one combat, but also to flaunt a psychological weapon in front of the enemy to intimidate him. Equestrian High School became an indispensable European cultural technique for rulers. While other dynasties needed their experts to be educated in Naples, the Casa de Austria enjoyed immediate access in the equestrian art via dynastic connections to Spain, and cultivated it as something private, apparently without need of written record. Absolutist rule and expected courtly decorum encouraged more and more subjects to emulate the Emperor's style.

1650: Galiberto's First Viennese Equestrian Treatise

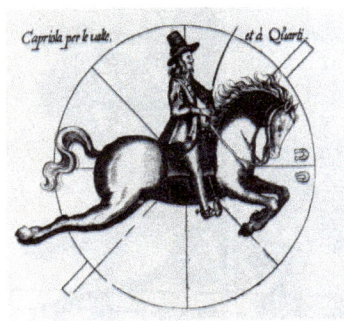

This demand was met by Vienna's first printed equestrian treatise, "IL CAVALLO DA MANEGGIO," written by the Neapolitan cavalry colonel GIOVANNI BATTISTA GALIBERTO. Beginning here, the features of Austrian equestrian art are described. Drafted in 1634, his volume serves both martial and artistic equitation, and a similar motto graces the famous plate in the Viennese Winter Riding School. Unlike many of his contemporaries, he requires horse-friendly procedures, strongly advising against brutality. He postulates the "thinking," "sensible," "reasonable" rider, and demands educational thoroughness without trivialization. He advises against severe bits and, about 100 years before Guérinière, describes the "shoulder-in," calling it "canton or angle."

1648-1789: Heyday of European Equestrian Art

Between 1648 and 1789, equestrian art as an expression of European culture reached its apex. Under Emperor Charles VI, the Austro-Hungarian Empire achieved its maximum expansion in land area, and reached the acme as the major cultural power. JOHANN GEORG VON HAMILTON (1672-1737) documented the supreme splendour of Austrian riding culture in his paintings, above all in his work "The Imperial Riding School" (1702). In particular, Count JOSEPH IGNAZ VON PAAR (1659-1735) was considered the continent's best rider, and his riding school is said to have been among the most pompous facilities in Vienna.

Austria's Classical Era in the 18th Century: Regenthal

The most influential figure to horsemanship was JOHANN CHRISTOPH VON REGENTHAL, Imperial Chief Rider 1709-30, riding instructor of the Emperors Charles VI and Francis I Stephen, and trainer of the riding masters SIND and EISENBERG. They spread his methods and fame in Europe. We have Regenthal's legacy, the manuscript only emerged in 1996, obviously dictated in a great, fast gesture that gives insight into the lifelong, profound experience and knowledge of this key figure in Austrian equestrian art. In his "Compendium," "The Primary Directives," he demands elegance, concentration, and practicable yet horse-friendly methods of the thinking rider, refusing brutality and impatience as well as self-aggrandizing theorization while despising draw reins and severe bits. The riding master must inform his student with "assurance and love." The horse is to be controlled by the completely immobile rider only by thoughts. He considers himself an inventor of the bridoon, practising "shoulder-in," which he calls "head in, croup out," not adopted from Guérinière. He does not approve of French equitation. Under Regenthal's direction and the Emperor's active interest, the Viennese riding school had become an internationally admired training establishment for Europe's nobility.

Austria's Classical Era in the 18th Century: Adam von Weyrother

Charles VI commissioned the construction of the most beautiful riding hall in the world as an architectural apotheosis of Austrian equestrian art: The Winter Riding School. Regenthal's successor, ADAM VON WEYROTHER (1696-1770) rode at its opening in 1735. He was an eminent rider and horseman of encyclopaedic dimension in the spirit of the Age of Enlightenment. He published his oeuvre "L'UTILE À TOUT LE MONDE OU LE PARFAIT ÉCUYER" (Useful for All the World or the Perfect Horseman) in Brussels, in 1767. He considers Joseph Ignaz von Paar the best and most virtuosic master horseman. Solleysel came next and subsequently Guérinière and Garsault, whom he may have known personally. For him, these masters' wisdom excelled anything of his epoch which he deemed "decadent." His principles mostly corresponded to Regenthal's.

For him, the horse is an intelligent creature, not a machine as in la Mettrie's sense. Riding must happen in a traditional, horse-friendly manner without pressure or anger. The master horseman shapes horse and man, leading the rider to self-knowledge. Hence, equestrian culture becomes an instrument of education for the entire character. Riding takes much time, taste, and intelligence. The most efficient riders learn every day.

The good horseman rides a horse trained by himself on a loose curb rein without bridoon using invisible aids. Hyper-flexion is a massive dressage error. As all authors of Austrian equestrian art before and after him, Adam von Weyrother demands cessation of the aids once they have worked. Regenthal's indispensable cavesson is replaced by the bridoon.

Austrian Equestrian Art Integrates the Cavalry's Mass Attack

With Regenthal, Paar, and Adam von Weyrother in Austria, and Guérinière in France, European equestrian art reached its apex. Nothing before or after could match this quality. Regenthal and Adam von Weyrother gave Austrian equestrian art an intellectual potential and charisma that only Podhajsky could attain. The success of the Prussian cavalry mass attack and the French Revolution led to a decline of equestrian art in Iberian-Neapolitan manner which survived only in Austria because there, it was applied as a supplement to the dominant "campaign school" until the 20th century. Highly gifted cavalry officers were always sent to the Spanish Riding School for training to pass on their knowledge to the mounted troops. And with this exchange, interdisciplinary contact with the military preserved equestrian art from artificiality.

1814 and 1836: Maximilian von Weyrother's Mechanistic Approach

MAXIMILIAN VON WEYROTHER (1783-1833), Chief Rider of both the Spanish Riding School and the Campaign Riding School, succeeded in maintaining acknowledgement of the High School in an age dominated by Anglomania. His booklet "THE BEST FITTING CURB BIT" (1814) was used as practical information even by the French cavalry. True child of his time, he wanted to explain the entirety of equitation by mechanics. He continues the idea of the thinking rider according to tradition. In cases of time constraints, he recommends "lifting and draw reins." As a connaisseur of Guérinière's École de cavalerie, he applied "l'épaule en dedans." The "FRAGMENTS" (1836), published after his death, demands that the "handler" "handles" horse and rider according to the rules of mechanics, physics, and anatomy.

The rider uses "not-so-visible" aids which he discontinues immediately after they work. Perfectly in the Austrian tradition, he demands horse-friendly treatment, but applies calculated, massive violence if needed. He does not see campaign riding as something different from High School, but as a necessary preliminary step toward it. His views influenced Seeger, Oeynhausen, Steinbrecht, Niedermaier, Holbein, Dreyhausen, and Podhajsky.

2nd half of the 19th Century: Rider's Spirit and Exercise Manual

Military circumstances in the middle of the 19th century led to a revision of the "EXERCISE MANUAL FOR THE IMPERIAL AND ROYAL CAVALRY," a task especially entrusted to LEOPOLD WILHELM VON EDELSHEIM-GYULAI (1826-93). This monument of best equestrian culture stayed in force until the era after the monarchy. Edelsheim emphasizes an always closed front of attack, endurance riding and terrain riding, riding over obstacles, and crossing of and swimming through waters in order to enhance the troop body's manoeuvrability. It is an explicit law to give leeway to the individuality of horse and rider, and to avoid pedantry.

The true cavalryman should be inspired by "rider's spirit." Horse training happens in a soft, humane, methodical, slow manner. Side reins only get used rarely and as a subordinate tool. Even the ordinary recruit's correct seat and soft, giving hand are cared for. Firearms are used solely when absolutely necessary. The cavalry relies on the devastating momentum of the compact assault. Until its doom, the Imperial and Royal Cavalry did not regard itself as a producer of cannon fodder but the cradle of military-chivalric elite. Emperor FRANCIS-JOSEPH I himself could be considered a model for every soldier because of his elegant equestrian appearance and courage, and no other side-saddle-rider could match the boldness and grace of Empress ELISABETH.

50 Years of Tradition: Mathäus von Niedermaier

Eyewitnesses described MATHÄUS VON NIEDERMAIER, active at the Spanish Riding School from 1837-87, Chief Rider since 1871, as a supreme horseman. He describes his training methods in the fragmentary manuscript "DRESSAGE OF THE GREEN HORSE. TREATMENT IN THE RIDING SCHOOL" (1885). Like Xenophon, he aims for the ideal of riding a horse in a way that allows it to move in a state of free spiritedness. The colt is intricately started with "care and love," with soft words, its poll being actively raised, while the trainer subtly uses a whip in order to activate the hindquarters.

The mouth must be in harmony with the body. "Shoulder-in" is the movement for the "thinking rider" who wants to educate his horse to "higher perfection." This can only be achieved by avoiding any superficiality. Principles of "never-exhausted patience" and "never punishment" make the horse fearless. Niedermaier offers most detailed insights into the training practice at the Spanish Riding School of Vienna up to the era of Holbein. Amidst a world of Anglomania and military and hunting equitation, the tradition of courtly-academic equestrian art survives at a paramount level.

1898: Holbein's Cavalry-Based Directives for the Spanish Riding School

A duumvirate of chief rider and cavalry officer for the management of Europe's last institution which cultivates academic equestrian art succeeds in the final symbiosis of two seemingly opposed spheres of riding. JOHANN MEIXNER works for the Spanish Riding School 1885-1916. The playful, brilliant calmness he rides his horses with brings him various awards. As its chief rider, he gives the first interview in the institute's history in 1914. FRANZ VON HOLBEIN (1832-1910), dragoon commander, and successful competition rider, becomes entrusted with the Spanish Riding School's general management. Together they publish "DIRECTIVES FOR THE IMPLEMENTATION OF THE METHODIC PROCEDURE OF TRAINING RIDER AND HORSE AT THE IMPERIAL AND ROYAL SPANISH COURT RIDING SCHOOL," the first official written instruction in the riding house's history. Equestrian art must be carried out "without pedantry" and schematics. Shoulder-in gets praised exuberantly as a universal remedy.

High School has two necessary preliminaries without which it cannot work: Natural straight-ahead-riding and campaign-riding in balance, for nature works without art, but art cannot work without nature. A High School horse must be apt as a campaign horse anytime. Cavalry riding is the indispensable basis for High School. Austrian equestrian art was always closely connected to military riding. Nevertheless, Holbein's horse training program clearly shows a big difference in comparison to Niedermaier's. Instead of an academic sense of detail, military principles dominate. One effect of Holbein's management still prevails: In Lipizza, he rejected almost all non-greys since he preferred the uniform carriage-horse white.

1914-38: Doom of the Austro-Hungarian Cavalry

If cavalrymen considered High School an anachronism, they had to have realized that classically trained cavalry could not perform effectively against the murderous machinery of mass-war. In 1917, the Austro-Hungarian cavalry was discontinued as a primary military force, and riders were sent into war on foot. The romantic ideas of rider's spirit, chic uniforms, energetic, elegant riding of great tradition, casually shown-off pride, and thoroughly trained horses – everything sank amidst blood, mud, and poisonous gas. The First Republic of Austria's cavalry with its remaining 1000 horses was taken over by the German army in 1938. Thus the specifically Austrian way of equitation ultimately survived solely at the Spanish Riding School of Vienna.

After 1918:
The Spanish Riding School Goes Public

Men of foresight and perseverance stood up for the school, above all Chief Rider MAURITIUS HEROLD (at the School from 1896-1925). He realized that after the doom of the Danube Monarchy, the previously private imperial institute would need professional publicity and advertisement. While Meixner had refused to write about the academic equestrian training, in 1923, Herold describes for the public how "THE CAREER OF A SCHOOLHORSE ACCORDING TO THE USUAL PROCEDURE AT THE SPANISH RIDING SCHOOL OF VIENNA" develops.

Between Two World Wars:
Hopeful Retrospections

That same year, the ingenious painter LUDWIG KOCH (1866-1934) and co-author SIGMUND VON JOSIPOVICH publish "THE EQUESTRIAN ART IN IMAGES," a book finally summarizing the Austro-Hungarian manner of equitation characterized by cultivated naturalness, impulsion, and self-evident elegance. GUSTAV VON

DREYHAUSEN issued "PRINCIPLES OF EQUESTRIAN ART" in 1936, which documents "the system of the Viennese school," or the "optimum impulsion with supreme softness and perfect form."

Alois Podhajsky (1898-1973):
A Life for Austrian Equestrian Art

The Spanish Riding School survived World War I (1914-18) and attained some fame. ALOIS PODHAIJSKY ran it from the beginning of World War II (1939-45) until 1964. The cavalry officer, an avid show jumper and hunt-horseman, won the dressage bronze medal at the 1936 Olympic Games despite German tactical tricks. His selfless, courageous actions saved from the barbarity of war the Spanish Riding School and the Lipizzaner breed as the remaining physical foundations of Austrian equestrian art. The riding school, always proving its unshakeable will to live, became a source of identity to the successfully restored Republic of Austria. Podhajsky succeeded in convincing the old chief riders – who thought of themselves as a vanishing breed – of their craft's future sustainability, to pass-on their savvy to the following young riders in order to preserve the high equestrian standard, and to maintain the traditions without compromise. He also became the first director in the Spanish Riding School's long history to publish a full-scale, detailed and philosophically enriched training manual in 1965: "CLASSICAL EQUESTRIAN ART. RIDING INSTRUCTION FROM THE BEGINNINGS TO PERFECTION." The book contains knowledge most of which has been characterizing Austrian equestrian art since its beginnings:

- Equestrian art aims to present a splendid, obedient horse that is a pleasure to ride.

- All the rider's aids are discontinued as soon as they work in order to increase the horse's sensitivity; a clear refusal of permanently knocking legs and constant pulling on the reins.

- Energetic riding forward is the basis of all movements.

- Admonishing the neck's hyper-flexion.

- Like a carefully observing psychologist, the thinking rider responds to each horse's individuality and character.

- Frequent and sensible praise is given with tenderness while punishment comes rarely, but with emphasis.

- Evil treatment of the horse reveals the rider's character.

- Equestrian art demands consequent, careful work without violating nature.

- Supreme standards are requested without irking the horse, without making him suffer mentally or physically, always aiming at trust, obedience and energetic gaits for a long, healthy, happy life for the horse.

- From the beginning, the correct seat is of paramount importance.

- The correct manner of handling the reins with curb bit and bridoon is 3:1.

- Riding with the reins in one hand, on the curb alone is the acme of equestrian art.

- Equitation as an art requires the ease of the horse and consistency of the rider.

- The horse shall "evoke in all his beauty, in all his movements, the impression of controlled power."

In other countries' and masters' equitation, these features may occur more or less, but not in such historic permanence over such a long period of time.

Worldwide Radiance

After the enormous material and mental destruction caused by World War II (1939-45), Austria perceived the Spanish Riding School's tradition as a source of identity it could rightly be proud of. Austrian equestrian art, incarnate at the Spanish Riding School of Vienna, was considered a significant part of Austria. Important persons brilliantly exported this art worldwide, for instance, Charles de Kunffy to the USA, Karl Mikolka to Brazil and the USA, and Franz Mairinger to Australia. And, one of the rare and fair coincidences in history is that Iberian equestrian art, preserved in Austria and developed further to something specifically Austrian, found its way back to its country of origin after several centuries, after it was about to fall into oblivion there in its purely classical form. Both the Spanish and Portuguese schools of equestrian art were founded in the 1970s following the model of the Viennese Spanish Riding School, closely observing the historic original.

Indescribable Playfulness

During the 20th century, thanks to the definite successes of Podhajsky, the Spanish Riding School of Vienna attained global renown. As unmistakable and unique as the sound, atmosphere, and ductus of the Vienna Philharmonic Orchestra is the unconstrained elegance of equestrian art epitomized by the Austrian Spanish Riding School. But what is it exactly, that makes these two artistic institutions so fascinating and distinctive? After all, these special traits evade any verbal description, for this speciality is indescribable and cannot be put into words. A metaphor can help us. Old masters' superb paintings radiate a depth effect not only due to the design visible on the surface. These old images feature layered structures. The layers latent behind the surface make the visible surface something special, sublime, and intriguing. Imitations usually lack such background, seldom displaying the charisma of the original. In this volume, we have witnessed approximately 500 years of Austrian equestrian history. This provides the highly complicated depth of structure for the riding practiced today at Vienna's Spanish Riding School. This picture would not have its indescribable quality and unmistakable originality without the historic background that it draws its energy from. Only upon such a background can a great chief rider state with relaxed charm that the School's riders "playfully prove that riding, if done really correctly, is definitely an art."[1]

Image 117 – Spanish Riding School in Graz 2005, Warming up. (Photo Poscharnigg.)

ENDNOTES

1. http://de.wikipedia.org/w/index.php?title=Attentat_von_Sarajevoandoldid=111312234.

2. Sigmund von Josipovich: Unsere Bilder und die Reitkunst in ihrem Zusammenhange mit der praktischen Reiterei. In: Ludwig Koch: Die Reitkunst im Bilde. Wien: Beck 1928, Reprint Olms, pp. 245-258, p. 253.

3. http://wiev1.orf.at/stories/141955, Jan. 7, .2012.

4. Cf. http://de.wikipedia.org/w/index.php?title=Maximilian_I._(HRR)andoldid=112246711.

5. Leopold von Heydebrand: Illustrirte Geschichte der Reiterei. Wien: Hartleben n. d., p. 90f. On knightly tournaments cf. pp. 73-108.

6. Ibid, p. 85.

7. Ibid, p. 101.

8. Cf. http://de.wikipedia.org/w/index.php?title=Triumphzug_Kaiser_Maximiliansandoldid=108248790.

9. Heydebrand, op. cit., p.103.

10. Cf. Marc Aurel: Des Kaisers Marcus Aurelius Antoninus Selbstbetrachtungen. Stuttgart: Reclam 1979, p. 5.

11. Cf. http://de.wikipedia.org/w/index.php?title=Baldassare_Castiglioneandoldid=96538664.

12. Baldesar Castiglione: Etiquette for Renaissance Gentlemen. London: Penguin 1995, p. 12f.

13. Castiglione, op. cit., p. 13f.

14. Cf. http://de.wikipedia.org/w/index.phptitle=Il_Libro_del_Cortegianoandoldid=96389622

15. Cf.. http://de.wikipedia.org/w/index.php?title=Ferdinand_II._(Neapel)andoldid=92860923

16. Cf. Alain Laurioux, Guillaume Henry: Die Schulen der Reitkunst: Wien, Saumur, Jerez, Lissabon. Schwarzenbeck: Cadmos 2009, pp. 9-13.

17. Cf. http://de.wikipedia.org/w/index.php?title=Andalusier_(Pferd)andoldid=95452581 .

18. Larioux, Henry, op. cit., p.9.

19. Ibid.

20. Cf. Ned and Jody Martin: Bit and Spur Makers in the Vaquero Tradition. Nicasio: Hill 1997, p. 30f.

21. Cf. Ed Connell: Reinsman of the West. Bridles and Bits. Hollywood: Wilshire 1964, pp. 24-26.

22. Cf. Patricio Estay and Pierre Delannoy: „Cavaliers des chevaux et des hommes." Solar 1994, pp. 42-51.

23. Cf. Fernando Sommer D'Andrade: La tauromachie équestre au Portugal. Paris: Chandeigne 1991, pp. 99-116.

24. Antoine de Pluvinel: L'Instruction du roy en exercice de monter à cheval. Neu-auffgerichte Reut-Kunst...Frankfurt: Merian 1690. Reprint Olms, p. 122.

25. Cf. http://de.wikipedia.org/w/index.php?title=Pistoleandoldid=98098863.

26. Heydebrand, op. cit., p. 113-

27. Ibid, p. 114.

28. Hernán Cortés: Die Eroberung Mexikos 1520-1524. München: Heyne 2001, p. 310.

29. Jakob Wassermann: Das Gold von Caxamalca. Erzählung. Stuttgart: Reclam 1971, p. 6f.

30. Cf. http://de.wikipedia.org/w/index.php?title=Neapelandoldid=112517313

31. Michaela Otte: Geschichte des Reitens von der Antike bis zur Neuzeit. Warendorf: FN-Verlag 1994, p. 58. Cf. also Heydebrand, p. 107.

32. Heydebrand, op. cit., p. 120.

33. Norbert Conrads: „Ritterakademien der frühen Neuzeit. Bildung als Standesprivileg im 16. und 17. Jahrhundert." Göttingen: Vandenhoek und Ruprecht, 1982, p. 16.

34. http://de.wikipedia.org/w/index.php?title=-No_Sportsandoldid=94403624.

35. Cf. Georg Kugler: Die Reitkunst der Neuzeit. In: Georg Kugler, Wolfdieter Bihl: Die Lipizzaner der Spanischen Hofreitschule. Wien: Pichler 2002, pp. 9-159, p. 19.

36. Laurioux, Henry, op. cit., p. 19

37. Federico Grisone: Künstlicher Bericht und allerzierlichste beschreybung...Augsburg: Fayser 1570, p. 86

38. Cf. Otte, op. cit., p. 62f.

39. Cf. Michel Henriquet: L'oeuvre des écuyers Francais. Paris: Belin 2010, p. 39.

40. Cf. Ibid., p. 27.

41. Grisone, op. cit. p. 119.

42. Ibid., p. 119f.

43. Ibid., p. 120.

44. Ibid., p. 122.

45. Ibid, Introduction.

46. Cf. ibid., p. 34.

47. Ibid., p. 54.

48. Ibid., p. 101.

49. Ibid., p. 118.

50. Cf. ibid., pp. 124ff.

51. Ibid., p. 128.

52. Ibid., p. 132.

53. Ibid., p. 147.

54. Cf. ibid., pp. 151ff.

55. Ibid., p. 155.

56. Ibid., pp. 189ff.

57. Ibid., p. 198.

58. Ibid.

59. Ibid., p. 199.

60. Ibid., p. 207.

61. Ibid., p. 209.

62. Ibid., p. 226.

63. Ibid., pp. 235ff.

64. www.opensourceshakespeare.org.

65. Cf. Henriquet, op. cit., pp. 32-39.

66. Cf. Silvia Loch: The Royal Horse of Europe. London: Allen 1986, p. 80f

67. Laurioux, Henry, op. cit., p. 13.

68. Kugler, op. cit., p. 99.

69. Ibid., p. 37.

70. Cf. ibid.

71. Christopher F. Laferl: Die Kultur der Spanier in Österreich unter Ferdinand I. 1522-1564. Wien 1997/google books, p. 144.

72. Ibid, p.116.

73. Cf. ibid., p. 122.

74. Ibid.

75. Cf. ibid., p. 145.

76. Cf. http://de.wikipedia.org/w/index.php?title=Maximilian_II._(HRR)andoldid=99795903

77. Kugler, op. cit., p. 39.

78. Laferl, op. cit., p. 129

79. Brigitte Vacha, ed.: Die Habsburger. Eine europäische Familiengeschichte. Graz: Styria 1992, p. 172.

80. Cf. Kugler, op. cit. , p.48.

81. A color of horses in the dun family, characterized by tan-gray or mouse-colored hairs on the body, often with shoulder and dorsal stripes and black barring on the lower legs.

82. Cf. Gustav René Hocke: Die Welt als Labyrinth. Manier und Manie in der europäischen Kunst. Von 1520 bis 1650 und in der Gegenwart. Hamburg, Rowohlt 1973, pp. 144ff.

83. Vacha, op. cit., p. 188.

84. Cf. Bernd Warlich, www.30jaehrigerkrieg.de/galiberto.

85. Ibid.

86. Ibid.

87. Ibid.

88. Ibid.

89. Cf. Vacha, op. cit., p.259.

90. Ibid., p. 223.

91. Vgl. http://de.wikipedia.org/w/index.php?title=Annibale_Gonzagaandoldid=109977995 .

92. Cf. Wolfdieter Bihl: Die Entwicklung der Spanischen Hofreitschule. In: Georg Kugler, Wolfdieter Bihl: Die Lipizzaner der Spanischen Hofreitschule. Wien: Pichler 2002, pp. 161-319, p. 192.

93. Cf. http://www.univie.ac.at/Geschichte/wienerhof/wienerhof2/grafiken/regio1.htm.

94. Cf. Antiquariat Christian M. Nebehay, www.find-a-book.com.

95. Kugler, op. cit., p. 99.

96. Johann Baptista Galiberti: Neugebahnter Tummel-platz…Wien: Rieger 1650.

97. Oulehla, Mazakarini, Brabec d'Ipra: Die Spanische Reitschule zu Wien. Wien: Orac 1986, S. 76.

98. Cf. Galiberto, op. cit., pp. 1-12.

99. Ibid., p. 5.

100. Ibid., p. 6.

101. Ibid.

102. Ibid., p. 7.

103. Ibid., p. 9.

104. Cf. ibid., pp.13ff.

105. Ibid., p. 104.

106. Ibid., p.15.

107. Ibid., p.16.

108. Ibid., p. 17f.

109. Ibid., p. 27.

110. Ibid., p. 27f.

111. Ibid., p. 37.

112. Ibid., p. 47f.

113. Ibid., p. 48.

114. Ibid.

115. Ibid., p. 51.

116. Ibid., p.57.

117. Ibid., p.58.

118. Ibid., p. 62.

119. Ibid., p. 66.

120. William Cavendish: A General System of Horsemanship. Facsimile reproduction of the edition of 1743. London: Allen 2000, p. 142.

121. Ludwig Hünersdorf: Anleitung zu der natürlichsten und leichtesten Art Pferde abzurichten. Marburg: Neue akademische Buchhandlung 1800, p. 210.

122. Dorian Williams: Der klassische Reitmeister. Die Eisenberg-Sammlung im Wilton House. Berlin: Parey 1980, Einleitung.

123. Cf. Vacha, op. cit., p.233.

124. Heydebrand, op. cit., p.130.

125. Ibid., p. 132.

126. Kugler, op. cit., p.67.

127. Cf. http://de.wikipedia.org/w/index.php?title=Georg_Simon_Winter_von_Adlersfl%C3%BCgelandoldid=89405799.

128. Cf. Bihl, op. cit., pp.172ff.

129. Cf. ADB.

130. http://de.wikipedia.org/w/index.php?title=Salomon_Kleinerandoldid=10778839.2

131. www.alservorstadt.at.

132. Baron de Sind: L'art du manège pris dans ses vrais principes…Wien, Paris: Desprez 1774, p. 8

133. Ibid., p. 3.

134. Ibid., p.70.

135. Cf. Sind, op. cit., p. 60

136. Ibid., p. 20.

137. (Johann Christoph von Regenthal): Unbekanntes aus der Spanischen Hofreitschule. Die Urdirektiven. Wiederentdeckte Handschrift eines Oberbereiters. Ed. Bertold Schirg. Hildesheim: Olms 1996, p. 231f.

138. Reis von Eisenberg: Wohleingerichtete Reitschule oder Beschreibung der allerneusten Reitkunst in ihrer
  Vollkommenheit. Zürich: Herrliberger 1748. Reprint Olms 1974, p. 37.

139. Ibid., p. 34.

140. Ibid., p. 48.

141. Ibid., p. 37.

142. Regenthal, op. cit., p. 4.

143. Vollständiges Diarium, alles dessen Was...in denen...Wahl- und Crönungs-Solennitäten des...Caroli des VI....Frkft:
  Zunner 1712, p. 84.

144. Ibid., p. 20.

145. Cf. Williams, op. cit., image 26.

146. Regenthal, op. cit., p. 5.

147. Cf. Holbein von Holbeinsberg and Johann Meixner: Die Direktiven für die Durchführung des methodischen Vorganges bei der Ausbildung von Pferd und Reiter in der k.u.k. Spanischen Reitschule (1898). In: Unbekanntes aus der
  Spanischen Hofreitschule. Hildesheim: Olms 1996, p. 17.

148. Regenthal, op. cit., p. 13.

149. Ibid., p. 15.

150. Ibid., p. 39.

151. Ibid., p. 37.

152. Cf.. Alexis Francois L'Hotte: Reitfragen. Questions Équestres. Transl. Bertold Schirg. Hildesheim: Olms 1977, p.
  153.

153. Regenthal, op. cit., p. 43

154. Ibid.

155. Ibid., p. 47.

156. Ibid., p.53.

157. Ibid., p. 59.

158. Ibid., p. 61.

159. Ibid., p. 69.

160. Ibid., p. 71.

161. Ibid., p. 73

162. Ibid., pp. 77-79.

163. Ibid., p. 95.

164. Ibid., p. 103f.

165. Ibid., p. 119.

166. Ibid., p. 129.

167. Ibid., p. 131.

168. Ibid., p. 143.

169. Cf. Francois Robichon de la Guérinière: Reitkunst oder gründliche Anweisung...Transl. J. Daniel Knöll. Marburg: Krieger 1817. Reprint Olms 1989, pp. 119-121.

170. Regenthal., op. cit., p. 145.

171. Ibid., p. 147.

172. Ibid., p. 149.

173. Ibid., p. 151.

174. Cf. Guérinière, op. cit., p. 121.

175. Regenthal, op. cit., p. 167.

176. Cavendish, op. cit., p. 56f.

177. Regenthal, op. cit., p. 185.

178. Ibid., p. 191.

179. Ibid., p. 197f.

180. Cf. ibid., p. 203.

181. Cf. Williams, op. cit., Image 37.

182. Regenthal, op. cit., p. 205.

183. Ibid., p. 209.

184. Ibid., p. 211.

185. Ibid., p. 213.

186. Ibid., p. 227.

187. Ibid., p, 239.

188. Ibid., p. 241.

189. Ibid., p. 243.

190. Cf. L. K. Glazovskaya: Akhalteke. A Great Racer of History. Ashgabat: TDH 2003, p. 175.

191. Regenthal, op. cit., p. 247.

192. Ibid., p. 249.

193. Ibid., p. 263f.

194. Ibid., p. 283f.

195. Ibid., p. 287.

196. Cf. Kugler, op. cit., p. 126

197. Cf. Neil Jeffares: Dictionary of pastellists before 1800. Online edition. - Baudez Basile: Un Français au pays du cheval. Vallin de La Mothe et Wilton House, 1755. In: *Livraisons d'histoire de l'architecture*. n°6, 2e semestre 2003. pp. 9-27. http://www.persee.fr/web/revues/home/prescript/article/lha_1627-4970_2003_num_6_1_945, pp. 12ff. – Dorian Williams, op. cit.

198. Eisenberg, op. cit., p.40.

199. Ibid., p. 10.

200. Ibid., p. 17.

201. Ibid., p. 11.

202. Ibid., p. 17.

203. Ibid., p. 27.

204. Ibid., p. 24.

205. Ibid., p. 11.

206. Ibid., p. 15.

207. Ibid., p. 18.

208. Ibid., p. 17.

209. Ibid., p. 43.

210. Sind, op. cit., p. v.

211. Ibid., p. 2f.

212. Ibid., p. 17.

213. Ibid., p. 20.

214. Ibid., pp. 44, 46.

215. Ibid., p. 73.

216. Cf. Henriquet, op. cit., pp. 145ff, 151ff.

217. Günter Zeman: Die Spanische Hofreitschule zu Wien. Geschichte und Architektur der Winterreitschule. In: www.freundeskreis-srs.at.

218. Kugler, op. cit., p. 124.

219. Adam von Weyrother, L'utile à tout le monde ou le parfait écuyer...Bruxelles: Boucherie 1767, vol. 1, 2; vol. 1, p. xiii f.

220. Ibid., p. xiv f.

221. Ibid., vol. 2, p. 3.

222. Ibid., p. 51f.

223. Ibid., p. 52.

224. Ibid., p. 52f.

225. Ibid., p. 55f.

226. Ibid., p. 57f.

227. Ibid., p. 61.

228. Ibid., p. 86.

229. Ibid., p. 96.

230. Ibid., vol. 1, p. 49.

231. Cf. Vacha, op. cit., p. 267.

232. www.literaturatlas.de. Von Hunden und Pferden des Freiherrn von Münchhausen.

233. Cited in Kugler, op. cit., p. 108.

234. Heydebrand, op. cit., p. 157f.

235. Cf. Kugler, op. cit., p. 109.

236. Cited in: Alphons Bernhard: Die öst.-ung. Kavallerie. Ein Nachruf. In: Militärwissenschaftliche Mitteilungen 1931, pp. 1-16, p. 5.

237. Vacha, op. cit., p. 319.

238. Cf. Heydebrand, op. cit., p. 177.

239. F. L. Wilder: Englischer Sport in alten Drucken. Wien: Schroll 1975, p. 142

240. Cited in: Henriquet, op. cit., p. 252.

241. Cf.. Philippe Karl: Reitkunst. Klassische Dressur bis zur Hohen Schule. München: BLV 2000, pp. 19ff.

242. Kugler, op. cit., p. 159.

243. Heydebrand, op. cit., p. 169.

244. Enrico Acerbi: The Austrian Imperial-Royal Army 1805-1809. www.napoleon-series.org.

245. Heydebrand, op. cit., p. 168.

246. Cf. ibid., p. 176.

247. Alois Podhajsky: Die klassische Reitkunst. Reitlehre von den Anfängen bis zur Vollendung. München: Nymphen- burger 1988, p. 18.

248. Maximilian von Weyrother: Anleitung wie man nach bestimmten Verhältnissen die passendste Stangen-Zäumung finden kann. Nebst einer einfachen Ansicht der Grundsätze der Zäumung. Wien: Schaumburg 1814.

249. Weyrother, Stangen-Zäumung, p. 7.

250. Ibid., p. 20.

251. Ibid., p. 29.

252. Ibid., p.38.

253. Ibid., p. 50.

254. Ibid., p. 53.

255. Ibid., p. 60.

256. Ibid., p.57f.

257. Ibid., p. 60.

258. Ibid., p. 64f.

259. Ibid., p. 69.

260. Ibid.

261. Ibid., p. 74f.

262. J.J.B.: De l'embouchure du cheval...In: Revue encyclopèdique ou analyse raisonnée...Paris 1828, vol. 39, p. 701. Google books.

263. Bulletin universel des sciences...Paris 1828, vol. 5, p. 485. google books.

264. Bruchstücke aus den hinterlassenen Schriften des k.k. österr. Oberbereiters Max Ritter von Weyrother. Gesammelt durch einige seiner Freunde. Mit dem Portrait des Verfassers. Wien: Heubner 1836.

265. Weyrother, Bruchstücke, p. 2.

266. Ibid., p. 80.

267. Cf. ibid., p. 1.

268. Ibid., p. 12.

269. Ibid., p. 17.

270. Ibid., p. 55.

271. Cf. ibid., p. 24.

272. Cf. ibid., p. 25f.

273. Ibid., p. 29.

274. Ibid., p. 43.

275. Ibid., p. 53.

276. Ibid., p. 30.

277. Cf. ibid., p. 41f.

278. Ibid., p. 46.

279. Ibid., p. 70.

280. Ibid., pp. 74-77.

281. Ibid., p. 78.

282. Heydebrand, op. cit., p. 164.

283. Weyrother, Bruchstücke, p. 79f.

284. Ibid., p. iv.

285. Ibid., p. 81.

286. Cited in: Podhajsky, op. cit., p. 19.

287. Louis Seeger: System der Reitkunst. Berlin: Herbig 1844. Reprint Olms, p. x.

288. Ibid., p. viii.

289. Ibid., p. xi.

290. Ibid.

291. Ibid., p. 135.

292. Cf. Francois Baucher: Méthode d'équitation…Paris: Place 1988.

293. Louis Seeger: Herr Baucher und seine Künste. Ein ernstes Wort an Deutschlands Reiter. Berlin: Herbig 1852. Digitalisat der Bayerischen Landesbibliothek, p. 18.

294. Weyrother, Bruchstücke, p. vi.

295. Podhajsky, op. cit., p. 20.

296. Cf. Heydebrand, op. cit., pp. 164ff.

297. Ibid., p. 172.

298. Cf. http://de.wikipedia.org/w/index.php?title=Maschinengewehrandoldid=112077765

299. Cf. http://de.wikipedia.org/w/index.php?title=Schlacht_bei_K%C3%B6niggr%C3%A4tzandoldid=112544107

300. Bernhard, op. cit., p. 6.

301. Ibid.

302. Ibid., p. 6f.

303. Heydebrand, op. cit., p. 164.

304. Cf. ibid. and Podhajsky, op. cit., p. 21.

305. Ibid., p. 20f.

306. Cf. http://de.wikipedia.org/w/index.php?title=-Leopold_Freiherr_von_Edelsheim-Gyulaiandoldid=105691341.

307. Exercier-Reglement für die k. u. k. Cavallerie. I. Theil. 4. Aufl. Wien: K.k. Hof- und Staatsdruckerei 1898, p. 8.

308. Ibid., p. 9.

309. Ibid.

310. Ibid., p. 62.

311. Stefan von Maday: Psychologie des Pferdes und der Dressur. Berlin: Parey 1912. Reprint Olms 1996.

312. Exercier-Reglement, op. cit., p. 66.

313. Ibid., p. 86.

314. Ibid., p. 79.

315. Ibid., p. 105.

316. Ibid., p. 165.

317. Ibid., p. 66.

318. Ibid., p. 68f.

319. Ibid., p. 74.

320. Ibid., p. 159.

321. Ibid., p. 159.

322. Ibid., p. 161.

323. Ibid., p. 95.

324. Cf. ibid., p. 164.

325. Ibid., p. 99.

326. Ibid., p. 107.

327. Ibid., p. 106.

328. Ibid., p. 108.

329. Ibid., p. 119f.

330. Ibid., p. 148f.

331. Ibid., pp. 159-161.

332. Ibid., p. 166.

333. Ibid., p. 166f.

334. Ibid., p. 167.

335. Ibid., p. 168.

336. Cf. Baucher, op. cit., pp. 25ff.

337. Heydebrand, op. cit., p. 172.

338. Ibid., p. 178f.

339. Ibid., p. 177.

340. Cf. Kugler, op. cit., p. 159. For Niedermaier's biographic data I owe thanks to Georg Kugler and Günter Zeman.

341. Waldemar Seunig: Von der Koppel bis zur Kapriole. Die Ausbildung des Reitpferdes. Berlin: Verlag Sankt Georg 1943. Reprint Olms, p. 346.

342. Cf. Sind, op. cit., p. 60.

343. Waldemar Seunig: Marginalien zu Pferd and Reiter. Heidenheim: Hoffmann 1961, Reprint wu-wei-verlag, p. 226f.

344. Cf. Alexis Francois l'Hotte: Reitfragen (Questions Èquestres). Transl. by Bertold Schirg. Hildesheim: Olms 1977, p. 152f.

345. Mathäus von Niedermaier: Dressur des rohen Pferdes. Behandlung auf der Reitschule. Manuscript 1885, Archive Lipizzanermuseum, quire 24, p. 2. This manuscript is now available in print: Matthäus Niedermeyer: Die Dressur des rohen Pferdes. Behandlung auf der Reitschule. Ed. Georg Kugler, Günter Zeman. Historica Austria, vol. 11. Vienna: Verlag für Wissenschaft, Forschung und Kultur des Österreichischen Archäologie-Bundes 2014.

346. Ibid., quire 2, p. 4.

347. Ibid., p. 2.

348. Ibid., quire 3, p. 1.

349. Ibid, quire 8, p. 4 – quire 9, p. 1.

350. Ibid., quire 9, p. 4.

351. Ibid., quire 10, p. 1.

352. Ibid., quire 10, p. 2f.

353. Ibid., quire 11, p. 3.

354. Ibid., p. 4.

355. Cf. ibid., quire 13f.

356. Ibid, quire 16, p. 1.

357. Ibid., quire 15, p. 3.

358. Ibid., quire 17, p. 1.

359. Ibid., quire 18, p. 1.

360. Ibid., p. 2.

361. Ibid., p. 4.

362. Ibid., quire 19., p. 2.

363. Ibid., quire 20, p. 2.

364. Ibid., quire 21, p. 1.

365. Ibid., p. 2.

366. Ibid., p. 3.

367. Ibid., quire 23, p. 1f.

368. Ibid., p. 2.

369. Ibid., quire 24, p. 1.

370. Ibid., p. 4.

371. Ibid., quire 25, p. 2f.

372. Ibid., p. 4.

373. Franz Thurn und Taxis: Pardubitz. Parforce-Jagd und Rennen. Wien: Böhlau 1990, p. 106.

374. Empress Elisabeth, quoted in: Egon Caesar Conte Corti: Elisabeth. Die seltsame Frau. Salzburg: Pustet 1934, p. 298.

375. Quoted in: ibid, p. 255f.

376. Ibid., p. 310.

377. Ibid., p. 313.

378. Ibid., p. 289.

379. Ibid., p. 275.

380. Ibid., p. 290.

381. Cf. Martin Haller: Pferde unter dem Doppeladler. Das Pferd als Kulturträger im Reiche der Habsburger. Graz and al.: Stocker, Olms 2002, p. 96.

382. Gustav Rau: Oberbereiter Meixner. Zu seinem Gedächtnis. In: St. Georg Nr. 44, 1922, pp. 33-36, p. 33.

383. Ibid.

384. Ibid., p. 34.

385. Ibid.

386. Cf. ibid.

387. Cf. James Fillis: Breaking and Riding. London: Reprint Allen 1986, Preface.

388. Rau, op. cit., p. 34.

389. Ibid.

390. Ibid.

391. Ibid., p. 35.

392. Ibid.

393. Ibid., p. 36.

394. http://de.wikipedia.org/w/index.php?title=Franz_von_Holbein-Holbeinsbergandoldid=96039689.

395. (Franz) Holbein von Holbeinsberg and Johann Meixner: Directiven für die Durchführung des methodischen Vorganges bei der Ausbildung von Reiter und Pferd in der k. u. k. Spanischen Hofreitschule. In: Unbekanntes aus der Spanischen Hofreitschule. Hildesheim: Olms 1996.

396. Ibid., p.3f

397. Ibid., p. 5.

398. Ibid., p. 7.

399. Ibid.

400. Ibid., p.8.

401. Ibid.

402. Ibid., pp. 9-11.

403. Ibid., p. 11f.

404. Ibid., p. 14f.

405. Ibid., pp. 15-17.

406. Ibid., p. 17f.

407. Ibid., p. 22f.

408. Franz von Holbein-Holbeinsberg: Vorhabensbericht „Programm für die Sommer-Arbeit des Jahres 1899 in der k.k. Spanischen Schule." Manuscript, 2 quires, 1899. Archiv Lipizzanermuseum, Stallburg, Wien.

409. Ibid., p. 1.

410. Ibid.

411. Ibid., p. 2.

412. Franz von Holbein: „Denkschrift" „Die Hofgestüte und ihre Aufgaben." (Manuscript, 2 quires, 6 written pages, Stallburg, Archiv Lipizzanermuseum); quire 1, p. 1.

413. Ibid., p. 2.

414. Ibid., p. 3.

415. Ibid., p. 4.

416. Ibid., quire 2, p. 1.

417. Ibid.

418. Ibid., p. 2.

419. Ibid.

420. Bernhard, op. cit., p. 9.

421. Cited in: Ulrike Weiss: Die Reiter von Graz. Die Geschichte der Grazer Reiterkasernen und der in ihnen untergebrachten Regimenter. Graz: Vehling 2005, p. 109.

422. Cited in: Ibid., p. 111.

423. Bernhard, op. cit., p. 7f.

424. Ibid., p. 8.

425. Weiss, op. cit., p. 111.

426. Bernhard, op. cit., p. 12.

427. Ibid., p. 9.

428. Ibid., p. 10f.

429. Ibid., p. 11.

430. Ibid., p. 14f.

431. Ibid., p. 15.

432. Alois Podhajsky: Ein Leben für die Lipizzaner. München: Nymphenburger (1960), p. 16.

433. Georg Nagyrévi v. Neppel: Husaren in der Weltgeschichte. Wiesbaden: Vollmer 1975, p. 69.

434. Cf. Kriegs Stammbuch der Stadt Wien. Wien: Gerlach and Wiedling (1917).

435. Nagyrévy, op. cit., p. 70f.

436. http://de.wikipedia.org/w/index.phptitle=Erster_Weltkriegandoldid=107437069.

437. Ibid.

438. Cf. ibid.

439. Bernhard, op. cit., p.1f.

440. Ibid., p. 16.

441. Cf. Arnold R. Rojas: These Were the Vaqueros. Bakersfield: Hall 1974, pp. 383ff.

442. Cf. http://de.wikipedia.org/w/index.php?title=Bundesheer_(1._Republik)andoldid=109810560.

443. Cf., Weiss, op. cit., p. 23.

444. Podhajsky, Leben für die Lipizzaner, p. 50.

445. Ibid., p. 49.

446. Ibid.

447. Ibid., p. 17f.

448. (Mauritius) Herold: Memorandum über die Entstehung, Verwendung und Zukunft der Spanischen Hofreitschule. Typoscript, 4 pages, Wien, Dec. 16, 1918, p. 1f. Dokumentationszentrum fuer altoesterreichische Pferderassen. A 2291 Schönfeld, Gutshofstr. 23.

449. Herold, Memorandum, p. 2.

450. (Mauritius) Herold: Der Werdegang eines Schulpferdes nach der in der Spanischen Reitschule zu Wien üblichen Methode. In: Sankt Georg, Apr. 15, 1923, p. 3f.

451. Ibid., p. 1.

452. Ibid.

453. Ibid., p.4.

454. Ibid.

455. Ibid.

456. Cf. Österreichisches Biographisches Lexikon 1815-1950.

457. Ludwig Koch: Die Reitkunst im Bilde. Wien: Beck 1928. Reprint Olms, p. 11.

458. Ibid., p. 13.

459. Ibid., p. 38.

460. Ibid., p. 139.

461. Ibid.

462. Ibid., p. 160.

463. Josipovich, op. cit., p. 248.

464. Ibid., p. 252.

465. Felix Dörmann, cited in: Stefan Gmünder: Wenn die Inflation Seelen frisst. In: derStandard.at, Dec. 5, 2012.

466. Josipovich, op. cit., p. 252.

467. Ibid., p. 253.

468. Ibid., p. 245.

469. Gustav von Dreyhausen: Grundzüge der Reitkunst. Wien: Selbstverlag der Österr. Renn- und Campagnereitergesellschaft 1936, p. 25f.

470. Ibid., p. 62.

471. Ibid., p. 49.

472. Ibid., p. 58.

473. Ibid., p. 49.

474. Ibid., p. 108.

475. Podhajsky, Ein Leben für die Lipizzaner, p. 36

476. Ibid., p. 73.

477. Gustav Rau, cited in: Ibid., p. 40.

478. Dresdner Nachrichten, Feb. 8, 1939, cited in: Ibid., p. 55.

479. Ibid., p. 66.

480. Cf. ibid., p.63f., p. 68.

481. Cf. Podhajsky, Reitkunst, p. 176.

482. Cf. ibid., pp. 15ff.

483. Cf. ibid., pp. 25-48.

484. Ibid., p. 51.

485. Ibid., p. 53.

486. Ibid., p. 55.

487. Ibid., p. 61.

488. Ibid., p. 63f.

489. Ibid., p. 65.

490. Ibid., p. 92.

491. Ibid., p. 94.

492. Ibid., p. 98.

493. Ibid., p. 110.

494. Ibid., p. 112.

495. Ibid., p. 122.

496. Ibid., p. 122.

497. Ibid., p. 152.

498. Ibid., p. 170.

499. Ibid., p. 175.

500. Ibid., p. 179; cf. ibid., pp. 177-183.

501. Ibid., p. 190.

502. Ibid.

503. Ibid., p. 199.

504. Ibid., p. 216.

505. Cf. ibid., pp. 221-225.

506. Ibid., p. 224.

507. Ibid., p. 224f.

508. Ibid., p. 225.

509. Ibid, p. 226.

510. Ibid.

511. Ibid., p. 239.

512. Ibid., p. 241.

513. Cf. ibid., pp. 244-257.

514. Ibid., p. 257.

515. Ibid., p. 261.

516. Ibid., p. 277.

517. Cf. Charles de Kunffy: Dressage Principles Illuminated. London: Allen 2002, p. 23.

518. Cf. www.mikolkadressage.com.

519. Richard I. Cashman: Franz Mairinger. In: Australian Dictionary of Biography. Adb.anu.edu.au.

520. Franz Mairinger: Horses are Made to be Horses. Adelaide: Howell Book House 1983.

521. Information by First Chief Rider Klaus Krzisch, Dec. 4, 2012.

522. Cf. www.realescuela.org.

523. Cf. Johann Riegler: Beruf Oberbereiter. Schondorf: wu-wei Verlag 2010, p. 106.

524. Escola Portuguesa de Arte Equestre, Folder.

525. Ana Oliveira Martins: Parks und Schlösser von Sintra. Sintra: Orgal 2012, p. 38f.

526. Werner Poscharnigg: Spielerisch vorführen, dass Reiten eine Kunst ist. Interview mit dem Ersten Oberbereiter Klaus Krzisch. In: Steirische Pferdewelt 1/2000, p. 12.